A THEOLOGY
OF READING

A THEOLOGY
OF READING

The Hermeneutics of Love

ALAN JACOBS

Westview PRESS
A Member of the Perseus Books Group

Copyright © 2001 by Westview Press, A Member of the Perseus Books Group

Westview Press books are available at special discounts for bulk purchases in the United States by corporations, institutions, and other organizations. For more information, please contact the Special Markets Department at The Perseus Books Group, 11 Cambridge Center, Cambridge MA 02142, or call (617) 252-5298.

Published in 2001 in the United States of America by Westview Press, 5500 Central Avenue, Boulder, Colorado 80301–2877, and in the United Kingdom by Westview Press, 12 Hid's Copse Road, Cumnor Hill, Oxford OX2 9JJ

Find us on the World Wide Web at www.westviewpress.com

A CIP Catalog record for this book is available from the Library of Congress.
ISBN 0-8133-6566-X; 0-8133-6577-5 (hc)

The paper used in this publication meets the requirements of the American National Standard for Permanence of Paper for Printed Library Materials Z39.48–1984.

10   9   8   7   6   5   4   3   2   1

The one thing that is true is love. To base a doctrine of language on this statement is to move towards a theological theory of language.

—**Gerhard Ebeling**

Theology consists precisely in saying that for which only another can answer—the Other above all, the Christ who himself does not speak in his own name, but in the name of his Father. Indeed, theological discourse offers its strange jubilation only to the strict extent that it permits and, dangerously, demands of its workman that he speak beyond his means, precisely because he does not speak of himself. Hence the danger of a speech that, in a sense, speaks against the one who lends himself to it. One must obtain forgiveness for every essay in theology.

—**Jean-Luc Marion**

O stand, stand at the window
As the tears scald and start;
You shall love your crooked neighbour
With your crooked heart.

—**W. H. Auden**

CONTENTS

ACKNOWLEDGMENTS

My heartiest and most sincere thanks to:

- my son Wesley, for joy
- my parents-in-law Lynn and Margaret Collins, for unceasing support, especially in prayer
- Wheaton College, for a sabbatical during which much of this book got written
- the Pew Charitable Trusts, for funding a seminar on christology and scholarship at Wheaton, directed by Mark Noll, which got me started thinking theologically about reading
- Roger Lundin, Mark Noll, and the late (and greatly lamented) Tim Phillips, for being my unofficial teachers in theology
- Paul Griffiths, Stanley Hauerwas, and Joel Weinsheimer, for honest and useful responses
- Gail Kienitz, David Jeffrey, Donald Marshall, and Ashley Woodiwiss, for reading portions of the manuscript, for providing acute comments and stimulating conversation, and, above all, for the sustenance of friendship
- Kelly Rae and (especially!) Laura Andersen, for outstanding assistance in research and preparation of the manuscript

Two expressions of thanks must be set apart from the rest.

First, I owe a special debt of gratitude to Charles and Karen Marsh, and to Theological Horizons, the organization they created and oversee. The support (of various kinds) and encouragement they have given me have been invaluable. Their confidence in the project, when it was still incipient, gave me the determination to pursue it when I could find plenty of reasons to set it aside or abandon it altogether. And Charles's efforts as my unofficial (yet extraordinarily competent) agent quite literally made publication of this book possible.

And to Teri, my wife of twenty years, let one simple public act stand for a world of meaning (of gratitude, of love) that neither can nor should speak in a public voice: I dedicate this book to you, without whom. . . .

PRELUDE

To read with intelligent charity. ("The only method," says T. S. Eliot, "is to be very intelligent." A sobering verdict, if true.) Once again to speak of works rather than texts, of personal acts—*answerable* acts, we will hear them called—rather than a proliferation of signs or verbal instantiations of ideological forces. To become confused, sometimes, about the difference between reading works and reading their authors. Iris Murdoch: "Coherence is not necessarily good, and one must question its cost. Better sometimes to remain confused" (*Metaphysics* 147). And Murdoch again: "Art and morals are one. . . . Love is the extremely difficult realisation that something other than oneself is real" (*Existentialists* xiv). To read lovingly because of and in the name of Jesus Christ, who is the author and guarantor of love. These are some of the purposes of this book.

The key questions of charitable interpretation—what it is, how to achieve it—will be treated here according to the canons of what Aristotelians call practical rationality rather than speculative philosophy. Though it will of course be necessary to consider many epistemological and theoretical questions along the way, I have focused much of my attention on works of literature that, in my view, provide richer, more nuanced, and more expansive accounts of what it might mean to read charitably than I have been able to discover elsewhere: I echo Martha Nussbaum's argument that literature, carefully read, is an irreplaceable tool in the development of discernment or practical wisdom. I also hope that my use of literary examples and models exhibits, in

1

however imperfect a way, the charity that I am recommending to all interpreters of written works.

There are other ways to explain the character of my pursuit: I might say that I am interested in *praktischen Vernunft* rather than *reinen Vernunft*, or that I am "Against Theory" in the sense made familiar to literary scholars by the essay of that name by Stephen Knapp and Walter Benn Michaels. For Knapp and Michaels, theory—defined as "the attempt to govern interpretations of particular texts by appealing to an account of interpretation in general"—is impossible insofar as it claims to be above, or separate from, or not implicated in, the practices it seeks to "govern." Theory is one of the forms of practice and doesn't rise above anything, as Stanley Fish argues in almost every essay in *Doing What Comes Naturally*. My reservations about theory, then, are almost identical to Bernard Williams's reservations about philosophy, and this is apt, given that Williams takes "philosophy" to mean detached reflection, or *theoria:*

> How truthfulness to an existing self or society is to be combined with reflection, self-understanding, and criticism is a question that philosophy, itself, cannot answer. It is the kind of question that has to be answered through reflective living. The answer has to be discovered, or established, as the result of a process, personal and social, which essentially cannot formulate the answer in advance, except in an unspecific way. Philosophy [or *theoria*] can play a part in the process, as it plays a part in identifying the question, but it cannot be a substitute for it. (*Ethics* 200)

This may help to explain my reliance on literary examples throughout this book (especially in the "Interludes"), a reliance curiously uncommon in books about literary hermeneutics.

I might also say—and this follows from my reservations about *theoria*—that I share the conviction of Karl Barth and John Milbank that theology should be essentially kerygmatic rather than dialectical, governed by Christ's commandment to proclaim the Gospel rather than by the natural impulse to argue and justify. But that means that the great challenge for me in writing this book has been to discover whether I can be "practical" (or Aristotelian, or dialectical) in my questions and yet fully theological (or kerygmatic) in my claims. After all, as Alasdair MacIntyre has rightly said, "Aristotle would certainly not have admired Jesus Christ and he would have been horrified by St. Paul" (*After* 184).[1] But I am encouraged in my endeavor by thinking often of a great predecessor in this enterprise: Jane Austen. And it is MacIntyre who has called attention to the importance of her example:

> When Jane Austen speaks of "happiness," she does so as an Aristotelian. Gilbert Ryle believed that her Aristotelianism—which he saw as the clue to the moral temper of her novels—may have derived from a reading of Shaftesbury. C. S. Lewis with equal justice saw in her an essentially Christian writer. It is her uniting of Christian and Aristotelian themes in a determinate social context that makes Jane Austen the last great effective imaginative voice of the tradition of thought about, and practice of, the virtues which I have tried to identify. She thus turns away from the competing catalogues of the virtues of the eighteenth century and restores a teleological perspective. (*After* 240)

For all the Aristotelian acuteness with which Austen delineates the virtues and vices distinctive to the tiny *polis* about which she writes— "three or four families in a country village is the very thing to work on," as she famously wrote in a letter—the *telos* of which MacIntyre speaks, and which informs all her work, is Christian charity.

*   *   *

Shakespeare, *Much Ado About Nothing*, act 4, scene 1. The plot of Don John the Bastard has come to fruition, and Claudio has repudiated Hero before the crowd gathered for their wedding, shouting for all to hear that, while her blushes would seem to be maidenly they are in fact tokens of guilt: "She knows the heat of a luxurious bed" (l. 40). He thinks he has—to borrow a term from *Othello*, a play that shares this theme—"ocular proof" for his charge;[2] we know he does not, and that he and his patron Don Pedro have been deceived. Among the characters, only Hero and Don John (the innocent victim and the villain) actually *know* that the charge of fornication is false.

Or do they alone know? That depends on what counts as knowledge. The first to speak on Hero's behalf—after even her own father, Leonato, has accepted the charges against her ("Would the two princes lie, and Claudio lie?" [l. 153])—is the Friar who was to officiate at the ceremony:

> *Hear me a little:*
> *For I have only been silent so long,*
> *And given way unto this course of fortune,*
> *By noting of this lady. I have mark'd*
> *A thousand blushing apparitions*
> *To start into her face, a thousand innocent shames*
> *In angel whiteness beat away those blushes,*
> *And in her eye there hath appear'd a fire*
> *To burn the errors that these princes hold*
> *Against her maiden truth. Call me a fool;*
> *Trust not my reading nor my observations,*
> *Which with experimental seal doth warrant*
> *The tenor of my book; trust not my age,*
> *My reverence, calling, nor divinity,*
> *If this sweet lady lie not guiltless here*
> *Under some biting error. (ll. 155–169)*

It should register with us that the Friar lays no claim to some intuited *gnosis* or supernatural revelation divorced from the realm of the senses. Like Claudio and Don Pedro, he derives his judgment from what he sees, and he sees what they do: Claudio, as noted, has spoken of Hero's blushes, but has *interpreted* them differently. And what the Friar calls attention to here is precisely the importance of interpreting the sensory phenomena correctly and, moreover, the need for the interpreter to possess certain virtues in order to "read" Hero's blushes as they should be read—which is to say, in accordance with the truth of the situation and of her character.

Claudio and Don Pedro possess what they think of as "ocular proof" of Hero's infidelity, and that alone serves to determine their reading of Hero's blushes. No other factors shape their interpretation, nor, indeed, could they; for Claudio and Don Pedro have no other knowledge relevant to the interpretive task with which they are faced.[3] Claudio's own account, given to Don Pedro, of how he came to love Hero is instructive:

> *O my lord,*
> *When you went onward on this ended action,*
> *I look'd upon her with a soldier's eye,*
> *That lik'd, but had a rougher task in hand*
> *Than to drive liking to the name of love:*

But now I am return'd, and that war-thoughts
Have left their places vacant, in their rooms
Come thronging soft and delicate desires,
All prompting me how fair young Hero is,
Saying I lik'd her ere I went to wars. (I.i.277–285)

From this speech we learn two important things: first, that Claudio's knowledge about Hero is almost totally *visual*, the product of his repeated "looking upon her"; and second, that the growth of "liking" into what Claudio calls love results not from some positive development of attention and appreciation but rather from the mere *absence* of martial thoughts, from the vacuum created in Claudio's mind by the conclusion of the recent battle. Therefore, when presented with putative visual evidence of Hero's faithlessness, Claudio cannot make recourse to any other knowledge that might incline him to question the trustworthiness of the spectacle Don John offers for his contemplation. And Don Pedro, who is not in love with Hero, has even less reason to doubt that "evidence."

The Friar, conversely, claims an authority that allows him to connect the visual phenomena—which, again, he *perceives* precisely as Claudio and Don Pedro do—more responsibly and in a way faithful to the true character of Hero. This authority has, he explains, multiple sources: his age and consequent seasoning in the world (including, we may presume, the social world, the world of men-and-women-together, which Claudio and Don Pedro as soldiers have mostly avoided); his calling by God to the cure of souls, a calling that to be properly fulfilled requires constant attentiveness to the niceties of human character; his reading in wise authors and Scripture. Moreover, he claims that the judgments to which his age, vocation, and learning lead him have been tested ("warranted") by experience ("experiment"), and that such judgments therefore deserve more credence than those of Claudio and Don Pedro.

But the Friar is not the only person present, other than Hero, who is confident of Hero's innocence: There is Beatrice, whose trust in her cousin and friend is implicit and unwavering. In some respects Beatrice's certainty differs from the Friar's confidence, and not just in that it *is* certainty rather than confidence (the Friar acknowledges the bare possibility of his being wrong, Beatrice never does): Beatrice claims neither age, religious calling, nor erudition. Her certainty stems rather from her intimate personal knowledge of Hero. At this point the English language, as it does so rarely, fails us: Whereas it enables, as French does not, Claudio's distinction between liking and loving, it cannot offer us what we need here, which is the distinction between *connaître* and *savoir*—roughly, "knowledge of" rather than "knowledge about." One of the most important and productive elements of the work of Martha Nussbaum has been her insistence, deriving from Aristotle, that love—especially *philia*, the kind of love that Beatrice and Hero feel for each other—is productive of this intimate knowledge, this *connaissance*.

> The Aristotelian view stresses that bonds of close friendship or love (such as those that connect members of a family, or close personal friends) are extremely important in the whole business of being a good perceiver. Trusting the guidance of a friend and allowing one's feelings to be engaged with that other person's life and choices, one learns to see aspects of the world that one had previously missed. One's desire to share a form of life with the friend motivates this process. (*Love's Knowledge* 44)

Beatrice then claims an authoritative experience of Hero's character that gives the lie to the princes' accusation—and, one might add, to Leonato's shockingly immediate acquiescence in his daughter's condemnation. Beatrice's claim comes not in the form of an argument but, instead, as a series of wounded and desperate cries that her beloved cousin has been wronged. The Friar indicates that he is confident rather than certain precisely by forming an argument, making a case. To doubt that Hero is pure is not possible for Beatrice; therefore, making a case for it is not possible.[4]

Of course, the kind of claim Beatrice implicitly makes for Hero—though again it's not really a "claim"—carries weight only if those who hear it approve the character of the one making it. There would be no reason to take such an avowal seriously if it came from the mouth of a habitually dishonest and morally slovenly person. This observation leads us to consider the one character on stage in this complex scene who is *not* sure about Hero, who is puzzled and confused: Benedick. He has been the companion, friend, and confidant of Claudio and Don Pedro, and yet, when they stride self-righteously offstage, he remains. But this does not in itself indicate his allegiance: Almost his first words after the denunciation of Hero are "For my part I am so attir'd in wonder, / I know not what to say" (IV.1.144–145)—he who has never lacked for something to say! On the one hand, he knows that Claudio and Don Pedro "have the very bent of honour," and that they would not destroy an innocent woman unless they were "deceived" (ll. 186–189). On the other hand, he knows that a practiced villain, Don John, accompanied Claudio and Don Pedro as they stalked away and, moreover, that those who are deceived are not always free from culpability for their state of misinformation (as he demonstrates in his stern treatment of both Claudio and Don Pedro later on).

But the deciding factor for Benedick derives from his love of Beatrice, which in turn depends largely upon his assessment of her character. Unlike Hero and Claudio, Beatrice and Benedick have known each other for many years. It appears that, before the "merry war" of wit (I.i.56) in which they have been for some time engaged, they had some sort of romantic relationship (II.i.261–264)—a relationship that, of course, this play sees them resume and nurture to fulfillment. Benedick's knowledge of Beatrice, therefore, is far from being merely visual: It is not the *savoir* of "ocular proof" but the *connaître* of love.

It is Beatrice who reminds Benedick that, even if the princes were deceived, they failed to seek confirmation for their belief from sources other than their own eyesight and, moreover, made a point of condemning Hero in the most humiliatingly public way imaginable: before a crowd of family and friends waiting to celebrate her marriage (IV.i.300–306). They have therefore behaved cruelly even if they were deceived. It seems to be this incontrovertible point that drives Benedick to ask the question the answer to which settles for him his responsibility:

> Benedick: Think you in your soul the Count Claudio hath wronged Hero?
> Beatrice: Yea, as sure as I have a thought, or a soul.
> Benedick: Enough! I am engaged, I will challenge him. (ll. 327–335)

A few moments earlier, when Beatrice had asked him to "[k]ill Claudio," Benedick had replied, "Not for the wide world" (ll. 289–290). But now her exposure of Claudio's cruelty and her absolute conviction that Hero has been wronged win him over. He can deny neither the justice of her argument nor the authority of her testimony to Hero's character. A discrimination must be made here: Benedick need not know anything of Beatrice in order to acknowledge that, *if* Claudio and Don Pedro are wrong in what they charge, they have behaved abominably. But it is only his love for her, based upon his knowledge of her character—her honesty, perceptiveness, and faithfulness—that resolves for him that momentous "if" that must be resolved if he is to act rightly in this agonizing situation. It is love's knowledge that puts into play the chain of arguments that determine that he challenge Claudio—which he soon does. Lacking the age, vocation, and learning of the Friar, lacking Beatrice's intimate personal *connaissance* of Hero, Benedick nevertheless comes to share their conviction by acknowledging their claims to interpretive and moral discernment. For even before Beatrice convicts him of his responsibility with regard to Claudio, he encourages the grieving Leonato to be guided by the Friar's advice (l. 244).

This scene from *Much Ado About Nothing* provides, even in its brevity, a remarkably comprehensive outline of a hermeneutics of love.

CONTEXTS AND
OBSTACLES

*We care whether love is or is not altogether forbidden to us,
whether we may not altogether be incapable of it, of admitting it
into our world. We wonder whether we may always go mad between the equal efforts and terrors at once of rejecting and of accepting love.*

—*Stanley Cavell* (Disowning, 72)

The Law of Love and Interpretation

When asked by a scribe to name the greatest of the commandments,
Jesus complies by citing two injunctions, one from Deuteronomy (6:5)
and one from Leviticus (19:18): "You shall love the Lord your God
with all your heart, and with all your soul, and with all your mind. This
is the great and first commandment. And a second is like it, You shall
love your neighbor as yourself" (Mt. 22:37–40, RSV). But he then goes
on to make the greater, and more startling, claim that upon these commandments "depend all the law and the prophets." That the one identified by the Christian Church as incarnate Love speaks these words
compels our closest attention to them.[1] To say that "all the law and the
prophets" "depend" upon these two commandments—or this twofold
commandment—is to say that the multitude of ordinances and exhortations in the Old Testament presuppose the love that Jesus enjoins.
No one can meet the demands of the Law who does not achieve such
love; conversely, those who achieve such love will, like the psalmist,
"delight in [God's] statutes" and find themselves "consumed with long-
ing for [God's] ordinances at all times" (Ps. 119:16, 20).

9

Moreover, since the ordinances of the law cover the whole range of human interactions with one another and with God, it follows that there can be no realm of distinctively human activity in which Jesus' great twofold commandment is not operative. As Kierkegaard says, "There are only a few acts which human language specifically and narrowly calls works of love, but heaven is such that no act can be pleasing there unless it is an act of love" (*Works* 20). And those Christians who regularly pray that God's will be done on earth as it is in heaven should hope to see, in the life of one who loves God and her neighbor, that love manifested in her work and her leisure, in her caregiving and her worship. We need not shy away from evaluating *any* everyday pursuit according to what the fourteenth-century English theologian Richard Rolle (along with many others) calls "the law of love." "That you may love [Jesus Christ] truly," says Rolle, "understand that his love is proved in three areas of your life—in your thinking, in your talking, and in your manner of working" (159). This division should be of particular interest to people engaged in academic pursuits, because our thinking (including reading) and talking (including writing) pretty much *are* our "manner of working." How might we begin to consider academic tasks in light of this "law of love"?

To consider the problem more specifically: My work, as a teacher and scholar of literature, is largely occupied with the interpretation of texts. What would interpretation governed by the law of love look like? This is a question that has all too rarely been considered; but it is raised by Augustine in his treatise *On Christian Doctrine* (*De Doctrina Christiana*). Near the end of the first book, Augustine sums up the argument he has been making by specifically linking Jesus' great double commandment with Paul's elaboration of its two facets in Romans: "It is to be understood that the plenitude and the end of the Law and of all the sacred Scriptures is the love of a Being [i.e., God] which is to be enjoyed and of a being [i.e., our neighbor] that can share that enjoyment with us" (30). He then applies this insight to the interpretation of the Scriptures for the purpose of edifying the faithful (the word *Doctrina* in this context means, primarily, "teaching"): "Whoever, therefore, thinks that he understands the divine Scriptures or any part of them in such a way that it [i.e., his interpretation] does not build the double love of God and of our neighbor does not understand [the Scriptures] at all. Whoever finds a lesson there useful to the building of charity, even though he has not said what the author may be shown to have intended in that place, has not been deceived, nor is he lying in any way."[2] This is an astonishing statement—hardly less astonishing, in its way, than the twofold commandment itself—but what does it mean? What would interpretation governed by the law of love look like? Strangely, Augustine does not say. One must presume that he sought to meet the charitable imperative in his own exegetical work, but it is surely legitimate to ask what, specifically, makes Augustine's interpretations charitable, and how they might be distinguished from uncharitable interpretations.

Moreover, Christian theology has neglected Augustine's provocative statement; there are, to my knowledge, no thorough accounts of loving interpretation. This failure is surprising, not only because so few Augustinian hints have remained untaken in the course of the centuries, but also because it seems so obvious, once Augustine points it out, that Christian interpreters—and I refer not just to interpreters of Scripture but to interpreters of any and every kind of text—are just as obliged to conduct their work according to the principles of Christian charity as any other workers. An account of the hermeneutics of love is one of the great unwritten chapters in the history of Christian theology.[3]

Though Augustine makes his suggestion about loving interpretation in the context of Biblical exegesis and exposition, I will consider other kinds of texts in the context of *agape*—as my opening treatment of Shakespeare may indicate. Of course, certain circumstances are relevant to every experience of reading; for instance, our education (in the broadest sense: *Bildung*, one might say) is always at work whenever we read. To persons who claim that their understanding of Scripture comes from God alone and not from mere humans, Augustine replies that God didn't teach them the letters of the alphabet (*On Christian Doctrine* 4). But as we consider the reading of specific kinds of texts—legal, literary, scriptural—we find varying conditions in effect. One may compare the reading of Scripture with the reading of a novel, or a legal document, and find many common hermeneutical conditions, but these different kinds of works make different kinds of claims upon their readers, and these differences must be acknowledged and understood. That said, the more important thing to note is this: The universal applicability of Jesus' twofold commandment makes Augustine's charitable imperative just as relevant to the interpretation of epic poems or national constitutions as it is to the reading of Holy Scripture. This is a point that Gerhard Ebeling almost reaches, but not quite: "A theological theory of language . . . is not relevant solely to the language of theology, that is, to the problem of formulating adequate theological concepts and judgments. The tasks of a theological theory of language of course include this, and yet it is not exclusively concerned with theological language, as a particular specialist language." So far so good: But Ebeling immediately continues, "Its principal relevance is to the language of faith. For this provides theology with its object, and poses its task" (186–187). That a "theological theory of language" should be concerned with faith as well as with theology *per se* is certainly true, indeed is unarguable. But does not theology have an interest in language even if it isn't the language of faith? Is there not a theological stake in language about money, or *eros*, or architecture? Ebeling is precisely right when he says that "the one thing that is true is love. To base a doctrine of language on this statement is to move towards a theological theory of language" (180). But only if we understand this love of God and neighbor as the first requirement in the reading of *any* text can we fulfill "the law of love" in our thinking, our talking, and our manner of working.[4]

Of course, it is not as though the Church has failed to reflect on the place of non-Christian literature in the Christian life. To the contrary, much patristic (and later) thought is thoroughly occupied with the question of how to use the poems and stories, as well as the philosophy, of the pagan world. In this sense literature is subsumed under Tertullian's famous question: "What has Athens to do with Jerusalem?"—though it was St. Jerome who shaped the question in specifically literary terms: "What has Horace to do with the Psalter? Or Virgil with the Gospel? Or Cicero with the Apostle?"[5] (Jerome's pairings are nicely genre-specific: first lyric poetry, then heroic narrative, then forensic rhetoric.) For those theologians who would utterly renounce the use of pagan literature, Jerome provides the rationale: "We should not drink at the same time from the cup of Christ and the cup of demons." But, as David Lyle Jeffrey rightly demonstrates, Jerome also, and with greater emphasis, provides a thorough justification for the reading and use of the pagan writers: He quotes Paul's assertion that "all things are clean to the clean" (Tit. 1:15) and provides a detailed account of the ways in which Christian readers can despoil the literary Egyptians of their precious gold (Jeffrey 76–78).

In practice, the chief means by which this gold was laid hold of was allegory. As Jeffrey shows, Jerome uses an allegorical interpretation of a passage from Scripture—the disturbing provision in Deuteronomy (21:10–13) that a woman taken captive in warfare may be ritually purified, shaved, and washed, and then taken as a wife—to explain how pagan literature may be made worthy of Christian use. But it was also common to employ allegorical interpretation of the pagan texts themselves in order to extract Christian meanings from them, as when Clement of Alexandria explicates the scene in the *Odyssey* in which Odysseus escapes the song of the Sirens, who are figured here as sin and error: "Sail past their music and leave it behind you, for it will bring about your death. But if you will, you can be the victor over the powers of destruction. Tied to the wood [of the cross], you shall be freed from destruction. The Logos of God will be your pilot, and the Holy Spirit [*pneuma*, wind] will bring you to anchor in the harbor of heaven."[6] A subtler version of the same tendency may be seen in Thomas Aquinas's appropriations of Aristotle, "the Philosopher," whom Thomas can often make to hold—at least by implication—specifically Christian positions. As David Knowles neatly put it, Thomas had "no hesitation in extending [Aristotle's] thought, in filling gaps within it and interpreting it in accord with Christian teaching" (257).

Such creative interpretations were often necessary, given the recurrent hostility toward pagan thought among many Christians. Thomas himself worked in a time when the works of Aristotle were almost always at risk of being placed under some local, or perhaps universal, interdict. Often, only what Jeffrey calls "an unabashedly ideological appropriation of the [pagan] text" (72) was possible. But such uses of non-Christian literature can scarcely be accommodated to what I am calling a hermeneutics of love. There are two chief reasons for this, reasons that I hope will become clear as my argument progresses.

The first is that, as my patristic quotations show, the Christian appropriation of pagan literature was understood to occur in the context of spiritual warfare: One can in good conscience spoil the Egyptians because they are the cruel enemies of the people of Israel. In Jeffrey's terms, the "secular scripture" that becomes a "beautiful captive" is a prisoner of war and, therefore, someone toward whom we do not have the obligations we have toward our neighbors. The captured pagan woman presumably is not asked whether she wants to marry. Given the uncertain cultural position of Christianity in its early centuries, this combative attitude may be comprehensible. But the hermeneutics of love requires that books and authors, however alien to the beliefs and practices of the Christian life, be understood and treated as neighbors: "*Neighbour* is what philosophers would call the *other*" (Kierkegaard, *Works* 37).

The second reason involves hermeneutical method: The allegorical approaches of the Fathers, and the "gap-filling" of Thomas, risk the erasure of difference. The function of allegory, in this context, is to isolate the gold of identity (the points at which Christian and pagan understandings can be made to converge) and to dispose of the dross of difference (all those elements that cannot be reconciled with Christian understanding). And yet, as we shall see repeatedly in this study, the preservation of difference is absolutely central to a hermeneutics of love. I am to love my neighbor *as* myself, but this is a challenge precisely because the neighbor is *not* myself. As John Milbank says, fundamental to "Christianity is . . . (in aspiration and faintly traceable actuality) something like 'the peaceful transmission of difference,' or 'differences in a continuous harmony'" (*Theology* 417); but without the preservation of difference there can be neither transmission nor harmony.

Love and Error

It will immediately be objected by some that this notion of charitable interpretation is intolerably mushy, replacing a substantive concern for objectivity, or at least accuracy and fidelity, with a warm flow of sentimentality. Much of this book will be devoted to correcting such unfortunate assumptions about the nature of love—by, for instance, showing how a genuinely Christian notion of love requires among other things a deep commitment to discriminating judgment—but for now let me just say this, by way of provocation. It is likely that those most quick to object will be theologians whose training encourages them to think of the chief task of hermeneutics as the avoidance of error. Avoiding error is a good thing, but it is probably not central to hermeneutics. As Hans-Georg Gadamer rightly says, "The legal historian . . . has his 'methods' of avoiding mistakes, and in such matters I agree entirely with the legal historian. But the hermeneutics interest of the philosopher begins precisely when error has been successfully avoided" (xxxiii).

Gadamer also provides the necessary theological context for understanding this fear of error: "Theological hermeneutics, as Dilthey showed, developed from the reformers' defense of their own understanding of Scripture against the attack of the Tridentine theologians and their appeal to the indispensability of tradition" (174). The Reformers found themselves obliged by their polemical situation to show that they could specify a set of reliable safeguards against error—safeguards which would serve a similar liminal function to the concept of "tradition" in the Roman Catholic Church—and this need to provide safeguards and eliminate error came to dominate the hermeneutical tradition for the next several centuries. The chief goal of theological hermeneutics naturally, then, comes to be associated more closely with "getting it right" than with a deepening of understanding or a growing in love. Thus theological hermeneutics inevitably becomes what Gerald Bruns—speaking specifically of Spinoza's claim to be interested not in the "truth" of the Biblical text but rather in its "meaning"—calls "Cartesian hermeneutics, or the allegory of suspicion, in which the text comes under the control of the reader as disengaged rational subject, unresponsive except to its own self-certitude. . . . The motive of Cartesian hermeneutics is to preserve alienation as a condition of freedom from the text" (149). A century and a half after Spinoza, Hegel would point out that the "demand for neutrality has generally no other meaning but that [the interpreter] is to act in expounding [the texts he interprets] as if he were dead" (quoted in Bruns 150).

Gadamer's (or rather Dilthey's) point about the historical origins of the discipline of hermeneutics helps to explain why people would make "alienation from the text" a positive good. In this context one can see more clearly why the early Reformers, though thoroughly Augustinian in so many other respects, found little use for the Augustinian emphasis on charity as the chief imperative for and most reliable guide to interpretation. Faced with claims from their Catholic counterparts that, lacking a commitment to tradition, they had no constraints upon their interpretive activity, they could scarcely appeal to a hermeneutic that shows little interest in safeguarding readers from error.

For, indeed, Augustine appears—in the passage I have been referring to, if not elsewhere—to disregard the problem of error. In order to explain his attitude toward error in *De Doctrina*, I must first note that Augustine is rather uncertain about the terminology he wishes to employ in describing the interpretive situation he envisions. In the passage quoted above, he considers a devout and faithful Christian reader who has found in Scripture a lesson that builds up charity but is not in keeping with the author's intention, and claims that not only is such a person not "lying," he or she is likewise "not deceived."[7] But in the very next section Augustine seems to reconsider his claim about deception:

> But anyone who understands in the Scriptures something other than that intended by them is deceived, although they do not lie [*illis non*

mentientibus fallitur].[8] However, as I began to explain, if he is deceived in an interpretation that builds up charity, which is the end of the commandments, he is deceived in the same way as a man who leaves a road by mistake but passes through a field to the same place toward which the road itself leads. But he is to be corrected and shown that it is more useful not to leave the road, lest the habit of deviating force him to take a crossroad or a perverse way. (31)

It is "more useful" to stick to the road of authorial intention because the would-be shortcut draws the reader into unfamiliar and potentially dangerous territory that can prevent him (for the moment we'll retain Augustine's masculine pronouns) from rejoining the main thoroughfare and reaching his desired destination. This often happens, says Augustine, in the following way. Disregarding the author's intentions, this hypothetical reader achieves an interpretation that pleases him or even seems to him to build up charity. But when he then reads in Scripture, "he may find many other passages which he cannot reconcile with his interpretation." And then this reader experiences a conflict in his will that results from his fallen nature. For when he finds passages that call his reading into question he is extremely reluctant to abandon his own interpretation, in which he takes prideful satisfaction, and "under these conditions it happens, I know not why, that, loving his own interpretation, he begins to become angrier with the Scriptures than he is with himself."

In short, Augustine contends that there is a part/whole problem here: One may disregard the intentions of the authors of Scripture and nevertheless achieve a genuinely charitable interpretation of a particular passage of Scripture; but in the long run this will not work, for, as God's purpose is one, so the meaning of the Biblical text as a whole is one. Ultimately, then, if not immediately, disregard of the intentions of the Biblical authors will lead to the failure of charity: Since we are fallen creatures, if we follow our own authority our self-love or *cupiditas* will usurp our commitment to *caritas*. If the reader "thirsts persistently for the error, he will be overcome by it." (We shall resume, later, a discussion of the problem of interpretive will.)

Perhaps, then, Augustine is actually more concerned about error than he would at first appear to be.[9] Certainly he is not claiming that the reader can simply assume an attitude of love and then sally boldly forth, like Don Quixote, to interpret Scripture without fear. But neither is he saying that one can read Scripture properly by attending only, or even chiefly, to the avoidance of error. The real argument here is that the pursuit of a thoroughgoing charitable hermeneutics is not as simple as it might seem, that such pursuit, properly understood, does not abrogate the need for attention to such matters as an author's intentions but, rather, situates them within a context or places them under the sovereignty of the law of love. In short, the determination to avoid error cannot substitute for a commitment to charitable reading, but must grow from it: One seeks to avoid error because one cannot love properly when confused or deceived. However, the avoidance of error—like attentiveness to authorial purposes—does not in itself achieve anything of intrinsic worth: It is at best propaedeutic to the task of reading lovingly. Therefore, Augustine's position is certainly congruent with Gadamer's claim that "the hermeneutic interest of the philosopher begins precisely when error has been successfully avoided," and with Bruns's insistence that the Reformers' neglect of Augustinian hermeneutics in favor of what would become "Cartesian hermeneutics" is a disastrous move (as we shall see). The important point here is that a strong emphasis on being hermeneutically "correct" tends to lose sight of the *purposes* of interpretation. Brian Stock provides a striking summary of Augustine's position: "It is not the purpose of love to generate interpretation, but vice versa" (*Augustine* 185).

Now, these considerations cannot immediately be translated into the realm of literary, or indeed any non-Biblical, scene of interpretation. For it is not at all clear that the intentions of a fallible and finite human author can in any circumstances have the same status as the intentions of a Divine, or divinely inspired, author; or, to put it another way, a text identified as sacred makes claims upon our responsive attention that texts not identified as sacred do not and (perhaps) cannot. In later chapters we will have to explore the kinds of moral obligations a reader incurs to the author of the text being interpreted, and to texts identified as belonging to different genres. But Augustine's nuanced position will be the place to begin these explorations: Repeatedly it will become evident that if we consider the purpose of interpretation to be the generation of love, we will not be deceived.

The Pleasures of Love in the Act of Reading

Other interpreters will criticize this hermeneutics of love for an almost opposite reason: Far from being concerned that it provides no safeguard against error, they fear that it turns interpretation into a drearily moralistic activity in which every text and every reading has to justify itself at the bar of a rigid criterion of charity that leaves no room for the *pleasures* of reading. I take this to be a weightier and more potent objection than the previous one, for it seems to me beyond question that modern interpretive theory has utterly lost sight of the distinctive, perhaps unique, delights of reading. This point is lent credence by the fact that critics as different as Roland Barthes and Robert Alter have, in their different ways, both proclaimed it.

Here again Augustine would seem to be a figure of particular importance, largely because of his famous distinction between *uti* and *frui*, use and enjoyment. The most concise expression of this comes also in the *De Doctrina* (Book 1, sections III–IV):

> Some things are to be enjoyed, others to be used, and there are others which are to be enjoyed and used. Those things which are to be enjoyed make us blessed. Those things which are to be used help and, as it were, sustain us as we move toward blessedness in order that we may gain and cling to those things which make us blessed. If we who enjoy and use things, being placed in the middle of things of both kinds, wish to enjoy those things which should be used, our course will be impeded and sometimes deflected, so that we are retarded in obtaining those things which are to be enjoyed, or even prevented altogether, shackled by an inferior love. (9)

As Augustine continues it becomes more clear that when we enjoy that which we should use, we are committing a kind of idolatry: "To enjoy something is to cling to it with love for its own sake."

Since we will be discussing the reading of literary texts in this book, it is particularly important to note that one of Augustine's criticisms of his education was its lack of this essential distinction between *uti* and *frui*, a lack that had great consequences for the young Augustine's reading of the *Aeneid*: "I was forced to learn all about the wanderings of a man called Aeneas, while quite oblivious of my own wanderings, and to weep for the death of Dido, because she killed herself for love, while all the time I could bear with dry eyes, O God of my life, the fact that I myself, poor wretch, was, among these things, dying far away from you" (*Confessions* I:13). This point is so striking to Augustine that he cannot refrain from repeating it several times in the same paragraph. He was encouraged by his teachers to enjoy this poem—though it was a strange sort of enjoyment, a kind of "madness," he says: "If I were forbidden to read these things, I would be sad at not being allowed to read what would make me sad."[10] But he was not taught to reflect on his reading in a way that would be useful to him: Only now, as an adult Christian, does he use his memory of his early reading experience as a tool for self-reflection and self-understanding.

A later section of *The Confessions* suggests that Augustine's schoolboy attentions to the *Aeneid* perhaps could be labeled an example of *curiositas*. This is not certain, because Augustine goes to some pains to distinguish curiosity from the desire for pleasure (*voluptas*): "Pleasure goes after what is beautiful to us, sweet to hear, to smell, to taste, to touch; but curiosity, for the sake of experiment, may go after the exact opposites of these, not in order to suffer discomfort, but simply because of the lust to find out and to know. What pleasure can there be in looking at a mangled corpse, which must excite our horror? Yet if there is one near, people flock to see it, so as to grow sad and pale at the sight" (X.35). But, though the young reader of Dido's tragedy in Book IV of the *Aeneid* may also grow "sad and pale," it is for very different reasons, since in reading such a story one experiences a distinctive kind of sadness that is also sweet: *trilce*, to use the Peruvian poet Cesar Vallejo's nonce-word (comprised of *triste*, sad, and *dulce*, sweet). This is quite unlike the horrified fascination that leads people to look upon mangled corpses.

Except in one sense. Both *curiositas* and *voluptas* are, for Augustine, versions of *cupiditas*, that is, disordered desire. Both represent a faulty attentiveness: attentiveness either to the wrong things or to potentially right things in a wrong way. Thus, whether we call Augustine's early fascination with the *Aeneid curiositas* or *voluptas*, it signifies one who has lost sight of God, who lacks *caritas*, the love of God, and who is thereby inclined to enjoy that which is properly to be used. But it is the notion of reading as *curiositas* that proves particularly fruitful, because, as Hans Blumenberg points out in his massive defense of autonomous "theoretical curiosity" in *The Legitimacy of the Modern Age*,

> in the tenth book of the *Confessions, curiositas* appears as the negative correlate of *memoria*. Only by memory can what gets lost in dispersion be grasped; memory gives man the authentic relation . . . to his origin, to his metaphysical "history," and thus to his transcendent contingency. *Memoria* and *curiositas* relate to one another like inwardness and outwardness, . . . in such a way that memory as actualization of one's essence is suppressed only by the forcefulness of the world's influence

upon one and can assert itself to the extent that this "overstimulation" can be warded off and dammed up. (315)

One sees this point perfectly dramatized in Augustine's adult reflections upon his childhood reading practices: *Then* he had been "overstimulated" by the charms of Virgil's poetry, but *now* the faculty of *memoria* enables him to reconfigure the experience and renew his understanding of his "transcendental contingency": "What indeed can be more pitiful than a wretch with no pity for himself, weeping at the death of Dido, which was caused by love for Aeneas, and not weeping at his own death, caused by lack of love for you, God, light of my heart, bread of the inner mouth of my soul, strength of my mind, and quickness of my thoughts? You I did not love" (I.13). For Wordsworth, the "spontaneous overflow of powerful emotion . . . recollected in tranquillity" produces poetry ("Preface" 297); for Augustine it produces sound judgment and, in this case, useful habits of reading.

Because of experiences such as his tearful sympathy with Dido, Augustine remains terribly fearful of curiosity, of anything that might threaten, even in the smallest way, to displace his attention to God— or, to put it another way, that might present itself as an object of enjoyment rather than usefulness. He berates himself for noting "a lizard catching flies or a spider entangling them in his web," even though he quickly moves to praise God as Creator of these beings, because God was not the first or primary reason for his attentiveness. "It is one thing to get up quickly and another thing not to fall down" (X.35).

It is hard to be sympathetic with such strictness, hard to feel that the Christian does any disservice to God by being caught up in or fascinated by the quiddity of the things of the created world. Even Jonathan Edwards, as Augustinian a thinker as one could plausibly expect to find, recorded in loving detail his observations of spiders, with a particular intent to describe the means by which certain spiders, though wingless, manage to spin webs between rather widely spaced tree branches. In his letter on this subject to a member of the Royal Society, he concluded, "I thought [this description] might at least give you occasion to make better observations on these wondrous animals . . . from whose glistening webs so much of the wisdom of the Creator shines" (7–8). This is a common, perhaps the normal, Christian view of the matter: In Milton's *Paradise Lost*, for instance, Raphael encourages Adam to attend properly to the created order, employing the favored metaphor of nature (in this case particularly the heavens) as one of God's two books:

> *To ask or search I blame thee not, for heaven*
> *Is as the book of God before thee set,*
> *Wherein to read his wondrous works, and learn*
> *His seasons, hours, or days, or months, or years: . . .*
> *And for the heaven's wide circuit, let it speak*
> *The maker's high magnificence, who built*
> *So spacious, and his line stretched out so far;*
> *That man may know he dwells not in his own;*
> *An edifice too large for him to fill,*
> *Lodged in a small partition, and the rest*
> *Ordained for uses to his Lord best known.*
> *(VIII.66–69, 100–106)*[11]

Augustine would have agreed wholly with this statement, but he would also have added a warning: If attention to God does not *precede* and *envelop* our observations of the world, then those observations are simply idolatrous. ("It is one thing to get up quickly and another thing not to fall down.") Augustine's attitude leaves little room for the observer being drawn toward God by observing the created order; his view seems timid and unhealthily trepidatious, as though the fear of idolatry was disabling him from the blessings arising from discerning perception.[12]

On the other hand, it is equally difficult for the Christian to countenance Blumenberg's legitimization of "theoretical curiosity" as an end in itself—for concrete historical reasons as well as abstractly theological ones. W. H. Auden puts the case well:

In our culture, we have all accepted the notion that the right to know is absolute and unlimited. The gossip column is one side of the medal; the cobalt bomb is the other. We are quite prepared to admit that, while food and sex are good in themselves, an uncontrolled pursuit of either is not, but it is difficult for us to believe that intellectual curiosity is a desire like any other, and to recognize that correct knowledge and truth are not identical. To apply a categorical imperative to knowing, so that, instead of asking, "What can I know?" we ask, "What, at this moment, am I meant to know?"—to entertain the possibility that the only knowledge which can be true for us is the knowledge that we can live up to—that seems to all of us crazy and almost immoral. (*Dyer's* 272)[13]

Or, one might say, the sovereignty of the "right to know" is incompatible with an insistence on our "transcendent contingency." Blumenberg fully realizes this, which is why he insists that we simultaneously choose the former and reject the latter. But do Augustine's excessive rigor and Blumenberg's bold autonomy exhaust the options for a theology of reading?

We must begin by practicing attentiveness to the *tendency* of a given work, the spiritual direction toward which it inclines, to which it directs us. If Auden's formulation is at all useful, then we must think of pleasure and curiosity alike as desires that can be healthy if properly bounded. And this, after all, is an Augustinian notion, the notion of the *ordo amoris:* There is an order or hierarchy of loves such that all things that deserve our love deserve it in proportion to their excellence: "Hence, as it seems to me, a brief and true definition of virtue is 'rightly ordered love'" (Augustine, *City* 637 [XV.32]).

Now, there are some written works that by this criterion should not give us any pleasure at all, just as there are some forms of ordinary human speech that should not give us pleasure. For instance, in Dante's *Inferno*, as the pilgrim and his guide Virgil—a choice of guide Augustine would doubtless disapprove of—visit the eighth circle of Hell, the tenth bolgia ("ditch" or "pouch") of that circle, they meet the Falsifiers. Among these sinners are a counterfeiter named Master Adam and a falsifier of words, the infamous Greek Sinon, who tricked the Trojans into allowing the fatal wooden horse into their city. Dante watches as Master Adam and Sinon fall into a bitter exchange of vituperative insult. For thirty lines of verse they snarl at one another, Dante (and we the readers) attending all the time. Then Virgil, the personification of human Reason, turns to Dante and says, "Now keep on looking a little longer and I quarrel with you." Why is he troubled? Because, as he later explains, "*Ché voler ciò udire è bassa voglia*": The very desire to listen to such bickering is itself base (Canto XXX, l. 148). Note the words *voler* and *voglia*, both of which derive from the Latin *voluntas*, will: Dante's interests themselves mark the depravity of his will, the necessary redirecting of which begins with his visit to Hell. There are certain events and actions, Virgil seems to say, to which the only proper response is to avert one's eyes and shut one's ears. There is nothing that such speech can teach us that we do not already know, and to take pleasure in such recriminations is always de-grading.

On the other hand, it is not clear that we should take no pleasure in this passage from the *Inferno*. For Virgil's explanation shows us that we have been duped: We, like the pilgrim, have been listening with rapt attention to these two damned souls curse each other, and our inter-est, we suddenly realize, has not been wholly healthy. Dante the poet has written the exchange in as vigorous a way as possible, so as to at-tract and keep our attention; but then he has Virgil offer an interpre-tation of the scene that enables us to do what Augustine's *memoria* en-abled him to do, which is to reconfigure a reading experience in order to profit, spiritually and morally, from it. Thus Dante begins by ex-ploiting our tendencies toward wrong-headed, sinful reading, but quickly provides a hermeneutical corrective to those tendencies.[14] We may now see the argument between Master Adam and Sinon in its proper context: To use yet another Augustinian contrast, our un-healthy *curiosity* (in a scene that bears some resemblance to the con-templation of a "mangled corpse") has been replaced by a healthy and useful studiousness.[15] When we revise our readings in this way, we achieve what Augustine achieved through *memoria*, as he looked back over the events of his life and reinterpreted them according to his hard-won understanding of God's purpose for his life.

A healthy studiousness is of course not pleasure. But might it be said that a certain kind of pleasure is the fruit of such studiousness? After all, it is only by adopting the appropriate hermeneutical stance that we are able truly to appreciate Dante's verbal skill, first in fashioning the curse-fest of Sinon and Master Adam and then in providing a context in which that curse-fest is transformed. In other words, the literary mastery that effects our "conversion" from curiosity to studiousness then offers itself for our pleasurable contemplation. Surely this is nei-ther unhealthy nor un-Christian, since it is only the Christian's desire to read in what one might call (following St. Paul) a spiritual rather than a carnal way that makes the pleasure available in the first place.

Note, however, that if we had to do the work of "conversion" our-selves—as Augustine felt he had to do in his determined transforma-tion of his first reading of the *Aeneid* into his mature one—the situa-tion would be very different. We might, for instance, read a work that offered to us characters like Sinon and Master Adam, engaged in their kind of mutual vituperation, that did not provide an ironizing or dis-tancing context allowing us to escape from their hateful world.

Perhaps we could wring from such a work some profitable lesson, but there should be no pleasure in it, at least not from the work itself: only satisfaction, perhaps, at successfully performing a necessary task.

But these are after all rather extreme cases. What remains to be considered, and justified, is the common pleasure we gain from reading a well-wrought lyric poem, or a well-told story, or a suspenseful play, since—for persons less rigorous than Augustine—these cannot be said to produce sin unless we pay so much attention to them that they disrupt our lives with respect to the *ordo amoris*.[16] It is tempting to settle for a strictly negative defense: A good poem does no harm. But it is important, I believe, to say more: The kind of pleasure we take in a well-crafted work of literary art is very like the pleasure we take in a well-cooked meal, in that it is something given to us by another person. It is a gift that we honor, and whose giver we honor, by receiving it with gratitude. It is not always appropriate, it is not always charitable, to take that which is offered to us in a spirit of pleasure and recreation and use it according to a rigid criterion of studious application.

I do not mean to suggest that *all* literary gifts must be accepted in the spirit in which they are given, according to criteria established by the giver. Charitable reading does not require the reader to abdicate personal responsibility in favor of authorial dictation. There are times when we are right to look a gift poem in the mouth; some gifts, as we all know, have a coercive aspect. For instance, Nietzsche claims that with *Thus Spoke Zarathustra* he "gave mankind the greatest gift that has ever been given it" (*Ecce Homo* 5). But it would not be wise simply to accept this gift on its giver's terms: At the very least the claim must be interrogated.

However, this is not to say—though many have said precisely this—that *all* gifts have such a dubious and coercive character. Some works of art are presented to us as opportunities for refreshment, recreation, and pleasure. Discernment is required to know what kind of gift one is being presented with, and in what spirit to accept it (if at all), but a universal suspicion of gifts and givers, like an indiscriminate acceptance of all gifts, constitutes an abdication of discernment in favor of a simplistic *a priorism* that smothers the spirit. Goethe once wrote in a letter that "there are three kinds of reader: one, who enjoys without judgment; a third, who judges without enjoyment; and one between them who judges as he enjoys and enjoys as he judges. This latter kind really reproduces the work of art anew" (quoted in Jauss, 36). Like all good theology, then, a theology of reading will require an emphasis on discerning judgment: But it will also find its place as part of a theology of gift and recreation. Development of these ideas will occupy much of Chapter 3.

Agape and the Other Loves

A third potential objection—and the last that I will treat here—is that I have begun my argument in a state of confusion about the nature of love. I announced that this study is to be conducted in the name of Jesus Christ, which is to say, according to a specifically Christian understanding of love; but then I immediately chose as my *exemplum* a scene from Shakespeare that gives but minimal attention to *agape*. After all, what Benedick feels for Beatrice is erotic love; what Beatrice feels for Hero is a combination of familial affection and friendship. Only the Friar could be said to be exercising charity in a specifically Christian sense. And it is not clear, or at any rate has not been clear to many commentators, that *agape* is closely related to these other forms of love, or even commensurable with them. This is an issue famously contested in the Lutheran tradition, as demonstrated most fully in Anders Nygren's *Agape and Eros*.[17]

The Lutheran tradition is of course deeply implicated in the Augustinian tradition, and we have already seen Augustine's concern that even the most trivial attention to worldly things—"a lizard catching flies or a spider entangling them in his web"—threatens to distract us from a proper devotion to God: How much more dangerous than such *curiositas*, then, are the powerful attractions of *eros*. An acute illustration of this problem may be found in George Eliot's *Adam Bede*, near the end of which the Methodist lay preacher Dinah Morris mistrusts her love for the carpenter Adam Bede precisely because she cannot reconcile it with her almost lifelong sense of calling as a preacher:

> Since my affections have been set above measure on you, I have had less peace and joy in God; I have felt as it were a division in my heart. And think how it is with me, Adam:—that life I have led is like a land I have trodden in blessedness since my childhood; and if I long for a moment to follow the voice which calls me to another land that I know not, I cannot but fear that my soul might hereafter yearn for that early blessedness which I had forsaken; and where doubt enters, there is not perfect love. . . . We are sometimes required to lay our natural, lawful affections on the altar. (554)

Note that Dinah does not believe her love for Adam, even if strong "above measure," to be intrinsically sinful: It is a "natural, lawful affection." And yet she feels that she may be called upon to forego that love for the sake of a specific calling from God, for the sake, then, of a higher love—and this not only the love of God, but the love of her neighbors, who might also be displaced by the avariciousness of *eros:* "I fear I should forget to rejoice and weep with others; nay, I fear I should forget the Divine presence, and seek no love but yours" (552). Adam's reply to these concerns is eloquent (and will prove to be important for this study in other ways):

> I don't believe your loving me could shut up your heart; it's only adding to what you've been before, not taking away from it; for it seems to me it's the same with love and happiness as with sorrow—the more we know of it the better we can feel what other people's lives are or might be, and so we shall only be more tender to 'em, and wishful to help 'em. The more knowledge a man has the better he'll do 's work; and feeling's a sort o' knowledge. (553)

In other words, Dinah's love of Adam and her love of God need not compete with one another, but can be complementary forces in the expansion of Dinah's character, the strengthening of the affections that bind our lives and our neighbors' in mutual help and regard. Conversely, were Dinah to "shut up her heart" to the love of Adam, she would be sealing off one entrance for knowledge—that is, wisdom—and this could scarcely be pleasing to God.[18]

There is no question that Adam here speaks for George Eliot herself. Before she became George Eliot, Marian Evans wrote a series of powerful articles for the *Westminster Review*, one of which (in October 1855) discussed a recent book by a Calvinist preacher in London, Dr. John Cumming.[19] In a brilliantly angry essay perhaps the angriest moment comes when Marian Evans evaluates what she thinks of as Cumming's key claim:

> Dr. Cumming's theory, as we have seen, is that actions are good or evil according as they are prompted or not prompted by an exclusive reference to the "glory of God." God, then, in Dr. Cumming's conception, is a being who has no pleasure in the exercise of love and truthfulness and justice, considered as effecting the well-being of his creatures; He has satisfaction in us only in so far as we exhaust our motives and disposi-

tions of all relation to our fellow-beings, and replace sympathy with men by anxiety for the "glory of God." (*Essays* 186)

Then follows a witty, indeed a gleefully malicious, catalogue of brave and noble deeds that in Dr. Cumming's scheme could give no pleasure to God. And one item in this list bears close affinity, not only in theme but also in language, to the dilemma of Dinah Morris, which George Eliot would delineate just three years later: "A wife is not to devote herself to her husband out of love to him and a sense of the duties implied by a close relation—she is to be a faithful wife for the glory of God; if she feels her natural affections welling up too strongly, she is to repress them; it will not do to act from natural affection—she must think of the glory of God." When Dinah Morris ultimately *does* agree to marry Adam Bede, then, she thereby repudiates any lingering hold upon her of a Cumming-like divorce between, on the one hand, the love of God and a highly generalized love of one's neighbors and, on the other hand, love for particular other people (the kind of divorce Marian Evans believed to be typical of the evangelicalism that she embraced as an adolescent and from which she felt she had been rescued by modern theology, especially the work of David Strauss and Feuerbach). Indeed, the words with which Dinah accepts Adam's proposal explicitly join, in a kind of marriage-before-the-marriage, the love of Adam and the love of God, while also claiming that the real divorce or split would arise from her refusal to marry Adam: "My soul is so knit with yours that it is but a divided life I live without you. And this moment, now you are with me, and I feel that our hearts are filled with the same love, I have a fulness of strength to bear and do our heavenly Father's will, that I had lost before" (576).

This is very beautiful, but the "Epilogue" to the novel, set seven years after the conclusion of the main narrative, reveals an interesting complication. In his wooing of Dinah, Adam had explicitly said that she need not think of marriage as an impediment to her career as a preacher (554), but now we find that she has after all ceased to preach. To be sure, this is not Adam's doing but the doing of the Methodist Conference, which in 1803 (really, not just in the novel) forbade women from preaching; however, Adam enthusiastically endorses Dinah's decision to obey the conference, rather than join another denomination and continue preaching, which Adam's brother Seth believes she should have done (583). It is not clear that devotion to God and devotion to Adam have proved utterly compatible after all. It may well be that Dinah's former quest for divine love has simply been absorbed into the concerns and affections of everyday life; that, faced with the joyful obligation to love Adam and their children, she has found less need to project a God as the ideal and source of love.

This scene is a complicated one for modern readers, because for us it pulls ideologically in two directions: Its attitude toward "the woman question" seems to conflict with its attitude toward religion. On the one hand, it could be read as a cautionary tale describing how marriage confines women and denies them the expression of their gifts and powers: Adam's repudiation of husbandly authority—"I don't put my soul above yours, as if my words was better for t' follow than your own conscience" (554)—becomes on a Foucauldian reading a kind of ruse, though perhaps not a conscious one, a subtle coercion of Dinah's inclinations and a subversion of her sense of calling. But the personal history of Marian Evans suggests another reading: In her mature theology, or rather anthropology, the whole purpose of belief in God is to enable us better to love those around us. In the previous paragraph I used the word *project*, which inevitably and rightly calls Feuerbach to mind. Marian Evans's critique of Dr. Cumming is conducted on purely Feuerbachian principles, and the closing paragraphs of her essay are almost a précis of *The Essence of Christianity*:

> The idea of God is really moral in its influence—it really cherishes all that is best and loveliest in man—only when God is contemplated as sympathizing with the pure elements of human feeling, as possessing infinitely all those attributes which we recognize to be moral in humanity. ... The idea of a God who not only sympathizes with all we feel and endure for our fellow-men, but who will pour new life into our too-languid love, and give firmness to our vacillating purpose, is an extension and multiplication of the effects produced by human sympathy. (*Essays* 187–188)

To this useful image Marian Evans contrasts Dr. Cumming's God, who, "instead of sharing and aiding our human sympathies, is directly in collision with them; who instead of strengthening the bond between man and man, by encouraging the sense that they are both alike the objects of His love and care, thrusts himself between them and forbids them to feel for each other except as they have relation to Him" (188).

Perhaps, then, the "Epilogue" to *Adam Bede* is to be read as documenting Dinah's escape from the clutches of this ugly and dangerous notion of God. If Dinah gives up preaching in order better to love her husband, children, and friends, she has simply demonstrated the moral self-sufficiency and maturity that Feuerbach and Marian Evans envision as the future of the human race. This view differs quite distinctly from that of Adam Bede himself: For Adam, the love of God and the love of others are mutually reinforcing, whereas for Marian Evans the love of God, or rather the whole notion of God, has a strictly instrumental function and can safely be abandoned when it is no longer needed as a stimulus to the love of one's fellow humans.

It seems to me that Adam's account is preferable to his creator's. I am in full agreement with (among others) Kierkegaard and Karl Barth that we must at all costs avoid the notion that there can be any genuine love that is not of and from God. Since God *is* love, that which is not of and from God cannot be love; conversely, real love always derives from the one divine Source of love. This position is easily and often misunderstood: Kierkegaard and Barth may be thought to say—like Dr. Cumming—that any love that does not invoke the Christian God as its authorizing guarantor is *ipso facto* idolatrous, a demonic counterfeit of genuine love. And of course it would be simply obtuse not to recognize what Marian Evans neglects in her article but George Eliot often depicts in her fiction, that some erotic attachments are indeed idolatrous, or ersatz: They embody (for instance) possessive desire rather than loving regard for the other. But many erotic attachments—like the attachments of family or friendship—are indeed healthy and full of regard for the other, and insofar as they embody *these* traits they draw upon the originary and sustaining love of God, even when the people involved do not know that they draw upon that primal Love. Any genuine love, no matter what we call it, is in fact a form of *agape* and thus comes from God, not from us. (Kierkegaard, like many before him, including Jeremy Taylor and Samuel Johnson, wants to contend that *agape* is fundamentally different from any of the other loves in that it is universal whereas they are preferential; but this distinction creates serious problems, as Barth demonstrates.[20])

In the prison writings of Dietrich Bonhoeffer we find the most profound, if not the clearest and most fully developed, indication that Dr. Cumming and Marian Evans provide us with false contrasts. Indeed,

Bonhoeffer's pursuit of a "this-worldly" Christianity reads like a theological exposition of Adam Bede's plea to Dinah Morris:

> God wants us to love him eternally with our whole hearts—not in such a way as to injure or weaken our earthly love, but to provide a kind of *cantus firmus* to which the other melodies of life provide the counterpoint. One of these contrapuntal themes (which have their own complete independence but are yet related to the *cantus firmus*) is earthly affection. Even in the Bible we have the Song of Songs; and really one can imagine no more ardent, passionate, sensual love than is portrayed there (see 7:6). It's a good thing that the book is in the Bible, in the face of all those who believe that the restraint of passion is Christian (where is there such restraint in the Old Testament?). Where the *cantus firmus* is clear and plain, the counterpoint can be developed to its limits. The two are "undivided and yet distinct," in the words of the Chalcedonian Definition, like Christ in his divine and human natures. May not the attraction and importance of polyphony in music consist in its being a musical reflection of this Christological fact and therefore of our *vita christiana?* (*Letters* 303)[21]

This is an astounding passage; it could take many pages to unpack. But let us simply note here that it marks a kind of inversion of Marian Evans's argument in her critique of Dr. Cumming: For her, the love of God has a purely instrumental function, and is to be measured by its usefulness in prompting the love of other people (love of whatever kind), whereas for Bonhoeffer, our love of God, and our recognition of God's love for us, is the one essential form of love: Only it liberates us to love others ever more fully and passionately. *Agape* thus justifies and enables all other loves, rather than competing with them. After all—a point so simple and obvious that it bears repeating—Jesus' commandment is twofold and implies a close connection between love of God and love of neighbor, which is what Adam emphasizes in his wooing of Dinah and what Bonhoeffer elaborates on in his letter.

In Bonhoeffer's this-worldly spirituality, any of our various human loves may be conducted under the tutelage, so to speak, of *agape*—my wife or friend or mother becomes in Kierkegaard's sense, which is the Gospel sense, also my neighbor—in which case those loves will be healthy and properly oriented. Conversely, those loves may be self-governed, in which case they will inevitably descend into some destructive counterfeit of love. Thus, when we read, we may treat a book as means for the gratification of our passions, or we may genuinely wish the best for that book (or its authors, or its characters—this is a point on which I counsel a Murdochian wise confusion).

But what makes the difference between a reading that is manipulative and selfish and one that is charitable? Though again at the risk of anticipating later arguments, it is unavoidable here to give a general or schematic answer (dry bones onto which flesh will be attached in subsequent chapters). Fundamentally, it is the reader's will that determines the moral form the reading takes: If the will is directed toward God and neighbor, it will in Augustinian terms exemplify *caritas*; if the will is directed toward the self, it will exemplify *cupiditas*. This terminology is of course Augustine's version of the Pauline distinction between living spiritually and living carnally. That one can read charitably only if one's will is guided by charity is a pretty obvious point, yet it is neglected in hermeneutical theory even more than the charitable imperative itself.

This is perhaps the time to consider the description of "charitable interpretation" offered by the philosopher Donald Davidson. But what Davidson means by charitable interpretation is very different from what Augustine means, and the distinction is, for the purposes of this study, and especially for understanding the significance of a will oriented toward charity, instructive. Davidson believes that we come to a conversation (reading being one form of conversation) with the assumption that our interlocutor speaks sensibly and intelligibly. Sometimes we end by abandoning that assumption—perhaps the person with whom we are talking turns out to be mad—but we do so with the greatest reluctance and only after striving to find some way to reconcile our interlocutor's words with what we take to be intelligible utterance. Only when our hermeneutical resourcefulness is exhausted do we, regretfully, accept unintelligibility. Note that for Davidson this "principle of charity," as he calls it, is not something we choose, or pursue, or cultivate. It's just what we do. We choose charitable interpretation only insofar as we choose to converse with people; but once we do choose to converse with people, this "charity" is immediately consequent. It is perhaps not even correct to call it something we "do," an action: It is more an environment in which we dwell. (It is, barely, possible to imagine someone who always conversed with the assumption that her interlocutors made no sense, but this would require a titanic act of will that no one could sustain over time.) In this matter Davidson's point resembles that made by Gadamer, who expresses his interest not in "what we do or what we ought to do, but [in] what happens to us over and above our wanting and doing" (Gadamer xxviii).

But this is precisely what distinguishes Davidsonian charity from Christian charity. Various Christian thinkers might characterize *agape* as the fruit of spiritual discipline, the achievement of moral labor, or the unearned gift of the Holy Spirit, but no one would say that the kind of love, of God or neighbor, that Jesus commands and Augustine endorses simply "happens to us." Rather, it is a matter of the will, and thus in the etymological sense voluntary, rather than given. How, and by what force, the will may be redirected is a matter of theological dispute, but that it requires redirection in order that we might meet Jesus' commandment is axiomatic for Christian theology. It is clear, then, that Davidson and the Christian tradition are talking about two wholly different spheres of action.

That Christian charity (as opposed to Davidsonian charity) is not a category for philosophical hermeneutics is obvious; and it is not difficult to explain why this is so. In the first place, love has no part in any scientific conception of knowledge, and there are many forms of philosophical hermeneutics that think of themselves in scientific or quasi-scientific terms. (The notion of science I have in mind here is not necessarily the relatively narrow one represented by the English word: What Bruns calls "Cartesian hermeneutics" could as well be called "scientific hermeneutics." The point remains the same even if one has in mind the broader meanings of the German word *Wissenschaft*.) But even a theorist such as Gadamer who situates his work within an Aristotelian tradition of practical understanding or *phronesis* will not include love as an element of his hermeneutical theory or practice, because neither will nor love—in any Christian sense of the terms—plays a part in the Aristotelian concept of what understanding is.[22] (This point will require further exploration in the next chapter.)

I will later claim that we may indeed love books as friends, though not quite in the neo-Aristotelian sense that Wayne Booth develops, and that that love guides our interpretations. But if our love is *only* preferential—if we select some books as the proper and worthy recipients of our love, while excluding others from that charmed circle, as is always the case with Aristotelian forms of love—it fails to achieve genuine Christian charity. Charity demands that we extend the gift of love to all books, and receive the gift of love when it is offered to us; in that sense Kierkegaard is right to contrast the preferentiality of friendship or *eros* with the expansiveness of *agape*. But (as we shall see in Chapter 3) there is no single form that either the giving or the receiving takes, and moreover there is no inconsistency in having certain favorite books while seeking to love all other books in the way appropriate to them. (This is Barth's point about the acceptability of friendship. Its ultimate source is perhaps in the Gospel of John, where we are told of the "disciple whom Jesus loved" without any implication that his particular attachment to this one man compromised his love for the other disciples.) But to read in this way requires a constant attention to an always rebellious and selfish will that wants merely to use books for gratification. We may indeed use books—it is right and proper that we do so—but we must use them in the way that Augustine counsels, which is to say, a way that recognizes their value as parts of God's world and that therefore loves them in an ordinate manner.

The Fear of Love and the Love of Death

Any notion of hermeneutics—or any other human activity—guided by love will always and inevitably meet with strong opposition. That does not mean, of course, that any opposition this particular argument receives can be attributed to the depraved natures of its readers (though authors have often been known to have recourse to such explanations). Rather, I am merely claiming that love, in any of its genuine forms, is a fearful thing. To love one's neighbor is always a risk, for whether that neighbor returns or shuns our love we will in the striving for charity reveal (to our neighbor and to ourselves) elements of our character that will not be pleasant to have revealed. Similarly, to love God means, in part, to love God's righteousness; and therefore if we wish to love God in the act of interpreting, we must be prepared to subject what we read, those who write what we read, and ourselves as readers to the authority of that righteousness. As interpreters of texts, then, we should "test the spirits" (1 John 4:1) present in what we read; but such testing will be nothing more or less than sin if we do not simultaneously offer up our own spirits to be tested, both by the works we read and by the righteousness of God that is our proper rule and standard. This is why Mikhail Bakhtin (as we shall see) insists that monological reading—reading the text in one's own voice, refusing to be put to the question by the voice of the other—is safer than dialogical reciprocity, but only because it does not risk anything in the act of reading. The reading self is preserved inviolate, but at the cost of being unable to learn anything from the reading experience. A similar point is made by Jacques Derrida: "There is always a surprise in store for the anatomy or physiology of any criticism that might think it had mastered the game, surveyed all the threads at once, deluding itself, too, in wanting to look at the text without touching it, without laying a hand on the 'object,' without risking—which is the only chance of entering the game, by getting a few fingers caught—the addition of some new thread" (*Dissemination* 63).

But what Derrida does not appear to understand (though Bakhtin does) is that our decisions about whether to enter the game are determined by our love—or lack thereof. The instinct for self-preservation that leads us to refuse the game, to look without touching, is what the philosopher Stanley Cavell, in a famous essay on *King Lear*, has called "The Avoidance of Love": It is a game in which one trades in the possibility of winning for the security of being immune to loss. This tendency—which is the key defining feature of "Cartesian hermeneutics"—marks, I would contend, a kind of hermeneutical Buddhism, since Buddhism also holds that the highest human achievement is the elimination of suffering. As Frederick Buechner has written, 'He who loves fifty has fifty woes . . . who loves none has no woe,' said the Buddha, and it is true. . . . [But] side by side with the Buddha's truth is the Gospel truth that "he who does not love remains in death" (55). The "Gospel truth" that Buechner cites (from 1 John 3:18) is no more true than the Buddha's statement, but it is a greater truth: The avoidance of love, in interpretation as in all other human activities, achieves an escape from pain only by embracing death.

An especially potent image of this fearful escapism can be found in Cervantes's great story "The Man of Glass" (or, as it is sometimes translated, "The Glass Licentiate"). Tomás Rodaja is a learned and virtuous young man, so devoted to his studies that he pays no attention when "a lady who was somewhat of a charmer and up to every trick" (153) attempts to win his love. She is so angered by his rejection of her that she administers to him a poisoned fruit, though she believes that she is "administering to him a drug that would compel him to love her" (154). Tomás is ill for a long time, and though he recovers physically, his mental faculties remain deranged: "When he appeared in good health he was still stricken with the strangest craze that ever yet had been seen. The unhappy man fancied that he was entirely made of glass, and under this delusion, whenever anyone came near him, he would utter the most piercing cries, begging and beseeching them not to come near him or they would surely break him to pieces, as he was not like other men, but was made of glass from head to foot." Faced with the terrifying claims that others can make upon the self, Tomás Rodaja finds a form of madness that evades the need to respond (whether positively or negatively) to such claims: His new fragility puts him both literally and metaphorically beyond the reach of other people.

But what is especially interesting about the licentiate's glassy state is that, according to Tomás, it also makes him preternaturally wise and discerning: "He begged them to speak to him at a distance and ask what questions they pleased, saying that he would answer them more intelligently because he was now a man of glass, and not of flesh and blood; for glass, being a subtle and delicate material, permits the soul to act through it with more efficacy and promptitude than through the body, which is heavy and earthy" (155). Most of the remainder of the story is devoted to recounting the sayings of Tomás Rodaja—in a style both humorously and suggestively reminiscent of the paratactic narratives of the Gospels—and Cervantes leaves it to the reader to decide whether Tomás has indeed acquired wisdom as a consequence of his vitreous metamorphosis. But this much is clear: If he indeed possesses such discernment, it is at the price of a complete severance from his lifeworld. In this sense Tomás is a predecessor of Swift's Gulliver, who, in imitation of the Houyhnhnms, canters whinnying about his pasture and converses with his horses, preferring them to the human society that he has come to find repulsive.

When Tomás is called to the court at Valladolid, he insists that the only way he can travel safely is to be "packed in large baskets of straw, such as those in which glass is carried" and simply carted to his destination like inanimate freight (158). He is, for all practical purposes, dead to the human realm, and thereby achieves the first desideratum of Cartesian hermeneutics. Therefore, if he speaks wisdom, it is only as a fortune cookie speaks wisdom. Conversely, an elementary principle of a hermeneutics of love is that any discernment gained by such means is not worth having: Understanding requires overcoming, as Nietzsche insisted, but above all what must be overcome is the love of death.

Interlude A:
The Illuminati

Many of Henry James's stories concern the various ways in which it is possible to be interested in a writer—or, to put it in terms amenable to this project, the ways in which attentiveness that seems loving may in fact have an altogether different character. The narrator of "The Aspern Papers" appears to be devoted to the late great poet Jeffrey Aspern; yet his lust to possess Aspern's secret letters may betray a wholly different set of motives. Similarly, Paul Overt in "The Lesson of the Master" reveres Henry St. George—but what does he revere? St. George's artistic achievement, or the financial rewards accompanying literary success? And though the narrator of "The Death of the Lion" makes himself indispensable to a dying writer, it is not clear that he does so out of genuine reverence: There are certain pleasures associated with the powers that accrue to a gatekeeper.[1]

But perhaps the most useful of these stories, for the purpose of our argument here, is "The Figure in the Carpet." The interest of this story's nameless narrator in the novelist Hugh Vereker is at first mild. He had thought Vereker "awfully clever" (*Complete* 573) but had devoted little attention to him, until he received two invitations almost simultaneously: first, to attend a party at which Vereker would be present and, second, to review Vereker's newest novel. Though the narrator does not bother to tell us what he said in his review, it was clearly written to elicit a response from an artist of some "renown." His real interest, and that of his friend George Corvick, in Vereker begins only when Vereker entrusts him with a confidence about the "little point" not just of this novel but of his entire body of work:

> "By my little point I mean—what shall I call it?—the particular thing I've written my books most *for*. . . .
>
> ". . . [T]here's an idea in my work without which I wouldn't have given a straw for the whole job. It's the finest fullest intention of the lot, and the application of it has been, I think, a triumph of patience, of ingenuity. I ought to leave that to somebody else to say; but that nobody does say it is precisely what we're talking about. It stretches, this little trick of mine, from book to book, and everything else, comparatively, plays over the surface of it. The order, the form, the texture of my books will perhaps some day constitute for the initiated a complete representation of it. So it's naturally the thing for the critic to look for. It strikes me," my visitor added, smiling, "even as the thing for the critic to find." (579)

From this point on the narrator's mild interest in Vereker blooms into compulsive fascination, as does that of his friend Corvick (who ultimately discovers the secret, or appears to). But this fascination has nothing at all to do with literature or reading as such. Vereker himself provides the terms in which it is more properly understood. At one point his face lights up when the narrator refers to his secret as "buried treasure," so the excitements of hiddenness and discovery loom fairly large here; but the still more important trope comes in the passage just quoted, when Vereker refers to the "initiated" who will see and understand. What he therefore holds out to the narrator is the possibility of becoming one of the *illuminati*, one of the adept: the possessor of a *gnosis* denied to the ordinary mortal. "The critic just isn't a plain man," Vereker says; "if he were, pray, what would he be doing in his neighbour's garden? You're anything but a plain man yourself, and the very *raison d'être* of you all is that you're little demons of subtlety" (580). The Gnostic can but consider this a wholly complimentary remark.

This unbridled desire for initiation into mystery comes to dominate the lives of the narrator and his friend. That the mystery is textually encoded means nothing; that it is a mystery, one that no one has penetrated, means everything. Vereker himself is insignificant except as the holder of the keys: Though the narrator finds him likable enough, he inspires neither personal nor artistic veneration.

One of the purposes of James's story is to interrogate the character of the critic, that little "demon of subtlety"—the critic as opposed to the reader, in George Steiner's polarity. "The critic functions at a certain distance," says Steiner ("Critic/Reader" 77), and needs to, because "the distances between himself and the text are of themselves fertile and problematical" (67). One could say, reverting to James's story, that the excitement of potential initiation rises as one perceives the achievement of initiation to be difficult—that is, not an option for the "plain man." The distance between the postulant and the mystery is indeed fertile precisely because it is problematical.

The reader, on the other hand, says Steiner, will seek what he or she knows to be a partial and always incomplete "negation of distance" (89), will at once absorb and be absorbed by the text. Steiner is not oblivious to the uses of a properly conducted criticism, but he doesn't think criticism is often properly done and believes that, as compared to proliferating critics, readers are always in short supply. The critic is a professional "epistemologist" (67), whereas the reader is, as Steiner says in another context, an "amateur" in the etymological sense, a lover of the work (*Real* 11). Readers may love; critics care nothing for love, desiring instead to be among the Few initiated into mysteries which for the Many will be ever inaccessible.

In "The Figure in the Carpet," those who know the secret die, it would appear, without passing it on. George Corvick, the narrator's friend who first discovers the "buried treasure," dies; then Vereker himself; then Gwendolyn Erme, a novelist who had married Corvick and (after Corvick's demise) another writer named Drayton Deane. At last only Deane himself is left as a possible initiate into the mystery from which the narrator is excluded: "Therefore from [Deane] I could never remove my eyes," the narrator says (605). Did Gwendolyn tell him? Or did she deem him too pedestrian a mind to be worthy of the secret? At length the narrator faces Deane, inquires, and discovers that he knows nothing. Here is the last paragraph of the story:

> I drew him to a sofa, I lighted another cigarette and, beginning with the anecdote of Vereker's one descent from the clouds, I gave him an account of the extraordinary chain of accidents that had in spite of it kept me till that hour in the dark. I told him in a word just what I've written out here. He listened with deepening attention, and I became aware, to my surprise, by his ejaculations, by his questions, that he would have been after all not unworthy to be trusted by his wife. So abrupt an

experience of her want of trust had an agitating effect on him; but I saw that immediate shock throb away little by little and then gather again into waves of wonder and curiosity—waves that promised, I could perfectly judge, to break in the end with the fury of my own highest tides. I may say that to-day as victims of unappeased desire there isn't a pin to choose between us. The poor man's state is almost my consolation; there are really moments when I feel it to be almost my revenge. (608)[2]

One thinks in this context of Frank Kermode's *The Genesis of Secrecy*, that finely nuanced study of interpretation as an activity for "those outside," the uninitiated, the unenlightened. Faced with the prospect of living out his life as one of "those outside," James's narrator finds satisfaction ("revenge") only in seducing someone else into his miserable condition. In this account, it is wholly insufficient that Deane be an outsider to the secret: He must also *know* himself to be an outsider, he must share with the narrator the condition not of ignorance but of "unappeased desire." In James's picture, then, "misery loves company" becomes the watchword of criticism, the categorical imperative of hermeneutics; and it is hard to tell what predominates in James's attitude toward these outsiders, pity or contempt.

To Kermode, as an interpreter rather than an artistic maker, the situation looks rather different. He is troubled and fascinated by Jesus' really quite shocking explanation of why he taught in parables: To his disciples he said, "To you has been given the secret of the kingdom of God, but for those outside everything is in parables; so that they may indeed see but not perceive, and may indeed hear but not understand; lest they should turn again, and be forgiven" (Mark 4:11–12 RSV). Kermode's account of Christian attempts to explain away this harshness—or, failing that, to declare the whole passage corrupt—is scathing. His preference is to face the story squarely, and to recognize in it a "formula of exclusion" (28): "Mark is a strong witness to the enigmatic and exclusive character of narrative, to its property of banishing interpreters from its secret places" (34). Jesus' strange words, on Kermode's account, tell us that there can be no end to interpretation; and therefore when Kermode dedicates his book "to those outside" he is dedicating it to all of us.

An account of interpretation like this makes nonsense of James's story, because "The Figure in the Carpet" assumes an epistemological environment in which there is indeed a figure in that carpet that some, but only some, observers are acute or lucky enough to identify. It also makes nonsense of Jesus' distinction between his understanding disciples and the uncomprehending ones who do not follow him. But for that very reason the account leaves us nothing to say about interpretation save that we all do it and we all remain outside the texts we wish we could know from the inside.

If, on the other hand, we retain in some form the distinction between insiders and outsiders—or, to put it in a less tendentious way, those who have relatively more and those who have relatively less comprehension of a spoken or written utterance—we are, or should be, led by Jesus' words to a question: What is the difference between those who understand and those who don't? It is significant in this regard that Matthew's version of Jesus' explanation is slightly different: "This is why I speak to them in parables, *because* seeing they do not see, and hearing they do not . . . understand" (Mt. 13:13 RSV, emphasis added). Kermode takes it for granted that this is Matthew's flinching from the harshness of the Jesus he inherited from Mark, but it may also be possible for Matthew's version to offer us another take on the passage from Mark. Why are the outsiders outside? Could it be possible that they bear some responsibility for their failure to understand? The narrator of "The Figure in the Carpet" does not know how Corvick found the secret he couldn't find—but then he wouldn't, would he? Perhaps Corvick ultimately developed an interest in something other than merely knowing secrets, merely being initiated into a mystery. Perhaps our narrator wants the epistemological benefits of illumination without the ethical commitments requisite to it.

Genuinely charitable reading will wish to expand its scope, in a generous reversal of James's narrator's hope to initiate Drayton Deane into his parodic mystery cult for "victims of unappeased desire": Charity seeks to produce a banquet to which all are invited, a feast from which none will depart unfulfilled. However, it must also be said that while charity can be extended, its reception cannot be compelled; and those who wish to eat from the banquet without knowing the host may remain ever discontented.

LOVE AND KNOWLEDGE

> *The more, then, the thing is known, yet not fully known, the more the mind desires to know concerning it what remains to be known. . . . He then who with ardent carefulness seeks to know this, and inflamed by studious zeal perseveres in the search; can such a one be said to be without love? What then does he love? For certainly nothing can be loved unless it is known.*
>
> —*Augustine*, **On the Trinity** *(X.1)*

In *Love's Knowledge* and elsewhere, Martha Nussbaum uses the fiction of Proust, Henry James, Dickens, and others to buttress her claim that emotion should not be set in opposition to reason—that, in fact, a truly rational person will experience certain emotions as the consequence of proper understanding. Moreover, Nussbaum argues, there are some kinds of knowledge that are accessible to us when and only when we experience certain emotions, for example, love. As we have heard Adam Bede say, "The more knowledge a man has the better he'll do 's work; and feeling's a sort o' knowledge" (Eliot, *Adam* 553). There is, then, a reciprocal relationship between love and knowledge: We love people because of what we know about them, to be sure, but we also come to know them more fully because we love them. Certain kinds of knowledge of people (*connaître* rather than *savoir*)—are available only to those who love them. This is perhaps the chief lesson to be learned from attending to the passage from *Much Ado About Nothing* that was featured in my Prelude. (Thus Nussbaum's work is scarcely original on this point; but it does explore the insight in philosophical terms that are amenable to hermeneutical and philosophical reflection. We will find it continually useful.)

The relation of love and knowledge is also the theme of Plato's *Symposium*, but that work, too, is a debate about the *form* of love that produces knowledge. This is the subject of Nussbaum's brilliant analysis in her book *The Fragility of Goodness* (ch. 6). To the conventionally trained philosopher, the sudden appearance of the drunken Athenian general Alcibiades just after Socrates finishes his speech seems to be little more than a way, perhaps a rather clumsy way, for Plato to bring the dialogue to an end. Indeed, in G. M. A. Grube's classic commentary, *Plato's Thought*—as in a number of other accounts—a detailed summary of the *Symposium* ends with Socrates' argument; one would never learn from Grube that Alcibiades had entered at all.

But why would Plato, who as a writer obviously knows what he is doing, use such an awkward contrivance to end his dialogue? And stranger still, why would he allow Alcibiades to go on for several pages in a rambling confession of his love for Socrates? Nussbaum contends that the speech of Alcibiades enacts a refutation of the speech that Socrates has just completed. For Socrates, true love is a matter of ascent (this is the famous *scala amoris*) from the physical and individual to the spiritual and universal: The purest love is love of the Forms, or of Being itself; love in its highest and best sense is undifferentiated and abstract. But for Alcibiades it is senseless to speak of love-in-general: The only way to talk meaningfully about love is to celebrate the particular person whom one loves, and in his case that's Socrates. "Feeling's a sort o' knowledge," especially feeling for one individual.

Plato, then—this is the heart of Nussbaum's argument—presents us with a "harsh and alarming" picture of love: "We see two kinds of value, two kinds of knowledge; and we see that we must choose. One sort of understanding blocks out the other. The pure light of the eternal form eclipses, or is eclipsed by, the flickering lightning of the . . . unstably moving body" (*Fragility* 198). The traditional philosophical interpreters of Plato, like Grube, do not see the choice because their disciplinary training has already eclipsed one of the possibilities.

Nussbaum, as can be seen in the passage from *Love's Knowledge* that I quote in my Prelude, explicitly identifies her position with the ethical thought of Aristotle—and, similarly, links Alcibiades' speech in the *Symposium* with the positions Aristotle would later articulate (365). And yet I have claimed, in Chapter 1, that nothing resembling a

Christian picture of love can be found in Aristotle. These statements require some reconciliatory exposition, so that Nussbaum's valuable insights can be appropriated by Christian theological discourse.

Love in the Christian sense is missing from the Aristotelian picture of understanding largely because Aristotle did not have available to him a Pauline-Augustinian concept of *will*. Alasdair MacIntyre explains very clearly and convincingly the way in which Augustine brings the notion of the will into philosophical discourse. One of the fundamental problems for any understanding of ethics is, according to MacIntyre,

> how someone who knows what is best for him or her to do, but nonetheless does not act accordingly, is to be explained. Within the framework successively sophisticated by Socrates, Plato, and Aristotle such failure must be explicable . . . *either* by some imperfection in that particular person's knowledge at that particular time of what is good and best *or* by some imperfection in the education and disciplining of the passions. There is no third possibility. (*Whose* 156)

It was Augustine's distinctive contribution to draw on Pauline theology and make a third possibility available for philosophical reflection: "Augustine held that it is possible for someone to know unqualifiedly what is best to do in a particular situation and for there to be no defect in the passions as such, except that they are misdirected by the will." Augustine understood both reason and passion to be subject to a moving force external to them, but it is particularly important, when contrasting Augustine to his Athenian predecessors, to emphasize the dependence of reason upon will:

> For both Plato and Aristotle reason is independently motivating; it has its own ends and it inclines those who possess it toward them, even if it is also necessary that the higher desires be educated into rationality and that the bodily appetites be subordinated to it. For Augustine intellect itself needs to be moved to activity by will. It is will which guides attention in one direction rather than another.[1]

For Augustine, moreover, the will is governed by what it loves: Love determines will, and will in turn (to extrapolate to our present concern) governs interpretation. This is a wholly un-Aristotelian picture, and therefore one who wishes to develop a hermeneutics of Christian love will have to part company (however reluctantly) with Gadamer and other Aristotelian hermeneutical thinkers, just as he or she will have to part company with those who would contend for a scientifically rationalized hermeneutics.

Let us return again to Nussbaum's claim that love is productive of knowledge. If she is right, then Gadamer is to be faulted for his failure to recognize this relationship: He correctly understands hermeneutics to require the exercise of Aristotelian practical rationality, but neglects to explain that practical rationality draws upon the epistemologically enabling powers of love. And I think that Nussbaum is right in this, though if we look at her most thorough exploration of this theme—the detailed reading in *The Fragility of Goodness* of Aristotle's view of friendship (*philia*), as articulated in the *Nicomachean Ethics* (henceforth simply the *Ethics*)—we will see that she is more explicit on these points than Aristotle is. That is to say, Nussbaum justifies her argument in part by appealing to the authority of Aristotle, but it is not clear that Aristotle understands and accounts for the role of love and will any more than Gadamer does. Gadamer may be more Aristotelian than Nussbaum, but Nussbaum is more correct on this point than Gadamer.

In the passage from *Love's Knowledge* that I quoted in my Prelude, Nussbaum uses a footnote to refer us to her *Fragility of Goodness*, implying that there we will find a defense of the claim that love is productive of knowledge. But what we really find is a detailed exposition of the claim that *philia* (usually if inadequately translated as "friendship"[2]) is productive of *eudaimonia*, "happiness" or "human flourishing." There actually isn't much in either the *Ethics* or in Nussbaum's reading of it that links love with knowledge as such. There is a little bit, though, as when Nussbaum explores Aristotle's view of how "people who love one another's character have a strong influence over one another's moral development" (*Fragility* 362). In Nussbaum's reading of Aristotle (*Ethics* 1172a), this happens in three ways:

1. "The first and most direct mechanism is that of advice and correction."
2. "The second mechanism is the leveling or assimilating influence of shared activity: if the person you love loves and values a certain pursuit, you will be inclined to try to spend time sharing in that."

3. "The third and final mechanism is one of emulation and imitation. The strong emotions of respect and esteem that are part of Aristotelian *philia* generate a desire to be more *like* the other person." (*Fragility* 363)

Certainly in each case knowledge of some kind—and not only knowledge of the moral life—is being imparted. Presumably, given Aristotle's emphasis on mutuality, each friend is learning from the other, though about different things, since we don't have precisely the same gifts and interests.

This is all wise and useful; but the question we must ask here is, Will everyone take Aristotle's good advice and seek to cultivate friendships of this kind? Sometimes Aristotle appears to say yes: "Nobody would choose to live without friends even if he had all the other good things" (1155a); "nobody would choose to have all the good things in the world by himself, because man is a social creature and naturally constituted to live in company" (1169b). But of course Aristotle is moved to say these things because he is aware of a strong tradition in the Platonic dialogues to define the perfectly happy (*makarios*) person, the flourishing person (the *eudaimon*), as "self-sufficient" (*auto kath' auto*). For Aristotle this view, as one can tell from the passages just quoted, is simply mistaken: Much of the ninth book of the *Ethics* is devoted to correcting that mistake. And Nussbaum, with considerable force, agrees: The great theme of *The Fragility of Goodness* is the moral, the *human*, gain to be achieved by understanding that *eudaimonia* requires not self-sufficiency but the recognition that each of us needs others for enrichment and completion. In the *Symposium*, this need is one of the key themes of Alcibiades' eloquent confession of love for Socrates—who, after all, is unlike Alcibiades in almost every way.

Supposing we agree—as we should—with Alcibiades, Aristotle, and Nussbaum on the value of relational goods, we still have another question to answer: Is there anything else, other than the mistaken view that self-sufficiency is possible and desirable, that prevents people from understanding that *philia* is necessary for *eudamonia*? Certainly, in Aristotle's picture, incontinent passions can stand in the way: For instance, people who love themselves in the wrong way or in the wrong degree will not understand why or how to cultivate friendships (1168b–1169b). But, to return to MacIntyre's general characterization of ancient ethical theories, if the reason is properly instructed and the passions are properly disciplined, then anyone confronted with the possibility of *philia* will certainly take advantage of it. The only real question—and this is a point that Nussbaum makes much of (*Fragility* 359–361)—is whether a given person will be *lucky* enough to find a true friend at a time in his or her life when circumstances allow for the development of the relationship.

At this point a theological appropriation of the Aristotelian picture must begin to distance itself from the ideas I have been explicating. For the Christian, especially the Augustinian Christian, what Aristotle and Nussbaum provide is simply an inadequate account of the barriers to friendship. We are prone to sin, and sin disables the instinct for friendship in any number of ways: We may be too proud to admit our dependence on others; we may want others to be dependent on us; we may enjoy the superiority of hearing confessions from others without revealing anything of ourselves; we may wish to conserve our free time so that we might devote it to various recreational pleasures rather than to the labor that is always involved, even if it is pleasant labor, in developing a friendship. In general, the Christian account of the disorder of the will means that we are always tempted to seek self-gratification in ways that are actually detrimental to the achievement of *eudaimonia*. The necessary mutuality of real friendship runs against that universal human tendency which George McDonald (in a phrase much loved by C. S. Lewis) called "the first principle of Hell": "I am my own."[3] The will must be rightly oriented—love must be rightly ordered, as Augustine puts it—so that we may practice the virtues necessary to acquire the knowledge that comes only from love.

In other respects, too, the Christian understanding of relational goods generally, and of the links between love and knowledge in particular, must distinguish itself from the Aristotelian understanding. For instance, though the Christian will agree with the Aristotelian that these goods may properly and successfully be pursued only within a well-ordered community—that the practice of necessary virtues I just mentioned requires a social framework that enables this practice—the *polis* and the *ekklesia* are very different sorts of communities. In Aristotle's *polis*, friendship—with all its attendant blessings—is an aristocratic virtue accessible only to those who are freed, by the labor of others, for its pursuit. Since such leisure is possible only for the few, friendship is possible only for the few. The Christian Church, by contrast, need not suspect the partiality of friendship, but it is not concerned with developing such relationships; rather, it is bound to weave a web of mutuality for everyone who participates in the community.

Whereas Aristotle's aristocrats seek out friends whose strengths complement their strengths—so that they help one another grow in power and excellence—Christians share one another's weaknesses and seek to serve one another: Thus we are told not only to "rejoice with those who rejoice" but also to "weep with those who weep" (Rom. 12:15). This commandment enforces a total anti-Stoicism, which is important because there is something implicitly Stoic in Aristotle's whole picture of virtue, concerned as it is with the acquisition and retention of strengths, of powers. This is the difference of the Christian Church: *Agape* rather than *philia* is the love that produces knowledge.

As John Milbank has convincingly argued, this difference may require a fundamental reconfiguration of the whole notion of virtue. It is not just that Christians will sometimes practice different virtues than Aristotelians, or that they will practice the same virtues in different ways, but that the very notion of virtue itself (*arete*) may not be commensurable with a properly Christian theological anthropology. Milbank's central point is that the sovereign Christian virtue is charity—an idea certainly essential to my argument—and that charity is simply not configurable according to any definition of *arete*. It is a "non-heroic" virtue, Milbank says, which is "almost a contradiction in terms" (*Theology* 331). "In a way, the virtue that is charity is *not* virtue in the antique sense, because the very formality of *arete* and *virtus* is itself permeated by the content of preferred virtues, which are mainly of a heroic kind, and therefore ultimately related to victory in some sort of conflict" (332). These antique conceptions of virtue are intrinsically violent: "The word *arete* is always the standard of a victory"—victory, as we have seen, over ignorance or passion—"and while conquest puts an end to war, it requires a preceding war, and only ends war by war" (363). But charity cannot be described in these terms, which raises the decisive question: "Is virtue that is in *no sense* fundamentally a victory, still virtue at all?" (332)

Milbank goes on to say that "the point is arguable," but the force of his exposition places the burden of proof on those who would reconcile antique and Christian concepts of virtue.[4] It may be that the Aristotelian and neo-Aristotelian concepts of virtue, of relational goods, and of the links between love and knowledge, have taken us as far as they can take us. In formulating a fully Christian understanding of "love's knowledge," we may need to draw on other resources.

Long before it was thought that a defense of Christianity could be given on "objective" or "rational" grounds, fully comprehensible by any rational person whether that person were experienced in the practices of the Christian faith or not, the early Church recognized that the Christian life was something explicable only to those who participated in the life of the Church. Robert Wilken cites Origen of Alexandria on this point:

> Commenting on John 8:19—"You know neither me nor my Father. If you knew me, you would know my Father also"—Origen explains how the term "know" is used in John and in the Bible as a whole. "One should take note," he says, "that the Scripture says that those who are united to something or participate in something are said to *know* that to which they are united or in which they participate. Before such union and fellowship, even if they understand the reasons given for something, they do not know it." (*Remembering* 58–59)[5]

And Wilken goes on to say, "No doubt this is one reason why the knowledge of God is always conjoined with the love of God in early Christian literature." It is love that both prompts the knowledge of intimate union and flows from it. One might say, using Cardinal Newman's terms, that without love one may achieve "notional" assent to some proposition but remain disabled from any "real" assent to the proposition's truth (*Essay*, ch. 4). And the achievement of real assent may require participation in a practice; in other words, what Peter Brown (referring to a theme in the sermons of Augustine) calls "the healing process by which love and knowledge are reintegrated" (374) may be accessible only to people who are living in certain communal structures provided by the Church—just as the virtue of friendship requires for its cultivation a properly functioning *polis*.

Any way you look at it, this is a daunting point. If Milbank is right it is probably inconsistent for me to consider the relationship between reading and charity in nonpolitical and nonecclesial terms, but I don't see a plausible alternative. Though I am also convinced by Milbank's argument that "charity has to be a *tradition*" (*Theology* 416)—which in his terms means an ecclesial tradition and in any case an endeavor that encompasses many people and much time—one jumps in where one can. The making of a healthily functioning Christian community and a vibrant tradition of charity are beyond the scope of this book—or any book—and though the achievement of charitable interpretation may be achievable only within the Church, it can to some degree be intelligibly described. And the figure who is most useful to Christians in the elucidation of this point is, strange to say, one who is better known for a Davidsonian or Gadamerian emphasis on the hermeneutical conditions that exist "over and above our wanting and doing": Mikhail Bakhtin.

It is true that the constant emphasis of Bakhtin's career lies upon dialogism as *the* form of consciousness: Each human mind is heteroglot, composed of multiple, overlapping, and often contradictory voices of others.[6] Bakhtin notes that we speak of monologues and monological thinking, but in the strict sense they cannot exist. Yet we *do* speak of monologue, and we do so because monologism is a potential ethical stance, if not a possible epistemological condition. Again and again in his work Bakhtin moves freely from the epistemological to the ethical, the descriptive to the prescriptive. See (this is but one example among a multitude) his critique of the "human sciences":

> The exact sciences constitute a monologic form of knowledge: the intellect contemplates a *thing* and expounds upon it. There is only one subject here—cognizing (contemplating) and speaking (expounding). In opposition to the subject there is only a *voiceless thing*. Any object of knowledge (including man) can be perceived and cognized as a thing. But a subject as such cannot be perceived and studied as a thing, for as a subject it cannot, while remaining a subject, become voiceless, and, consequently, cognition of it can only be *dialogic*. (*Speech* 161)

Here we see Bakhtin treating simultaneously of that which is epistemologically necessary ("it cannot, while remaining a subject, become voiceless") and that which is the object of willed ethical choice ("[man] can be perceived and cognized as a thing"). Similar arguments recur throughout Bakhtin's work. But that such hermeneutical choices involve the love of others, or the failure to love them—this is a point that finds clear expression only in the early Bakhtin, in his fragmentary *Toward a Philosophy of the Act* and "Author and Hero in Aesthetic Activity" (though, as we shall see, it makes a less overt reappearance late in his career). Indeed, these incomplete works, though they make no reference whatever to Augustine, provide the best unfolding we have of the gnomic and cryptic Augustinian injunction to interpret lovingly. Bakhtin suggests the outline of a truly charitable hermeneutics that helps to bridge the chasm between the Aristotelian notions I have been sketching and the distinctively Christian concerns raised by Milbank.

I do not simply mean to say that Bakhtin's early philosophical thought is specifically Christian—though certain elements of it, as we shall see, may well be. I am sensitive to the validity of the charge Gary Saul Morson and Caryl Emerson have brought against Katerina Clark and Michael Holquist—namely, that they tend to see Bakhtin's philosophy as "disguised theology" even when there is no compelling reason to do so (Morson and Emerson 111–114). Similarly, Alexandar Mihailovic explores Bakhtin's constant reliance on the language and some of the conceptual apparatus of Christian theology—especially the Chalcedonian christological formulation—but is properly circumspect about drawing conclusions from that reliance: "A certain irony underlies Bakhtin's use of christology. Even allowing for the discretion needed in devotional matters during the Soviet period, he appears to be inordinately interested in its imagery and metaphors, perhaps even at the expense of its substance or status as credo" (43). Indeed, by taking theological concepts originally used in describing the nature(s) of the unique God-man, Jesus Christ, and applying them to ordinary human beings, Bakhtin is surely "playing noncanonical variations on christological themes" (24).

But there is another way to think about the theological significance of Bakhtin's work. It may represent neither the coded inscription of theology proper nor the excavation of a theological mine for nuggets of metaphor but, rather, the articulation of a philosophy of discourse that is not *necessarily* Christian but fully compatible with Christian theology. Moreover, it may be that Bakhtin's early account of interpretation both reinforces and is reinforced by Christian theology—in other words, that Bakhtin's charitable hermeneutics is justified by an appeal to the key convictions of the Christian faith, whereas, conversely, those convictions may best be put into hermeneutical practice by Bakhtin's prescriptions. The remainder of this chapter will be guided by such conjectures.

For the early Bakhtin, the initial trait of charitable hermeneutics is *attentiveness*. Nothing can compensate for a failure to attend to what is being indicated. Recall that, in the scene from *Much Ado About Nothing* with which I began this book, the Friar speaks of what he has learned "by noting of the lady"; more than one critic has linked this word "noting"—which appears elsewhere in the play—with the title: much ado about noting, "marking" (as the Friar also says), attending. Claudio and the Prince are insufficiently attentive to what they see; they perceive, but abdicate the responsibility of scrutinizing their perceptions, and they fail in this way because they are not motivated by love. Bakhtin says, "The valued manifoldness of Being as human (as correlated with the human being) can present itself only to loving contemplation. . . . Lovelessness, indifference, will never be able to generate sufficient attention to slow down and *linger intently* over an object, to hold and sculpt every detail and particular in it, however minute" (*Toward* 64).[7] An indifferent reading, then, will neglect particulars, will be content to acquire a general or (as Bakhtin puts it) a "schematized" overview of the work or the person. And the particulars it does happen to pick up will remain fragmented, disconnected from one another: "An indifferent or hostile reaction . . . always . . . impoverishes and decomposes its object."

(The claim that hostility can disable understanding, though important, must be clearly distinguished from the far more radical claim that love can enable understanding. In the Enlightenment's epistemological paradigm, hostility endangers knowledge because it is an unmastered passion: Thus Edward Gibbon's insistence that "the enemies of a religion never know it, because they hate it, and often they hate it because they do not know it" (quoted in Gay 210). But Gibbon would never say that the lovers of a religion know it because they love it. Love, too, would be a passion that had to be mastered before knowledge could be achieved. Bakhtin's view is very different; and it may well be that what Gibbon would call "disinterest"—he would not have said "objectivity," which is a nineteenth-century coinage—Bakhtin would call "indifference.")

Thus lovelessness fails to account either for plurality or unity, whereas loving attention always recognizes the "manifoldness"—that is, the irreducibly complex wholeness of a work (or a person, or an event)—that Bakhtin would much later in his career call its "open unity" or "open totality" (*Speech* 6, 7). One thinks also of Stephen Crites's shrewd comment about Augustine: "Augustine is a thinker for whom awe and close analysis are intensified together" (73)—awe being an encounter with something or someone in which one is fully aware of incomprehension. Loving contemplation, then, is best described through specifying what it does *not* do: It neither circumscribes a work within rigid boundaries, ignoring all elements of the work that cannot be assimilated to a presupposed theoretical schema, nor does it enumerate a mere chaos of details. Both positions exemplify what Morson and Emerson call "semiotic totalitarianism" (28), because both claim to be able to say all there is to say about the object of their attention: Either there is a definitive code that explains all, or there is an utter absence of pattern that is equally definitive and therefore equally omnipotent in its explanatory power. "Art and life are not one," Bakhtin writes in the early essay "Art and Answerability": "Semiotic totalitarianism" is the attempt to impose from "outside," by means of "authoritative discourse" (Bakhtin, *Dialogic* 342ff), a false oneness. Conversely, to acquiesce in the entropic and fissiparous rupturing of art and life into a chaotic "weightlessness" is a failure of responsibility: "Art and life are not one, but they must become united in me, in the unity of my responsibility" (*Art* 2). Through the assumption of the responsibility that is "assigned" to us (see Mihailovic 74), we ensure that words take on their proper weight: In the responsible or answerable consciousness, words have substantial heft but are mobile and usable. To use terms Bakhtin would have favored in the 1930s when he was working on the essays now collected in *The Dialogic Imagination*, loving contemplation keeps centrifugal and centripetal forces in balance with one another (*Dialogic* 272–273; see also Morson and Emerson 30).

But what, specifically, makes this kind of attention a *loving* attention? After all, one can be attentive for reasons other than love: No reader is more attentive than Jacques Derrida, and yet, as Geoffrey Bennington has pointed out, Derrida's scrupulous care may be understood either as humble studiousness or "immodesty itself."[8] Indeed, there is something ambiguous and potentially disturbing about all close attention: Celebrities love to have dedicated fans, but they dread the fan who becomes obsessed—fulfilling the etymology of the word "fan" (= fanatic)—and turns into a stalker. The malevolence of attention is one of the myths of our age, and a familiar literary theme as well, having its origins perhaps in the second part of *Don Quixote* and its apotheosis (as we shall see) in Nabokov's *Pale Fire*. This complication makes it rather frustrating that Bakhtin does not explicitly distinguish loving from unloving attention. Still, the attentive—not to say overly or improperly attentive—reader may discern a fairly clear picture emerging from Bakhtin's early works. This picture may profitably be contrasted with that of another thinker, Simone Weil, who stands as an exemplar of certain potent traditions regarding love and ethics that Bakhtin sometimes rejoins and sometimes rejects.

In a lecture for schoolchildren on the spiritual value of academic work, Weil claims that the habit of attending to anything aids the cultivation of the discipline of prayer. Moreover, she continues, with her characteristic emphasis on those who suffer,

> [n]ot only does the love of God have attention for its substance; the love of our neighbor, which we know [through Christ's answer to the scribe's question] to be the same love, is made of this same substance. Those who are unhappy have no need for anything in this world but people capable of giving them their attention. . . .
>
> The love of our neighbor in all its fullness simply means being able to say to him: "What are you going through?" It is a recognition that the sufferer exists, not only as a unit in a collection, or a specimen from the social category labeled "unfortunate," but as a man, exactly like us, who was one day stamped with a special mark by affliction. For this reason it is enough, but it is indispensable, to know how to look at him in a certain way.
>
> This way of looking is first of all attentive. (114–115)[9]

Weil echoes Bakhtin's rejection of the schematic in her identification of the dangers of categories; moreover, her emphasis on attention as a way of *looking* at someone rejoins the relentlessly visual language of *Toward a Philosophy of the Act* and its companion text, "Author and Hero in Aesthetic Activity" (*Art* 4–256).[10] Indeed, Weil may fairly be said to represent a main current in Christian (and Jewish) tradition about how to love one's neighbor. But in some quite important respects Bakhtin's view differs from Weil's and from this main current of Christian thought, and these differences are notably instructive if we wish to understand the potential theological significance of Bakhtin's charitable hermeneutics.

First of all, though Weil discounts certain schematic categories, she retains one: the notion of "man," or human being. We should see the other as a human being, "exactly like us." It is interesting how absent the notion of a common or universal humanity is from Bakhtin's work, early and late—not that he rejects it explicitly but, rather, that he doesn't seem to think it does much useful work. One reason for his skepticism is that to invoke a general category ("humanity") as a justification for an ethical action is to abstract oneself out of the particular, unique moment of ethical decision, and for Bakhtin this distancing abstraction is ethically disastrous. As Mihailovic notes, for Bakhtin "such hackneyed abstractions as 'humanity' or 'man' have little resonance for the incarnated consciousness; for such a person, the distinc-

tion between *I* and *Other* is far more important than such generalities"
(59–60). Let us recall at this point Kierkegaard's insistence that
"[n]eighbour is what philosophers would call the *other*" (*Works* 37).

Bakhtin would hold to this position throughout his career, but his
implicit critique of a generalized ethical humanism can best be understood through a passage in the revised version of his book on Dostoevsky. He refers to a passage in *The Brothers Karamazov* in which
Alyosha, who has just tried without success to give two hundred rubles
to Captain Snegiryov, tells Lise ("in a sort of rapture") that he is certain the Captain will take the money the next day. It is Lise's response
that interests Bakhtin:

> Listen, Alexei Fyodorovich, isn't there something in all this reasoning of
> ours, I mean, of yours . . . no, better of ours . . . isn't there some con-
> tempt for him, for this wretched man . . . that we're examining his soul
> like this as if we were looking down on him? That we have decided so
> certainly, now, that he will accept the money? (217)

Bakhtin forcefully contends that Lise is precisely right, because
such confident judgment is a sin against what Bakhtin called the "unfinalizability" of the person, even if that judgment turns out to be right:
"The truth about a man in the mouths of others, not directed to him
dialogically and therefore a *secondhand* truth, becomes a *lie* degrading
and deadening him, if it touches upon his 'holy of holies,' that is, 'the
man in man'" (*Problems* 59). Bakhtin implicitly, but clearly, attributes
this viewpoint to Dostoevsky himself, as does Gary Saul Morson
("Bakhtin" 215). But it is not evident that Dostoevsky endorses Lise's
judgment—if one calls it a judgment; it takes the form of a question—
given Alyosha's response, which is quoted by neither Bakhtin nor
Morson:

> "No, Lise, there is no contempt in it," Alyosha answered firmly, as if he
> were already prepared for the question. "I thought it over myself, on the
> way here. Consider, what contempt can there be if we ourselves are just
> the same as he is, if everyone is just the same as he is? Because we are
> just the same, not better. And even if we were better, we would still be
> the same in his place. . . . I don't know about you, Lise, but for myself I
> consider that my soul is petty in many ways. And his is not petty, on the
> contrary, it is very sensitive. . . . No, Lise, there is no contempt for him!"

Dostoevsky of course does not explicitly endorse this claim, any more than he ever endorses his characters' claims, but he does doubly emphasize (through his narrator's introductory comment and Alyosha's own statement that he has already considered Lise's objection) that this is a thoughtful response by someone we already know to be an intelligent, humble, and above all charitable young man. The response, then, carries ethical weight, and should not be ignored in the way that Bakhtin and Morson ignore it. Dostoevsky is appealing here—again, not with conclusive affirmation—to precisely the universal or common humanity that Weil appeals to and that has two sources in Christian thought: the doctrine of creation *in imago dei* ("Let us make man in our own image") and the doctrine of universal sinfulness ("All have sinned and fallen short of the glory of God").

If this way of thinking—that one can grow in love of one's neighbor by reminding oneself that the neighbor is another human being "exactly like us"—why is Bakhtin uncomfortable with it? Because even that category can become dangerously schematic: It provides an analogical framework ("you are like me") that, like all analogies, can be applied overly rigidly; my own limitations, especially the limitations of my self-understanding, can build a procrustean bed that I cut others to fit. (Matters are of course complicated still more if there are temporal or cultural gaps separating me from the person whom I am trying to understand.) For Bakhtin the "secondhandedness" of the knowledge of others generates this temptation, since we see only what others do before us and hear only what they say to us. Even that kind of knowledge might be reliable were it not that "a man never coincides with himself. One cannot apply to him the formula of identity A = A" (*Problems* 59). What Bakhtin called the "unfinalizability" of persons means that any attempt to understand them in light of a prefabricated category—even one so broad as "humanity"—sets limits to their potential development. Better to remain immersed in the particulars of their case.[11]

There is another way in which Bakhtin distances himself from Weil and the widely held position she represents. Underlying Weil's comments are a version of the Golden Rule: See others as you would be seen by them. (Or, to connect with the previous point, recognize their humanity as you would have your own humanity recognized.) Thus love of one's neighbor, love of the Other, is comprehensible to us by virtue of our prior self-love. And in the Pauline-Augustinian tradition of Christianity, nothing about human beings is more certain and obvious, more *given*, than this *amour-propre:* Augustine dryly notes that "there is no need for a precept that anyone should love himself" (*On Christian Doctrine* 30), and confidently states that "this principle was never questioned by any sect" (20). Yet this "unquestionable" assertion is bluntly denied by Bakhtin: "I love another, but cannot love myself" (*Toward* 46). What can this mean?

Bakhtin does not explain his statement in *Toward a Philosophy of the Act*, but "Author and Hero in Aesthetic Activity"—which is a continuation of the project for which *Act* is a kind of prologue—offers something like a full exposition of this claim. Bakhtin raises the question of why it is so difficult "to visualize one's own outward image in imagination, to 'feel' oneself from outside" (29). He then goes on to contend that even when such an effort is partially successful, it fails to yield the satisfaction the visualizer is seeking:

> And when we succeed in doing this, we shall be struck by the peculiar *emptiness, ghostliness*, and an eerie, frightening *solitariness* of this outward image of ourselves. What accounts for this? It is explained by the fact that we lack any emotional and volitional approach to this outward image that could vivify it and include or incorporate it axiologically within the outward unity of the plastic-pictorial world. All of my emotional and volitional reactions that apprehend and axiologically structure another person's outward expressedness in being (admiration, love, tenderness, compassion, hostility, hatred, and the like) are directed ahead of myself out into the world and are not immediately applicable to myself as I experience myself from within. My own inner *I*—that wills, loves, feels, sees, and knows—I structure from within myself in terms of entirely different value-categories, and these are not directly applicable to the outward expressedness of myself. (30)

Now, Bakhtin believes that in the purely *intellectual* sphere we have "no difficulty at all" in abstracting ourselves from our concrete historical place in order to recognize ourselves as human beings among other human beings. In that sense the general category of "human being" is both familiar and useful. But in the *aesthetic* and *ethical* spheres this self-abstraction is, for the reasons just noted, difficult and in the strict sense impossible. One can go through the motions, as it were, of some objectifying self-contemplation, seeing ourselves as though through the eyes of "a possible other," but the very attempt "introduces a certain spurious element that is absolutely alien to the ethical event of being. For, inasmuch as it lacks any independent value of its own, what is engendered is not something productive and enriching, but a hollow fictitious product that clouds the optical purity of being. . . . [T]hrough the eyes of this fictitious other one cannot see one's true face, but only one's mask-face" (32).[12] Therefore, I cannot love myself because it is not possible for me to formulate or imagine a self, as object of love, distinct from the I who loves; whereas I *can* so understand the otherness of my neighbor so as to love her. (It should be clear that the dynamic and sympathetic outsidedness that Bakhtin prizes has nothing in common with the Cartesian "alienation from the text," though Steiner's notion of the fertile "distance" of the critic, as he develops it in "Critic/Reader," is rather closer.) Bakhtin thus summarize his argument:

> I may be solicitous for myself and I may be equally solicitous for someone I love, but this does not justify the conclusion that my emotional-volitional relationship to myself and to the other is similar in kind—or, in other words, that I love myself the way I love the other. For the emotional-volitional tones that lead in both cases to the same actions of solicitude are radically dissimilar. I cannot love my fellow being as myself or, rather, I cannot *love* myself as a fellow being. (48)

Bakhtin throughout this discussion operates under the assumption that selves are essentially monadic, that the boundaries between self and other are fixed. He has not yet reached the conviction that would animate so much of his later work, that such boundaries are fluid and that each self is a composite of the voices of others—though at times, in "Author and Hero," he (as it were) thinks his way toward that position:

> [O]ne can speak of a human being's absolute need for the other, for the other's seeing, remembering, gathering, and unifying self-activity—the only self-activity capable of producing his outwardly finished personality. This outward personality could not exist, if the other did not create it: aesthetic memory is *productive*—it gives birth, for the first time, to the *outward* human being on a new plane of being. (36)

Bakhtin's stress on "outward" here suggests that he still wants to maintain a distinction between an external or superficial self, whose shape and form are molded by others, and a core inner self that retains its integrity. But when Bakhtin returns to the impossibility of self-love in his notes "Toward a Reworking of the Dostoevsky Book" (see *Problems* 287–288), he abandons this distinction altogether in favor of an utter or complete dependence of the self upon the other, the constant interpenetration of what appear to be two different beings:

> I cannot manage without another, I cannot become myself without another; I must find myself in another by finding another in myself (in mutual reflection and mutual acceptance). Justification cannot be *self*-justification, recognition cannot be *self*-recognition. I receive my name from others, and it exists for others (self-nomination is imposture). Even love towards one's own self is impossible.

By this point Bakhtin has long held his key conviction that consciousness is always-already dialogical and heteroglot, built from and constantly dependent upon other voices. Early in his career he was still under the strong influence of a Cartesian-Kantian (in short, modern) notion of selfhood with which he was struggling mightily, trying to find a vocabulary capable of expressing his instinctive dissent.

Given, then, that the early Bakhtin's notion of selfhood is still modern, and given that self-experience has an ineradicably different phenomenological character than other-experience—a difference that makes self-love impossible—what exactly is the nature of one's responsibility to oneself and others, in aesthetics and ethics? In *Toward a Philosophy of the Act*, the key phrase that expresses Bakhtin's imperative is "I-for-myself." What does Bakhtin mean by this? He complicates the matter at one point by making this distinction: "To live from within oneself does not mean to live for oneself, but means to be an answerable participant from within oneself, to affirm one's compellent, actual non-alibi in Being" (49). (Again note the presence of fixed boundaries, the within and without.) But when, elsewhere in the essay, Bakhtin refers to "I-for-myself," he does not mean "living for oneself" but rather "living from within oneself." It is tempting here to recall Sartre's famous categories of *en-soi* and *pour-soi*, but Bakhtin is talking about something very different. "Living for oneself," as Bakhtin uses the phrase here, means something very close to what it does in ordinary usage: It is selfishness, egotism; it involves treating others as objects and oneself as the only subject (I-it versus I-thou relations); it is, to use a term Bakhtin would favor later, monological consciousness, or consciousness trying to be monological.

The "I-for-myself," to the contrary, belongs to authentic living, and is for Bakhtin an *achievement*, as he indicates by his identification of it as one of the "emotional-volitional moments" that it is the task of moral philosophy to describe and the task of the moral life to achieve:

> These basic moments are I-for-myself, the other-for-me, and I-for-the-other. All the values of actual life and culture are arranged around the basic architectonic points of the actual world of the performed act or deed: scientific values, aesthetic values, political values (including both ethical and social values), and, finally, religious values. All spatial-temporal values and all sense-content values are drawn toward and concentrated around these central emotional-volitional moments: I, the other [for me], and I-for-the-other. (54)

The authentic answerable act (*postupok*) will take one of these three forms, and insofar as I am able fully to incarnate and comprehend all three forms of answerable action, I achieve "self-activity." As Mihailovic says,

> What is given in any life is the fact of existence, a state that requires no effort or work and which is simply *there*. . . . The true realization of the uniqueness of one's existence comes about through work or "activeness" (what Liapunov sometimes translates as "self-activity" [*activnost*]); the fulfillment of the ethical imperative is assigned (*zadana*) rather than given. (74)

We can see here again that Bakhtin has not yet managed to deconstruct the Cartesian-Kantian self: He still understands the labor of achieving answerability as something one achieves from within oneself and, in a sense, for oneself. Even the achievement of living as I-for-another is one's own achievement, not the other's. But what remains perfectly clear, and essential for our purposes, is the obligation to achieve, though "self-activity," a genuinely answerable "I-for-myself."

What means, though, suffice to distinguish the genuine "I-for-myself" from our ordinary quotidian egoism? Mihailovic offers a compelling answer to this question:

Crucial here is the distinction that Bakhtin draws between incarnation and embodiment. The former is the fullest flowering of the act in all of its ramifications whereas the latter represents a partial realization of the act. When we incarnate rather than merely embody the act in our lives we put our signature on it (*podpisat'sia pod nim*), which is to say that it in a certain sense has the stamp of our individuality on it. . . . Embodiment (*vopolshchenie*) refers only to the change that an individual undergoes when he or she becomes consciously aware of the fact that all human lives are different; the actual deed of ethically integrating with others follows after this awareness, and is described by Bakhtin as both a partaking . . . and an incarnation. (68–69)

And it is not only "all human lives" that are different: Every moment of each life is different from all others, and makes a distinctive demand upon me. Bakhtin laments the "unfortunate misunderstanding" that leads people to think that "the truth of a situation is precisely that which is repeatable and constant in it" (*Toward* 37). The truly answerable deed, in his view, is one that focuses all its attention on the "unique context," the "unique moment" with its utterly particular demands. Some people live in generality, and their lives are "fortuitous and incapable of being rooted" (56); to recognize the fact of uniqueness is embodiment, and is a necessary but not sufficient step toward answerability; but true answerability is achieved only when I recognize that this "fact of uniqueness" imposes a responsibility upon me that I cannot avert. When I acknowledge my responsibility and act upon it—whether in a conversation with a friend or in reading a novel—I realize the authentic "I-for-myself" and "I-for-another." This is true love; this is the incarnated deed.

Let it not be thought that the uniqueness of the moment and of the person deprives the ethical life of coherence and continuity. To the contrary, one of the reasons *this* moment is unique is that it succeeds *previous* moments in which I was also called to incarnational "self-activity"; and if I responded appropriately *then* by "undersigning" my deed I commit myself still more to a similar acknowledgment *now*:

It is not the content of an obligation that obligates me, but my signature below it—the fact that I at one time acknowledged or undersigned the given acknowledgment. And what compelled me to sign at the moment of the undersigning was not the content of the given performed act or deed. . . . And in this performed act the content-aspect was also but a

constituent moment, and what decided the matter was the acknowledgment or affirmation—the answerable deed—that had actually been performed at a previous time, etc. What we shall find everywhere is a constant unity of answerability . . . .(*Toward* 38–39)

Here we see one of the first appearances of that characteristic
Bakhtinian notion of an "open unity," of that which coheres without
being fixed, schematized, or finalized. And the term that Bakhtin uses
to describe this open yet "constant unity of answerability" is simple,
familiar, and quite beautiful: He calls it *faithfulness* (38).

We began this survey of Bakhtin's thought by noting the necessity
of attentiveness: This faithfulness is merely attentiveness that is both
loving and constant. The Russian word translated as "faithfulness"
means literally "being-true-to"; when one attends to the life or work
of another lovingly and with constancy, one is being true to her; that
is, one is doing justice to who she is. And in the context of the Orthodox Christianity that, as we have seen, shapes Bakhtin's thinking on
these issues, "who she is" is a being made in the image of God, an image defaced by sin but (one hopes) in the process of being restored. In
the Orthodox view, one of the best descriptions of salvation is as the
process by which the image of God in us is restored: Perhaps the most
characteristic idea of Orthodoxy is its conviction that salvation is *theo-
sis* (see Pelikan, *Christian* 10–12).

Moreover—and this is a still more important point for our purposes
here—the God in whose image we were made and are being remade is
a Trinity, that is, an intrinsically *relational* being. Here again we must
invoke a doctrine that, although not unique to Orthodoxy, is characteristic of it: *perichoresis*, the eternal loving dance in which the persons
of the Trinity are intertwined. To become deified—or, to put it in a
less exalted language more familiar to Western Christians, to imitate
Christ—is to learn to practice with our neighbors the perichoretic
movements that are so awkward for fallen human beings. This practice does proper honor not only to our neighbors but also to us: We
may offer loving and constant attention to them, but in return we receive from them the gift of their otherness, the "outsidedness" that
makes it possible for us to understand and to achieve "self-activity,"
"answerability," the "incarnated deed."

This gracious exchange of gifts, this dance of faithfulness, is of
course something that achieves its fullest flowering only within the

life of the Church, but it can (indeed must) be practiced anywhere and with anyone. (We owe love to all our neighbors, not just to fellow members of what St. Paul calls "the household of God.") It is a kind of love that is always productive of some degree of knowledge. Here is where Bakhtin's account parts company most forcefully with the Aristotelian picture, in which love can be productive of knowledge only within a certain political context, and only if one is lucky enough to find an other receptive to one's own virtues and in possession of virtues that one lacks (or possesses in lesser measure). The Christian love that Bakhtin counsels is both an always compelling obligation and an always available opportunity.

It is this commitment to faithfulness that we must bring to our lives as readers if we would govern our reading by the law of love. This is a debt that we owe to all the books we read, because those books become, for the duration of our reading and perhaps long afterward, our neighbors—as do, in subtly differing ways, the books' characters and authors. Bakhtin's account of faithful attentiveness demonstrates that Wayne Booth's wise and noble treatment of "books as friends," in his wonderful book *The Company We Keep*, is not quite adequate to its subject, because the very notion of friendship that Booth employs is tainted by the exclusionary and agonistic character of the virtue of friendship as he has inherited it.

To some degree Booth recognizes this problem. He tries to address it early in his treatment of the subject by insisting that Aristotle's *philia* encompasses not only "what we would call close friends but [also] all bonds of affection or reliance between parents and children, kings and subjects, neighbors and citizens, husbands and wives, and so on" (*Company* 173). This definition of *philia* goes even further than Martha Nussbaum's, and in my view stretches Aristotle's term beyond recognition and coherence; but even if we grant a great deal of what Booth says, there remains an element of choice and hence exclusion in *philia* with which Booth is not altogether comfortable. In a footnote on the same page he writes:

> In what follows I do not mean to suggest that I find Aristotle's rational account of friendship the only or the best account of human affection. The chief "rival" is obviously the Christian command to love our enemies—love them in a mysterious, gratuitous way that takes no account of what they might offer us. Applied to our relations to implied authors, the command would yield a "golden rule" that I hope informs this whole

book: "Read as you would have others read you; listen as you would have others listen."

How odd that Booth would write a large and copious book based largely on an account of human relations that he cannot or will not endorse! How odd also that Booth fails to note that Christianity, in "rivaling" the Aristotelian emphasis on friends, teaches us to love not just our enemies but all of our neighbors (many of whom are neither friends nor enemies). Also worth considering—though we will not explore this issue right now—is Booth's assumption that the love of enemies is necessarily "gratuitous."

Booth's uneasiness returns much later in the book, when he outlines "two strong ethical traditions" that give us seemingly contradictory advice about how to respond to inimical or deceptive books (and characters)—that is, about how we are to put into practice our "golden rule." One of them is "the tradition of exclusion or denial," which "advises a purifying caution and restraint, a defensive drawing of lines and boundaries" (485). Booth seems to associate this way of thinking primarily with modern American (including, or perhaps especially, American Christian) attitudes toward censorship, immigration, the control of schools and neighborhoods, and so on; but he also recognizes that it is deeply imbedded in the Aristotelian tradition:

> [I]n the classical way of talking about friendship . . . some friends are useful and some are harmful; some pleasant friends are likely to corrupt us; most would-be friends will prove to be inferior or dangerous influences. In fact in that tradition we can hope at best for a very small number of true friends, perhaps finally, as Montaigne would have it, only one. All "others" are at least partially suspect. (486)

The "opposing tradition," as Booth describes it, derives primarily from the practices of Jesus, even if it is not often found among Christians: It "urges an openness to the world, including even that part of it that looks like vice or corruption. . . . The tradition is perhaps best represented by Christ's seeming willingness, nay, eagerness, to consort with sinners and by the 'imitations' of his all-embracing practice by saints like Francis of Assisi" (487).

Having described these two traditions, Booth admits that "at any one moment, facing any particular piece of otherness, one cannot follow both at once: I cannot both ostracize dubious friends and cultivate them for the good they might do me as challenges, or the good I might do them" (488). But he nevertheless wants to insist that "in ethical criticism of narratives" we need not "make a hard and fast choice between the excluding and embracing modes. . . . The only fully general advice inherent in all this is that by taking thought about *who* and *where we are*, and about *when it is*, we may improve our chances of finding and dwelling with those others who are in fact our true friends" (488–489). This is a limp conclusion indeed, but the limpness is inevitable given the choices that Booth has evolved for himself. He wants neither to abdicate judgment nor to enact it: Having conceived of an ethical practice of reading in strictly Aristotelian terms, he flinches from the agonistic and exclusionary character of the *arete* that enables *philia*.

If, however, we think of books as our neighbors rather than as our friends, and *agape* rather than *philia* as the model for our affectus, the impasse dissolves. Not that we must reject the notion that our relationships with books can be friendly: As I pointed out in the previous chapter, theologians of friendship have often noted the references in the Gospel of John to "the disciple whom Jesus loved," one who was his particular friend, and this can be read as testimony that friendship, though inherently preferential, need not be sinful because it need not be strictly exclusionary. As C. S. Lewis says, in a passage inflected by Aristotle and yet fully Christian,

> [T]rue friendship is the least jealous of loves. Two friends delight to be joined by a third, and three by a fourth, if only the newcomer is qualified to become a real friend. They can then say, as the blessed souls say in Dante, "here comes one who will augment our loves." For in this love "to divide is not to take away." Of course the scarcity of kindred souls . . . sets limits to the enlargement of the circle; but within those limits we possess each friend not less but more as the number of those with whom we share him increases. In this, Friendship exhibits a glorious "nearness by resemblance" to Heaven itself where the very multitude of the blessed (which no man can number) increases the fruition which each has of God. (*Four* 59)

One could say that this passage recognizes the difference between finitude and fallenness: Our finitude—the limited scope of our acquaintance, of our intellectual and moral resources—ensures that our capability for friendship is likewise finite; but this is simply the consequence of being created beings, not the consequence of a sinful desire to exclude (though most of us possess that too).

Similarly, we will not read all books with full sympathy, with a sense of kinship, with an awareness of expanded understanding, with the conviction that this book teaches me what I need to know and could not have learned from another book. In short, not all the books we read will become our friends. But if we consider that we owe a debt of loving and constant attentiveness (of faithfulness) to all the books we read—whether they be friends, foes, or neighbors—we provide for ourselves what Bonhoeffer calls the *cantus firmus*, the ground over which variations can be elaborated and developed. Those "variations" are the products of discernment, and Chapter 3 will consider that topic—first distinguishing the Christian virtue of loving discernment from its ever-present shadow: suspicion.

Interlude B: Transfer of Charisma

In the previous interlude I relied rather heavily on George Steiner's distinction between critic and reader. That this distinction is not wholly adequate may be demonstrated by a look at Nabokov's *Pale Fire*. Charles Kinbote, the narrator of this story, fits neither of Steiner's categories. He is certainly no critic of John Shade's work, since he deems "distance" between reader and author, at least in this case, problematic and hence infertile: He does not disguise his disappointment that Shade's poem "Pale Fire" turned out to be something other than what he had expected. Indeed, he makes haste to save and then hide the manuscript, rather than attend to the bleeding, dying Shade, only because he is convinced that the poem is about him, Kinbote, and his native country, Zembla: Had he known that it had nothing to do with him he would scarcely have bothered. Having saved the poem, he then determines to construct a theory that will account for its *lack* of reference to Kinbote and Zembla, and to discover that Kinbote and Zembla constitute the hidden subtext of the poem—a subtext partially but imperfectly covered by Shade in his attempts to placate his wife Sybil's irrational hostility toward Kinbote.

Therefore Kinbote could scarcely be called a reader, either, since he loves not Shade's work itself but, rather, the mirror of himself into which he has (as far as he can) transformed the poem.[1] Indeed, Kinbote's only real mistake is to provide us with the poem about which he writes his commentary: Even if the commentary is ten times the length of the poem, the poem remains as a witness to Kinbote's meta-

69

morphosis of it. No matter how fervently Kinbote insists upon his reverence for John Shade, no matter how passionately he declares that he and he alone is the fit custodian and guardian of Shade's literary reputation, the only genuine love here is Kinbote's narcissism. Kinbote understands himself to be the still point of the turning world: Thus he is convinced, even when he can no longer sustain the belief that "Pale Fire" is about him and his country, that Shade's killer was nonetheless a Zemblan assassin seeking his, Kinbote's, life.

This is Nabokov's picture of the critic: not an epistemologist so much as a textbook passive-aggressive, proclaiming himself (like Dickens's Uriah Heep) a humble servant but in fact seeking the constant expansion of his own ego. Gerald Bruns, in a passage I cited in Chapter 1, summarizes Steiner's view of the critic in his description of "Cartesian hermeneutics," the impulse of which "is to preserve alienation as a condition of freedom from the text" (149). But Nabokov's Kinbotean critic seeks not freedom from the text but mastery over it, and absorbs it into his own being. ("Freedom from" and "mastery of" are related but not identical concepts.) What is vital to note here is the elimination, in each case, of an ongoing dialogical encounter with the text, in which the reader and the text subject each other to scrutiny: Steiner's critic builds a wall between him- or herself and the text, Nabokov's critic eats the text. In neither case is there anything like real reverence, love, or friendship—in Bakhtin's term, *faithfulness* is lacking—and thus, in neither case is the readerly/critical experience productive of genuine knowledge (of the self or the other).

"Friendship" is one of the themes of a book that paints a subtler picture of the relationship between a reader and a writer, Nicholson Baker's account of his ongoing fascination with John Updike in *U and I*. Baker refers to Nabokov repeatedly in his book, since Nabokov is his other chief influence besides Updike: "I had said that he and Nabokov were heroes in several interviews" (175). At times Baker suggests a kind of trinity: "Ahh!—another link between Nabokov and Updike and Updike and me: insomnia!" (144). And yet there is only one reference to *Pale Fire*, not actually by Baker, but by Updike as quoted by Baker in an *en passant* phrase: Reviewing *Despair* Updike had imagined, or hoped (fruitlessly) for, "the delightful, devilish, and unimaginable successor to *Pale Fire*" (118).

The only reason Baker might be expected to say something about *Pale Fire* is that at one point he gives a list of books that are relevant when an essay's "subject is a writer thinking about an older writer," a list that includes (among other things) James's "The Figure in the Carpet"—a doubly inappropriate example, since, as I have noted, the story really isn't about reading and writing at all, and the narrator isn't a writer, just an occasional reviewer. It is rather odd, then, that Baker never considers whether his obsession with Updike might resemble Kinbote's with John Shade.

One might immediately protest here—Baker, especially, might protest—that Baker bears no resemblance to Kinbote, who is no more a writer than James's narrator (but *what* he is, is difficult to say), and who uses or tries to use Shade in a way that Baker couldn't and wouldn't use Updike. But this point requires more reflection, and a further consideration of *Pale Fire*.

Kinbote isn't a writer, but he becomes one by making himself the official editor of and commentator on John Shade's poem. Of course, Shade's reputation and the public interest in his work is what makes it possible for Kinbote to come before the public with his commentary. But this secondary, derivative, or parasitical role is intolerable to Kinbote, who proceeds in his commentary to make the Socratic/Platonic argument that his spoken tales of Zemblan culture and history inspire the written (and hence secondary, derivative) "Pale Fire":

> By the end of May I could make out the outlines of some of my images in the shape his genius might give them; by mid-June I felt sure at last that he would recreate in a poem the dazzling Zembla burning in my brain. I mesmerized him with it, I saturated him with my vision, I pressed upon him, with a drunkard's wild generosity, all that I was helpless myself to put into verse. . . . At length I knew he was ripe with my Zembla, bursting with suitable rhymes, ready to spurt at the brush of an eyelash. (80)

Shade is a "genius" and Kinbote "helpless," but only in technique: Shade has the know-how of a poetic engineer, but Kinbote the "vision" of an architect. The poem ultimately produced would be a skillful imitation, but only an imitation, a "recreation," of the "dazzling Zembla burning in [Kinbote's] brain."

Of course, upon first reading the poem Kinbote suffered "horrible disappointment" (296) that it was not the gorgeous romance of Zembla that he had been expecting; but later, when he "reread" the poem "more carefully," he was pleased by his discoveries:

Here and there I discovered in it and especially, especially in the invaluable variants [i.e., Shade's discarded drafts], echoes and spangles of my mind, a long ripplewake of my glory. . . . My commentary to this poem, now in the hands of my readers, represents an attempt to sort out those echoes and wavelets of fire, and pale phosphorescent hints, and all the many subliminal debts to me. (297)

By positioning himself and his story both *prior* to the poem as inspiration, and *succeeding* the poem as commentary, Kinbote hopes to redescribe the poem's power as his emanation. Thus the statement at the end of his "Foreward" to the poem (the poem that is immediately succeeded by Kinbote's lengthy "Commentary"):

Although these notes, in conformity with custom, come after the poem, the reader is advised [note the divine passive] to consult them first and then study the poem with their help, rereading them of course as he goes through its text, and perhaps, after having done with the poem, consulting them a third time so as to complete the picture. . . . Let me state that without my notes Shade's text simply has no human reality at all. . . . To this statement my dear poet would probably not have subscribed, but, for better or worse, it is the commentator who has the last word. (28)

Kinbote gives, or tries to give, himself the first and last words—words that deserve rapt attention and repeated engagements—and to reduce Shade's poem to a wan reflection of his own mind. (As Brian Boyd points out [443], in Jonathan Swift's *Battle of the Books* we hear that "a malignant deity, call'd *Criticism* . . . dwelt on the top of a snowy mountain in Nova Zembla.")

Kinbote cannot find in Shakespeare the reference that provides Shade's poem its title, though as he writes his commentary the only Shakespearean play he has access to is a Zemblan translation of the very play from which the title is drawn: *Timon of Athens*. "It certainly contains nothing that could be regarded as an equivalent of 'pale fire' (if it had, my luck would have been a statistical monster)" (285). Indeed his luck was great, though not matched by his discernment. Earlier in the book Kinbote unwittingly quotes the relevant passage, translating it from Zemblan back into English: "The moon is a thief:/he steals his silvery light from the sun" (80). Shakespeare has it thus: "The moon's an arrant thief, / And her pale fire she snatches from the sun." So Timon says in his discourse on the ubiquity of thievery (IV.iii.420–445). This is of course a perfect image of Kinbote's relation to Shade, Shade being (in a punning paradox) the sun, and Kinbote the moon—though the whole of Kinbote's commentary is a passionate and desperate claim to the contrary.[2]

In short, what Kinbote wants from John Shade is a transfer of charisma: to be not the recipient of energy but the source of energy, not the reflector of light but the generator of light. Kinbote recalls the moment of Shade's murder by Jack Grey: "I felt—I still feel—John's hand fumbling at mine, seeking my fingertips, finding them, only to abandon them at once as if passing to me, in a sublime relay race, the baton of life" (294). Shade, dead, can generate no more light or force: But Kinbote still breathes.

Baker's relation to Updike is different—he certainly doesn't want Updike dead—but not wholly different, and the lineaments of this likeness need to be discerned. The book starts by being about an almost obsessive admiration: His early notes for the project, he says, were along these lines: "'I should,' I typed that morning, 'write some appreciation of Updike.' 'Make a whole book about my obsession with Updike,' I typed" (13).

And occasionally throughout the book that note returns: Rereading *Of the Farm*, he says near the end, "More than once I yelled 'He's a fucking maestro!'" (171). But in general terms there's a shift in emphasis: More and more what Baker wants is what he calls "friendship" with Updike, by which he means a particular kind of reciprocity. Let's remember in this context that for Aristotle reciprocity or mutuality is what distinguishes genuine friendship from good will or benevolence or, for that matter, admiration. And friendship is what Baker wants from—or, to be precise, *with*—Updike. For many years as a reader he had been receiving gifts *from* Updike; now he wants to be able to give something in return. That's why he toys with what he calls his "half-nuts" theory that he (who had met Updike briefly, twice, before he wrote *U and I*) was the physical and vocal model for the character of Dale in Updike's *Roger's Version* (178).

Baker's exposition gets rather delicate on this point. He begins with his reaction when the novelist Tim O'Brien revealed that he sometimes played golf with Updike:

> I was of course very hurt that out of all the youngish writers living in the
> Boston area Updike has chosen Tim O'Brien and not me as his golfing

partner. It didn't matter that I hadn't written a book that had won a National Book Award, hadn't written a book of any kind, and didn't know
how to golf; still, I felt strongly that Updike should have asked me and
not Tim O'Brien. (50)

But the more Baker reflects on the potential pleasures of golfing
with Updike, the more he fears that their conversation would be dis-
rupted by a mutual fear—Baker *hopes* it would be mutual—of revealing some tidbit of wit or eloquence that the other would steal (54–57).

This concern for unhealthy competitiveness makes Baker conclude
that "literary friendship is impossible, it seems; at least, it is impossible
for me" (57). And yet, almost immediately Baker senses the impoverishment of such a stance: "And yet I want to be Updike's friend now!
Forget the guardedness!" (58). Moreover, he continues, "I *am* friends
with Updike—that's what I really feel—I have, as I never had when I
was a child, this imaginary friend I have constructed out of sodden
crisscrossing strips of rivalry and gratefulness over an armature of remembered misquotation" (59).

That's a valuable discriminating phrase: "crisscrossing strips of rivalry and gratefulness"—much richer than Harold Bloom's "anxiety of
influence" (which Baker made a point of not reading about until he
had finished his book). But this notion of friendship is still trying to do
without reciprocity: Baker may have *said* "Forget the guardedness,"
but he has clearly discarded fantasies of golfing with Updike in favor
of settling for a purely imaginary friendship.

Eventually, though, he realizes that this imaginary friend isn't really
a friend at all: Thus his manifest pleasure—in the scene that concludes
U and I—in discovering (he thinks it's a discovery anyway) that he has
"communicated with [Updike] in a permanent way" (178). Baker believes that a brief passage in Updike's 1984 novel *The Witches of East-
wick* echoes a passage in a story Baker published in 1981, a story that
in their second meeting Updike told Baker he had read and liked.
Thus the last words of *U and I*: "Because I exist in print, Updike's
book is, I think, ever so slightly different. For a minute or two, sometime in 1983, the direction of indebtedness was reversed. *I* have influ-
enced *him*. And that's all the imaginary friendship I need" (179).

It seems clear from this conclusion that, however wonderful it may
be to admire Updike, friendship requires something more. If Kinbote—who relentlessly invokes the *language* of friendship—really
sought a *transfer* of charisma, Baker wants an *exchange* of charisma.

The exchange is not and need not be an equal one: Baker makes it manifest throughout the book that he knows Updike "has it" (126)—"genius" he even calls it—whereas he, Baker, still needs confirmation of some kind. But if there can be even an unequal exchange of charisma, this must confirm that Baker has something to offer–some gift, however meager, to return to one who has given him so much.

Are there rivalry and competitiveness in this "imaginary friendship"? Of course. But that is not the whole story. In Aristotelian terms, the friendship is flawed because it is based on instrumental rather than intrinsic goods. But I think that, in the literary and hermeneutical terms of this study, what Baker desires and imagines is a genuine friendship—as opposed to the trivial, unfruitful gnosticism of the narrator of "The Figure in the Carpet" or the cannibalistic annotations of Nabokov's Kinbote. Baker is willing to receive gifts of style and insight, and eager to give them—from motives that are by his own admission impure, but what of that? As someone (Rebecca West, I believe) once said, there is no such thing as an unmixed motive. There is health in Baker's admiration of Updike, especially in this admission, one that comes after a period in his life when he was eager to have his girlfriend tell him he was a better writer than Updike or, failing that, a more intelligent person: "Updike is a better writer than I am *and* he is smarter than I am" (134).

The significance of this admission can readily be seen by anyone who tries to remember the last time he or she read a critical essay, or review, or book, in which a critic said such a thing. Baker puts us on the road to understanding the role that humility—or, to be more specific, an honest recognition of another's gifts—can play in reading. Surely such honesty and humility are necessary in a reader who would love God and her neighbor through the act of reading.

But still richer models are available.

L OVE AND THE
S USPICIOUS S PIRIT

*"And love?"—what! Even an act performed out of love is sup-
posed to be "un-egoistic"? But you blockheads—!*

—*Nietzsche* (Beyond #220)

Earlier, in Chapter 1, I spoke of reading as the reception of a gift, and promised fuller explorations later on. Such explorations are necessary because the notion of gift is one of the most contested in contemporary thought. I have already indicated my position in this contest: "Discernment is required to know what kind of gift one is being presented with, and in what spirit to accept it (if at all), but a universal suspicion of gifts and givers, like an indiscriminate acceptance of all gifts, constitutes an abdication of discernment in favor of a simplistic *a priorism* that smothers the spirit."

I have also noted that we can and often do love a particular book in a way that is very like—almost indistinguishable from—the love we give to persons, and yet that love is not precisely to be equated with love for the author or any particular character. This topic has great significance for how we read books, and yet has scarcely been considered. One possible way to approach it is by considering a historical development noted by Marcel Mauss in his classic work *The Gift* and developed by Lewis Hyde in his book of the same title: the distinction that arose in Roman law between, as Hyde puts it,

> "real" and "personal" law—between, that is, a law of things and a law of persons. . . . In antiquity the Roman *familia* was not simply people but

the entire "household," including the objects in the home down to the food and the means of livelihood. Later Roman law, however, increasingly distinguished economic and ritual interest; it divided the *familia* into *res* and *personae*. (86)

Hyde is interested in this legal development because it goes a long way toward transforming many forms of human creativity—including, especially, works of art—from *gifts* that bind people together to *commodities* that divide them. In other words, the legal distinction between persons and things marks the transformation from a "gift economy" to a "market economy." If Hyde is right, then any attempt to think of a work of art as a gift—and I contend that it is only as a gift that the work of art can become available for serious theological reflection and use—requires as a first step the interrogation of the distinction between things and persons. In other words, to think of a book as a thing is to commodify it in ways that deny it human significance: Conversely, to think of it as a gift, as a human *activity*, may create confusion—How can a book be a person? How could we think of a fictional character in the same way that we think of that character's author?—but it is a productive and enabling confusion. This is why in my Prelude I quoted Iris Murdoch: "Coherence is not necessarily good, and one must question its cost. Better sometimes to remain confused" (*Metaphysics* 147).

But how can we think of a book as a gift?

The gift assumed its status as a topic of controversy with the publication, in 1925, of Mauss's "Essai sur le don," later published in book form and translated into English as *The Gift*.[1] Mauss's brief essay has spawned an enormous literature of response and counter-response chiefly because of one claim: that the gift as such, a free offering of something valuable to another, does not exist. Every gift, argues Mauss, not only expects but demands some return: Exchange and reciprocity are at the heart of every gift-giving practice. (The prominence of the terms *exchange* and *negotiation* in the vocabulary of the New Historicism, especially in Stephen Greenblatt's work, is an inheritance from Mauss—as mediated by Claude Levi-Strauss and Clifford Geertz, among others.) In short, Mauss subjects the gift to a rigorous hermeneutics of suspicion, a suspicion that is *a priori* and absolute. (In this he is almost the opposite of Lewis Hyde, who, as he admits, does not "take up the negative side of gift exchange" [xvi].)

That is, Mauss does not conclude on the basis of serious and extended fieldwork that gifts are never "free"—Mauss actually did almost no fieldwork in his entire career—but rather brings to his cultural reflections that conviction. The origin of Mauss's conviction may well be found in the work of Nietzsche, to the reader of whose work such notions will be familiar: For instance, "the disinterested act is a very interesting and interested act. . . . [H]e who has really made sacrifices knows that he wanted and received something in return—perhaps something of himself in exchange for something of himself—that he gave away here in order to have more there, perhaps in general to be more or to feel himself 'more'" (*Beyond* 221). But to Nietzsche we will return later.

This *a priorism* of Mauss, and Nietzsche, raises problems to which we will also return later, but the most important point to consider in reflecting on Mauss's work, and the response to it, is a particular ethical assumption: that a gift is truly a gift—which is to say, an admirable and generous act—only if it is accompanied by no expectation of reciprocity or exchange. (This is also nearly explicit in Nietzsche's comment on the one who sacrifices.) Perhaps the most interesting element of the long controversy over Mauss's little book is the agreement of almost all parties to this point: The arguments tend to be about whether any particular gift can be truly "gratuitous" or free from expectation, not about whether such a gratuitous offering is indeed ethically superior to an offering made with an eye toward reciprocation. *That* everyone seems to assume. Thus Jacques Derrida, one of the most important commentators on the theme given us by Mauss, speaks for the tradition (though in his discourse he seeks to overcome the tradition): "For there to be a gift, it is necessary that the donee not give back, amortize, reimburse, acquit himself, enter into a contract, and that he never have contracted a debt" (*Given* 13). As Stephen Webb puts it, "Even (perhaps especially) gratitude destroys the gift" (69). And yet Derrida goes farther. Not only must the receiver of the gift return nothing for it, the giver must, to sustain the gift in its purity, erase all traces of it from his memory: "For there to be [a] gift, not only must the donor or donee not perceive or receive the gift as such, have no consciousness of it, no memory, no recognition; he or she must also forget it right away and moreover this forgetting must be so radical that it exceeds even the psychoanalytic categorality of forgetting" (*Given* 16). If the receiver were to remember the gift, she might feel obligation, which according to this view would cancel the giftness of the gift; likewise, if the giver were to remember the gift, she might consider potential reciprocations, which also would cancel the giftness of the gift.

And yet is the assumption valid? Is the gift immediately erased from consciousness ethically superior to the gift presented in a spirit of reciprocity and mutual accountability? Is only the forgotten gift genuine? This can be so only under the Platonic (or, to invoke a slightly different historical framework, the Cartesian) assumption that the strong and virtuous person is self-sufficient. As so often, Ralph Waldo Emerson makes Platonic assumptions ingenuously explicit: "It is not the office of a man to receive gifts. How dare you give them? We wish to be self-sustained. We do not quite forgive a giver. The hand that feeds us is in some danger of being bitten" (536). The one who offers gifts presumes that we are deficient; if we accept them we confirm that deficiency, that failure to achieve self-sustained "manhood."

This critical interrogation of the gift provides a summary of and model for what is usually called the hermeneutics of suspicion. That phrase, coming from Paul Ricoeur's critique of Freud and applied by him also to Marx and Nietzsche, has naturally been associated with the collapse of religious authority in the nineteenth century, but the notions of gift we have just explored indicate that the roots of hermeneutical suspicion lie much farther back. Thus once again Gerald Bruns on Spinoza's separation of textual meaning from truth: "Call this Cartesian hermeneutics, or the allegory of suspicion, in which the text comes under the control of the reader as disengaged rational subject, unresponsive except to its own self-certitude. . . . The motive of Cartesian hermeneutics is to preserve alienation as a condition of freedom from the text" (149). Likewise, we suspect gifts, and deny forgiveness to their givers, because we dislike being obliged to another: We do not wish it even to be suggested that we are in another's debt, or owe her reciprocation.

But this dislike, this discomfort, may not be praiseworthy. What if in fact we *are* obliged to others, what if we do indeed owe something to them? In such a case Derrida's chimerical beast, the gift instantly forgotten by both giver and receiver, would become ethically dubious because it would sustain us in a fictional self-sufficiency and deny us the possibility of reflecting on what happens to that which we tender to others. Conversely, the gift remembered by both giver and receiver could serve as a reminder of our incompleteness and need for others to supplement and enrich our lives; moreover, it could serve as a useful provocation to reflection upon the debts we owe one another.

Another way to put the same point: The Derridean position regarding gifts reinforces the Platonic view of selfhood, whereas the alternative position I have sketched out appeals to the account of "relational goods" developed in Chapter 2. Relational goods are not available to the isolated self but only to the person in relation to, with, others: As we saw in Chapter 2, neither the *eudaimon* in Aristotle's philosophy nor the Christian living in ecclesial community proclaims, or even seeks, self-sufficiency, but rather situates herself in healthy relation to others. What I hope to do at this point is to connect this picture of relational goods, or, more precisely, the *willingness* to admit the human need for reciprocity, with the willingness to receive and give gifts. For no one can practice hermeneutical charity who is unwilling to receive a poem, a story—a work—as a gift.

In each of us, of course, there dwells a tension between the desire for self-sufficiency and the desire for meaningful relations with others. We understand Aristotle when he says that "nobody would choose to live without friends even if he had all the other good things" (*Ethics* 1155a3). But perhaps we also understand Nietzsche when he says, as he often does, that "solitude is with us a virtue"—one of the four in his later taxonomy, along with courage, insight, and sympathy (*Beyond* 284). Still, Nietzsche's exposition of the "virtue" of solitude is problematic, and reveals the impasse confronting one who would elevate suspicion into the cardinal principle of hermeneutics. For our purposes, the most important service Nietzsche performs is to pursue more fully than anyone previously had done the implications of the Platonic doctrine that the *eudaimon* is self-sufficient: In particular, Nietzsche describes the role that *other people* play in the life of one who would be self-sufficient.

Nietzsche's understanding of virtue is strictly Athenian in that he shares the view (unquestioned by any ancient Greek thinker, as far as I know) that *arete* is achieved through struggle, contestation, the *agon:* As we noted in an earlier chapter, ignorance and the passions are the opponents with which one who wishes to be virtuous, excellent, must contend. Let us recall again John Milbank's claim that in the antique order "the word *arete* (virtue) is always the standard of victory, and while conquest puts an end to war, it requires a preceding war, and only ends war by war" (*Theology* 363). And likewise recall Milbank's crucial question: If "the virtue that is [Christian] charity is *not* virtue in the antique sense . . . [then] is virtue that is in *no sense* fundamentally a victory, still virtue at all?" (332). But for now I wish merely to note that Nietzsche clearly endorses this agonistic understanding of virtue, and most especially the view that the crucial *agon* pits one against internal enemies: "One must test oneself to see whether one is destined for independence and command. . . . One should not avoid one's tests, although they are perhaps the most dangerous game one could play and are in the end tests which are taken before ourselves and before no other judge" (*Beyond* 41).[2]

From these two convictions—that the happy person is self-sufficient and that virtue is the product of struggle—almost everything in Nietsche's later thought derives, by an iron and implacable logic. Given these two convictions, hell is indeed (in Sartre's famous phrase) other people, for the only possible role other people can play in this scheme is to impede your pursuit of *eudaimonia* or distract you from it: Each person you meet is your satan, your adversary. "Not to cleave to another person, though he be the one you love most—every person is a prison, also a nook and corner" (*Beyond* 41). Nooks and corners offer, or seem to offer, protection, but they also impede if not thwart movement. Moreover, the presence of others in one's life brings something worse than impediment: defilement. "Solitude is with us a virtue: it is a sublime urge and inclination for cleanliness which divines that all contact between man and man—'in society'—must inevitably be unclean. All community makes somehow, somewhere, sometime—'common'" (284).

Thus Paul Ricoeur speaks of Nietzsche's Brahminical "urge and inclination for cleanliness": "Dread of the impure is, in fact, no more a physical fear than defilement is a stain or spot. Dread of the impure is like fear, but already it faces a threat which, beyond the threat of suffering and death, aims at a diminution of existence, a loss of the personal core of one's being" (*Symbolism* 41). Solitude is a key virtue, then, because it preserves the integrity of the omnicompetent self: It serves as a prophylactic against the "loss of the personal core of one's being" that arises when one is in contact, in "community," with others. And how do others defile one? Clearly, for Nietzsche, by achieving, or even by pretending to achieve, understanding: "Every profound thinker is more afraid of being understood than of being misunderstood" (*Beyond* 290). Or, again, Emerson: "To be great is to be misunderstood" (265).

From this dread, Ricoeur says, "suspicion is born" (*Symbolism* 41). One suspects others: One preserves oneself from the defilement of their attention, of their potential comprehension. "Every profound thinker is more afraid of being understood than of being misunderstood" because any thinker understood by the herd is *ipso facto* not profound. "That which can be made Explicit to the Idiot is not worth my care," says Blake (676). And here, perhaps, is the point at which Nietzsche's self-sufficiency comes unraveled. As we saw earlier, for Nietzsche the key "tests" in the *agon*, which produces *arete*, are those "which are taken before ourselves and before no other judge"; yet clearly, this other rhetoric indicates, the approval or disapproval of others is an even more important test, an infallible indicator of profundity or shallowness. The response of others is a requirement for genuine self-understanding: Thus Zarathustra, for all his incomparable arrogance, constantly assesses the quality of his audience's response to him: "They do not understand me, I am not the mouth for these ears," he thinks to himself (*Zarathustra* 45).[3]

The above passage from the prologue to *Zarathustra* is particularly important, because it complicates our pursuit of this topic. Zarathustra is contemptuous of the crowds who attend to him: He tells them stories that he knows they will misunderstand. For instance, he weaves the tale of the "Ultimate Man," who is of course far inferior to the "Superman," being cautious, timid, and obedient, but appealing to the people: "'O Zarathustra'—so they cried—'make us into this Ultimate Man! You can have the Superman!'" (47) Zarathustra, in silent reply, repeats to himself his previous comment: "They do not understand me, I am not the mouth for these ears." But Nietzsche prefaces this repetition of the comment with a most important sentence: "Zarathustra grew sad." Having deliberately offered to them a misleading discourse, he is distressed that they do misunderstand him, that they do not see the folly of the Ultimate Man. Similarly, in one of the passages about Jesus that are scattered through Nietzsche's later work—and we may take it as axiomatic that all of Nietzsche's comments about Jesus himself are autobiographical—he considers Jesus' whole career as a response to the world's failure to love (which is also to say, to understand) him! The colossal failure, the weakness of human love and human understanding prompted Jesus' teaching and (one infers) Nietzsche's philosophy—but they were also what prompted Jesus to choose death: "He whose feelings are like this, he who *knows* about love to this extent—*seeks* death.—But why reflect on such painful things? As long as one does not have to." (*Beyond* 269). It is difficult not to think that in the same way Nietzsche "seeks" madness, and finds it, torn as he is between contempt for all those beneath him and desire for their understanding and approval.

(An agonistic conception of virtue, especially in the extreme form of it presented by Nietzsche, only exacerbates the tension of self-evaluation, because in the relentless testing of the *agon*, the only reliable conclusion is failure. If one passes the test, one passes only *for now*—one could still fail the next one. As in a scientific experiment, the only perfectly reliable result is disconfirmation, disproof: A hypothesis borne out by experimental trial is never thereby *proved*, it simply remains adequate for now, remains a valid explanation without necessarily being *the* correct explanation. This is the problem of Othello: Desdemona can never be proved faithful, only not yet unfaithful. It is also the problem of Nietzsche's self-testing.)

I have noted that for the later Nietzsche solitude is one of the four virtues. Perhaps it is the key virtue. It is the one he emphasizes in the passage in which he lists four, and Zarathustra makes it clear that virtues war against one another for pride of place: "Each of your virtues . . . wants your spirit to be its herald, it wants your entire strength in anger, hate, and love" (64). But to raise solitude to this pinnacle is, in the long run, to elevate paranoia to the status of a categorical imperative. This paranoia underlies Nietzsche's peculiar fascination with giving, "the gift-giving virtue," or "the bestowing virtue"—*Die schenkende Tugend*—which as I noted earlier seems to underlie Marcel Mauss's influential treatment of the topic.

These thoughts of Zarathustra-Nietzsche's can best be understood by assimilating them to an ethical category best known to us from Aristotle: magnanimity (*megalopsychia*) or great-souledness. Indeed, what Nietzsche calls solitude simply *is* magnanimity in the Aristotelian sense. For the magnanimous man—the reader of Aristotle cannot quite imagine a magnanimous woman—is rightly conscious of his virtues and therefore unwilling to be in the debt of anyone:

The magnanimous man . . . is disposed to confer benefits, but is ashamed to accept them, because the one is the act of a superior and the other that of an inferior. When he repays a service he does so with interest, because in this way the original benefactor will become his debtor and beneficiary. People of this kind are thought to remember the benefits they have conferred, but not those that they have received (because the beneficiary is inferior to the benefactor, and the magnanimous man wants to be superior), and to enjoy being reminded of the former, but not of the latter. (*Ethics* 1124b14)[4]

And yet how difficult it is to avoid altogether being in a position to receive gifts. Even Zarathustra receives a gift from his disciples, "a staff, upon the golden haft of which a serpent was coiled about a sun," and moreover, he "was delighted with the staff and leaned upon it" (*Zarathustra* 100). The pleasure with which he receives it may be surprising, but perhaps less so once Zarathustra establishes the context of his reception.

"Tell me," he says to his disciples, "how did gold come to have the highest value? Because it is uncommon and useless and shining and mellow in lustre: it always bestows itself." Of particular importance here is Zarathustra's claim that gold is "useless": Likewise, the staff is useless, for Zarathustra does not need a staff, and walks perfectly well without one. Indeed, it is only because he does *not* need a staff that he takes this one, only because he does *not* require its strength that he is willing to lean upon it. Similarly, it is significant that he does not ask the disciples the purpose of their gift, nor the meaning they assign to the iconography of the staff: Instead he immediately offers his own interpretation of their gift, as though to forestall any explanation they might offer. Thus a few lines further into his discourse he says of his disciples—not describing them but rather exhorting them—"You compel all things to come to you and into you, that they may flow back from your fountain as gifts of your love." Note this hermeneutical transformation of the gift: If you gave something to me, Zarathustra says to his disciples, it is only because I "compelled" this to come unto me. Having then *seized* rather than *received* it, I have interpreted it and returned it to you in this transmogrified form. The staff is therefore my gift to you rather than yours to me, and what I am really giving you is myself in the form of my hermeneutical energy. On this point Emerson provides the best commentary: "You cannot give anything to a magnanimous person. After you have served him, he at once puts you in debt by his magnanimity" (537). Which is to say, he re-establishes his superiority to you: Disciples must remain disciples, and rise to no higher place.

It is important that the staff Zarathustra's disciples give him figures a serpent, for along with the eagle the serpent is Zarathustra's totem:

"the proudest animal under the sun and the wisest animal under the sun" (*Zarathustra* 53). In Heidegger's reading of Nietzsche these totemic animals, or the virtues they represent, are essential to an understanding of the doctrine of the *übermensch*. Explicating the significance of these animals for Zarathustra, Heidegger quotes from notes Nietzsche made during the period in which *Zarathustra* was composed:

> People talk so stupidly about *pride*—and Christianity even tried to make us feel *sinful* about it! The point is that whoever *demands great things of himself, and achieves those things*, must feel quite remote from those who do not. Such *distance* will be interpreted by others as a "putting on airs"; but he knows it only as continuous toil, war, victory, by day and by night. The others have no inkling of all this! (quoted in Heidegger 231)

Though Heidegger does not note it, this passage is merely a paraphrase of Aristotle's description of the magnanimous man, down to the point about putting on airs: Aristotle says that "magnanimous people are thought to be supercilious" (1124a). For Aristotle, "a person is considered to be magnanimous if he thinks he is worthy of great things, provided that he *is* worthy of them" (1123b): In other words, magnanimity requires both the pride of the eagle and the discernment, in this case self-discernment, of the serpent. (This is why the translation of *megalopsychia* simply as "pride" is wrong.) When Zarathustra identifies the eagle and the serpent as his totems, he is simply laying claim to Aristotelian magnanimity—and, by implication but equally important, *denying* that status to his disciples.

"Ultimately 'love of one's neighbour' is always something secondary, in part conventional and arbitrarily illusory, when compared with *fear of one's neighbour*," says Nietzsche in *Beyond Good and Evil* (201). And the content of this fear is precisely that some other could *be* one's neighbor, rather than one's disciple: an equal from whom one might receive gifts—with whom one might be in a position of reciprocity, of friendship—rather than an inferior to whom one gives, at one's own discretion and out of one's natural capaciousness (the interior "fountain"). One could say that Nietzsche is afraid that Kierkegaard's Christian definition is correct: "The concept of *neighbor* really means a duplicating of one's own self. *Neighbor* is what philosophers would call the *other*" (*Works* 37). If my neighbor really is the "other"—keeping in mind the limited usefulness of that formulation, which we saw in Chapter 2—then any claim I make to Zarathustra's hyper-magnanimity is baseless, and what I now have to fear is mockery, since, as Aristotle explains, the person who erroneously thinks himself magnanimous is "conceited" and, ultimately, "foolish" (*Ethics* 1123b): a figure of fun. To receive gifts from others would be to admit that one's claims to magnanimity are ill-founded, and to transform oneself thereby into a buffoon.[5] The solitude that makes the reception of gifts impossible may at times be painful, but it preserves the claim to self-sufficiency, to greatness, to the status of *Übermensch*.

Of course, solitude is more than just painful, it is psychically disfiguring. Thus the phenomena I have already indicated: Zarathustra's obsessive interest in how people respond to him, Nietzsche's half-hidden confession of the mortal agony of being misunderstood and unloved. (It is worth noting that Aristotle's magnanimous person is concerned—some critics say obsessed—with receiving proper honor, though to be sure he does not want honor from just anyone, or the wrong degree of honor.) The subtitle of *Thus Spoke Zarathustra* is immensely relevant here: "A Book for Everyone and No One." Equally important are the words with which I introduced Chapter 1 of this book: "We care whether love is or is not altogether forbidden to us, whether we may not altogether be incapable of it, of admitting it into our world. We wonder whether we may always go mad between the equal efforts and terrors at once of rejecting and of accepting love" (Cavell, *Disowning* 72). Nietzsche went mad.

All that we have done so far in the present chapter has, I hope, cleared the way for an understanding of the necessity of gifts—both the offering and receiving of them—in the moral life and in interpretation. The wise and charitable reader will understand the importance of receiving in the appropriate way the gifts that are offered to her, and will be willing to offer gifts herself, to authors (the gift of attention) and perhaps to other readers (the gift of criticism or commentary—which is also a gift to an author). But of course, knowing that the circulation of gifts is essential to a healthy society of interpreters is only the beginning: It is necessary to explore the kinds of discernment that are needed in order to know the spirit in which to receive a literary gift and the ways in which that gift should be assessed. It is after all the *a priorism* of Nietzsche's suspicion that I have questioned, not suspicion itself. In the Christian understanding, each of us is the other's neighbor, but of course that does not abrogate the distinction between good and bad neighbors, nor does it suggest that all my neighbors must become my friends. A healthy suspicion, bounded by a commitment to the love of my neighbor, is more properly called discernment: not the discernment of Nietzsche's serpent, which can *only* suspect and therefore is not discernment at all—since its conclusions are preestablished—but the discernment that is prepared to find blessings and cultivate friendships; in short, to receive gifts. There are enormous risks involved in such an enterprise, precisely the risks that Nietzsche was at the utmost pains to avoid. As he says in *The Anti-Christ*, "Love is the state in which man sees things most of all as they are *not*" (*Twilight* 145): In this scheme love—any form of love—far from being productive of knowledge, is the ultimate impediment to knowledge. We have already seen the extent to which Nietzsche's later thought is driven by fear, but above all else he fears being deceived in faith, hope, and love—after all, all three states of mind open one to deception—and would rather suffer anything than the humiliation of being fooled. This may be said to be the very origin of the hermeneutics of suspicion, the adolescent fear of being caught believing in that which others have ceased to believe in. Nietzsche is so often praised for the *daring* of his thought, and this is not wholly inaccurate, but whatever daring his *thought* may have is, paradoxically enough, produced by his exceptional timidity in *living*. Reinhold Niebuhr points out that love's disregard for justifying itself prudentially, its actual *inability* to justify itself prudentially, is just what gives it the power to build communities—it achieves much by risking much (*Nature* II:80–85). In this light, Nietzsche, with his refusal of all investments not calculated to affirm the self, can be seen as the most risk-averse of thinkers. As Paul Ricoeur shows, any positive (as opposed to purely suspicious) hermeneutics involves a Pascalian wager:

> I wager that I shall have a better understanding of man and of the bond between the being of man and the being of all beings if I follow the *indication* of symbolic thought. That wager then becomes the task of *verifying* my wager and saturating it, so to speak, with intelligibility. In return, the task transforms my wager: in betting *on* the significance of the symbolic world, I bet at the same time *that* my wager will be restored to in power of reflection, in the element of coherent discourse. (*Symbolism* 355)

Ricoeur gives the gift of his attention and reflection to the "symbolic world." Is it any less a gift because he hopes to receive some-

thing in return? We need not think so. But it is a valuable and necessary wager in any case, because without it understanding is impossible.
Of course, it remains a wager: There is no way to know in advance
whether anything will be returned. Niebuhr makes the same point yet
more strongly: "The [potential, envisioned] consequence of mutuality
must . . . be the unintended rather than purposed consequence of the
[loving] action. For it is too uncertain a consequence to encourage the
venture towards the life of the other." This uncertainty, this likelihood
that one's offer of love and trust will *not* be reciprocated, makes it important that "according to the ethic of Jesus the actual motive of *agape*
is always conformity to the will of God" (*Nature* II:84). One takes the
risk in obedience, not in expectation, thus protecting oneself from disappointment and, ultimately, cynicism.

And yet I have just said that Ricoeur makes this wager in part because he hopes to receive something in return, and hope is a virtue:
Indeed, hope is the virtue by means of which suspicion can be overcome. The charitable reader offers the gift of constant and loving attention—faithfulness—to a story, to a poem, to an argument, in hope
that it will be rewarded. But this hope involves neither *demand* nor *expectation*; indeed, if it demanded or expected it would not be hope.

An absolute suspicion—one that always and on principle refuses Ricoeur's wager—is the natural outworking of despair; and despair, or
desperatio, as Josef Pieper, drawing heavily on Aquinas, has usefully
shown, is one of the two forms of hopelessness (*On Hope* 47). The
other, presumption (*praesumptio*), which in its triumphalist confidence
sees no need for hope, would seem to be far less common in our time,
but should be kept in mind even as we think of despair and suspicion:
As Jürgen Moltmann notes, "Both forms of hopelessness, by anticipating the fulfillment or by giving up hope, cancel the wayfaring character of hope" (23).[6] That is a fine and important phrase—"the wayfaring character of hope"—and it reminds us that Augustine, as he
envisions the charitable interpreter, employs a similar metaphor. Here
is a passage that I quoted much earlier:

> But anyone who understands in the Scriptures something other than
> that intended by them is deceived, although they do not lie. However, as
> I began to explain, if he is deceived in an interpretation that builds up
> charity, which is the end of the commandments, he is deceived in the
> same way as a man who leaves a road by mistake but passes through a
> field to the same place toward which the road itself leads. But he is to be

corrected and shown that it is more useful not to leave the road, lest the habit of deviating force him to take a crossroad or a perverse way. (*On Christian Doctrine* 31)

The interpreter who seeks to know the purposed meaning of Scripture (or, my argument claims, anything else) is the wayfarer who stays to the well-made road; the less shrewd and patient interpreter risks the impediments of the field. But both are true interpreters because they set forth toward a goal: They are teleologically minded, they are wayfarers—they are hopeful. It is important to note that Moltmann derives his language of wayfaring from Pieper, who makes this key point: "The concept of the *status viatoris* is one of the basic concepts of every Christian rule of life. To be a 'viator' means 'one on the way.' The *status viatoris* is, then, the 'condition or state of being on the way.' Its proper antonym is *status comprehensoris*. One who has comprehended, encompassed, arrived, is no longer a *viator*, but a *comprehensor*" (11). The presumptuous and the despairing are not on the way to anywhere: Though they would disagree about what can be understood (comprehended), they agree that they understand all that there is to be understood. They have come to the end of interpretation. Suspicion elevated to a cardinal principle is not just arrogant—not merely the assertion of an antique and pagan magnanimity, though that is bad enough—it is also, and more troublingly, still the annulment of hope. The hopeless interpreter, in the lassitude of despair, can neither receive nor offer gifts: Having petrified the *personae* of human discourse and thereby transformed them into the *res* of commodified "texts," he or she has nothing left to love, and in the end lacks even the consolations of interpretation itself.

Interlude C:
Quixotic Reading

The Quixotic reader dwells in a world of mirrors: Looking into a book or a poem, the Quixotic reader sees himself or herself reflected. Don Quixote is the patron and exemplar of this kind of reading, because he is able to comprehend every experience—or almost every experience—within the context of his imagined chivalric world. Every innkeeper can be a castellan, every whore a princess, every windmill a giant; no challenge—or almost no challenge—is too great for Quixote's hermeneutical resourcefulness.

Charles Kinbote is nearly a Quixotic reader, but he fails to achieve that imaginative power: He cannot see "Pale Fire" as a poem about Zembla, though he does imagine that Shade *wanted* to write a poem about Zembla but was forcibly deflected from that enterprise by his jealous wife Sybil; he finds shards and fragments of Shade's "original design" in the poet's rejected variants. Don Quixote himself shuns such maladroit conjuring in favor of a more decisive and sweeping interpretive *diktat*. Perhaps it is an insult to Quixote's kindness to say so, but one is reminded here of Nietzsche: "In this condition one enriches everything out of one's own abundance: what one sees, what one desires, one sees swollen, pressing, strong, overladen with energy. The man in this condition transforms things until they mirror his power—until they are reflections of his perfection. This *compulsion* to transform into the perfect is—art" (*Twilight* 83; original emphasis). Kinbote by this standard fails of art, lacking the inner resource to transform the obviously flawed into "reflections of his perfection," as Zarathustra transformed the gift of the staff.

But of course, it is not only the powerful who transform books into mirrors; surely more common is the reader who discovers reflections of his or her weaknesses, struggles, and puzzlements. Every hermeneutics of suspicion is also a problematizing hermeneutics: Thwarted by its own *aporias*, it must find them always repeated in the texts it encounters. And when such problematizing readers indeed find what they knew they would find, their reactions are simultaneously triumphant and sorrowful; misery may love company, but it's misery all the same.

This is the dismal side of Quixotic reading: Its mirroring can be coercive and arrogant, as others are continually metamorphosed into copies of oneself. The great prophet of this dark Quixotism is not so much Nietzsche as Emerson: "Speak your latent conviction, and it shall be the universal sense; for the utmost in due time becomes the outmost,—and our first thought is rendered back to us by the trumpets of the Last Judgment. . . . In every work of genius we recognize our own rejected thoughts: they come back to us with a certain alienated majesty" (*Essays* 259). Even works of genius, then, cannot truly be gifts to us: They are merely our own possessions returned to their rightful owner. In this model otherness, difference, cannot be tolerated: "History"—and anything else—"is an impertinence and an injury, if it be any thing more than a cheerful apologue and parable of my being and becoming" (*Essays* 270). This variety of Quixotism is, in Pieper's term, presumptuous, and what it always presumes is *identity*.

The better angel of Quixotism's nature is its generosity, its willingness to seek and recognize value in unlikely and unfamiliar forms. This beneficent Quixotism does not revel in the distance that, as Steiner says, the critic finds "fertile and [excitingly] problematical" ("Critic" 67); the Quixotic reader cares nothing for the splendid alienation celebrated by Cartesian hermeneutics. One who reads in this way builds, or seeks to build, an imagined local culture, a tiny *polis* of like-minded people.

It is often hard to distinguish these two kinds of reading. Quixotic reading is always highly attentive, and we noted back in Chapter 1, with reference to Derrida, that attention tends also to be of this ambiguous character—which perhaps accounts for the radically different views readers have of Don Quixote himself: Is he a tyrant of fantasy, bending the world around him into conformity with his hermeneutical will to power, or is he a generous and playful giver of the gift of his imagination?

In contemplating this difficult notion, let us turn to a celebrated essay, Adrienne Rich's meditation on Emily Dickinson, "Vesuvius at Home"; it illustrates, perhaps, both sides of this hermeneutical Quixotism, which constitutes our closest approximation yet to genuinely charitable reading.

The first words of the essay do not state but rather enact a repudiation of the Cartesian models of alienation and objectivity:

> I am traveling at the speed of time, along the Massachusetts Turnpike. For months, for years, for most of my life, I have been hovering like an insect against the screens of an existence which inhabited Amherst, Massachusetts, between 1830 and 1886. The methods, the exclusions, of Emily Dickinson's existence could not have been my own; yet more and more, as a woman poet finding my own methods, I have come to understand her necessities, could have been witness in her defense. (158)

The whole of Rich's approach to Dickinson can be discerned from this opening paragraph. First, the persistent attention that will not rest content with distance and alienation, but that wants meaningful human contact: A little later Rich says, "For years I have been not so much envisioning Emily Dickinson as trying to visit, to enter her mind, through her poems and letters" (159). And when she enters Dickinson's bedroom, she writes, "Here I become, again, an insect, vibrating at the frames of windows, clinging to panes of glass, trying to connect" (161). As Patrocinio Schweickart has noted, the metaphors here are carefully chosen: Visitors and insects are outsiders, and not always welcome—to Dickinson perhaps not welcome at all. "The reader is a visitor and, as such, must observe the necessary courtesies. She must avoid unwarranted intrusions—she must be careful not to impose herself on the other woman" (Schweickart 48). Rich, then, recognizes her outsider's status and does not wholly regret it: She does not *become* Dickinson—"The methods, the exclusions, of Emily Dickinson's existence could not have been my own"—but she comes to "understand her necessities." She does not take Dickinson's place in the defendant's chair—"viewed by her bemused contemporary Thomas Higginson as 'partially cracked,' by the twentieth century as fey or pathological" (Rich 160)—but offers herself to Dickinson as a friendly "witness in her defense."

Moreover, there is humility here. It is implicit in Rich's comparison of herself to an insect, an unimportant creature, like the visitor often bothersome; but it is evident elsewhere in the essay too. At the end she disavows any complete or decisive reading of Dickinson: "There are many more Emily Dickinsons than I have tried to call up here. Wherever you take hold of her, she proliferates" (183). Like Bakhtin, though her pronouns differ in gender, she refuses to "finalize" the object of her attention: "The truth about a man in the mouths of others, not directed to him dialogically and therefore a *secondhand* truth, becomes a *lie* degrading and deadening him, if it touches upon his 'holy of holies,' that is, 'the man in man'" (*Problems* 59). Likewise, Rich concludes her reading of "My life had stood—a Loaded Gun" by insisting that the poem, too, evades finalization: "I do not pretend to have—I don't even wish to have—explained this poem, accounted for its every image; it will reverberate with new tones long after my words about it have ceased to matter" (174). The woman in the house—though she may have said that she heard a fly buzz when she died—will long outlive the insect beating at her door's screen, and so will her poems.[1]

All this is important, but what Rich is up to in "Vesuvius at Home" cannot properly be understood unless it is situated in a far larger project than Rich's attempt to connect with Dickinson. In a prefatory note to the essay, Rich describes a criticism that will ask of a given woman writer "how she came to be for-herself and how she identified with and was able to use women's culture, a women's tradition; and what the presence of other women meant in her life. . . . And this process will make women artists of the past—and present—available in ways we cannot yet predict or imagine" (158). In short, "Vesuvius at Home" participates in an undertaking first described by Virginia Woolf in her decisive book *A Room's of One's Own*.

In describing both the obstacles to and the possibilities of women's writing, Woolf makes a vital (and now famous) historical point:

> Towards the end of the eighteenth century a change came about which, if I were rewriting history, I should describe more fully and think of greater importance than the Crusades or the Wars of the Roses. The middle-class woman began to write. . . . Without these forerunners, Jane Austen and the Brontës and George Eliot could no more have written than Shakespeare could have written without Marlowe, or Marlowe without Chaucer, or Chaucer without those forgotten poets who paved

the ways and tamed the natural savagery of the tongue. For masterpieces are not single and solitary births; they are the outcome of many years of thinking in common, of thinking by the body of the people, so that the experience of the mass is behind the single voice. (65)

Woolf contends that it is necessary for women writers to discover and immerse themselves in this tradition. "It is useless to go to the great men writers for help" on this matter, "however much one may go to them for pleasure. . . . The weight, the pace, the stride of a man's mind are too unlike her own for her to lift anything substantial from him successfully" (76). And Woolf's references to weight, pace, and stride are not wholly metaphorical: A little later she argues that "the book has somehow to be adapted to the body" (78), women's books to women's bodies. If women cultivate the tradition of women's writing that first emerged in the eighteenth century, and emplace themselves in its discursive world—a world owing its whole character to distinctively female bodies, minds, and experiences—then, in "another hundred years" perhaps (94), the tradition will be long and powerful enough to produce true greatness. Women writers will be able to possess "the unconscious bearing of long descent which makes the least turn of the pen of a Thackeray or a Lamb delightful to the ear" (92); more important still, "the dead poet who was Shakespeare's sister will put on the body which she has so often laid down. Drawing her life from the lives of the unknown who were her forerunners, as her brother did before her, she will be born" (114).

It is this enterprise, this building or discovery of a tradition, in which Rich seeks to participate through her essay "Vesuvius at Home." The enterprise itself dictates the key features of Rich's approach that we have noted: The humility, the desire to connect, the refraining from imposition, the acknowledgment of outsidedness, all derive naturally from the task of tradition-building. And this point is vital to an understanding of the Quixotic tradition, because, unlike many of the counterfeits of charitable reading that we have seen, the beneficent form of Quixotic reading seeks not only to connect with an author but also to build a community of like-minded readers. Indeed, Schweickart says just this about Rich's essay: "To read a text and then to write about it is to seek to connect not only with the author of the original text, but also with a community of readers" (56).[2]

At its best, then, Quixotic reading invites the author and other readers to participate in a common venture. This invitation is hopeful: It anticipates an expanding circle of participants. Schweickart calls such hopefulness a "utopian" vision, but it might better be termed eschatological. (Moltmann and Pieper are both properly concerned to distinguish utopian dreaming from eschatological hope.) Thus the relevance of this passage from Bakhtin's last notebook:

> There is neither a first nor a last word and there are no limits to the dialogic context (it extends into the boundless past and the boundless future). Even past meanings, that is, those born in the dialogue of past centuries, can never be stable (finalized, ended once and for all)—they will always change (be renewed) in the process of subsequent, future development of the dialogue. At any moment in the development of the dialogue there are immense, boundless masses of forgotten contextual meanings, but at certain moments of the dialogue's subsequent development along the way they are recalled and invigorated in renewed form (in a new context). Nothing is absolutely dead: every meaning will have its homecoming festival. (*Speech* 170)

Such hopefulness distinguishes both a distinctively Christian charitable interpretation and the feminist model of reading shared by Woolf, Rich, and Schweickart from the kind of "conversational" model of interpretation associated, in various ways, with Richard Rorty, Stanley Fish, and (far less accurately) Gadamer. The *locus classicus* for this "conversationalism"—and still its most elegant expression—may be found in Kenneth Burke's vital book *The Philosophy of Literary Form:*

> Where does the drama [of history] get its materials? From the "unending conversation" that is going on at the point in history when we are born. Imagine that you enter a parlor. You come late. When you arrive, others have long preceded you, and they are engaged in a heated discussion, a discussion too heated for them to pause and tell you exactly what it is about. In fact, the discussion had already begun long before any of them got there, so that no one present is qualified to retrace for you all the steps that had gone before. You listen for a while, until you decide that you have caught the tenor of the argument; then you put in your oar. Someone answers; you answer him; another comes to your defense; another aligns himself against you, to either the embarrassment or gratification of your opponent, depending upon the quality of your ally's assistance. However, the discussion is interminable. The hour grows late,

you must depart. And you do depart, with the discussion still vigorously in progress.

It is from this "unending conversation" . . . that the materials of your drama arise. (110–111)

Bakhtin adds to Burke's appealingly humane but incomplete conversational model the necessary eschatological context: For Bakhtin, God is the Father who waits patiently but hopefully for the world's prodigal meanings to return to him and receive his blessing. Bakhtin implicitly invites us as readers to wait in patient hope for that consummation, and to participate, at first proleptically and then fully, in the "homecoming festival."

But—and here our argument must pivot to a new direction—it must be said that Rich is never as expansive as this in her invitation. Though, as we have seen, her approach to Dickinson acknowledges her status as a "visitor," an outsider, it nevertheless assumes that her threefold status as woman, lesbian, and poet enables her to understand Dickinson in ways that others cannot. It is significant that when Rich gets to the heart of her argument—which is a reading of some Dickinson poems that refer to an unnamed "he" who has some vital role to play in the poet's life—she simply claims privileged knowledge:

Much energy has been invested in trying to identify a concrete, flesh-and-blood male lover whom Dickinson is supposed to have renounced, and to the loss of whom can be traced the secret of her seclusion and the vein of much of her poetry. But the real question, given that the art of poetry is the art of transformation, is how this woman's mind and imagination may have used the masculine element in the world at large, or those elements personified as masculine—including the men she knew; how her relationship to this reveals itself in her images and language. (164–165)

Having posited this view of poetry as transformation, Rich suggests a sequence of changes. First, the images of the masculine human lover must be translated into religious language: In the "patriarchal . . . Judeo-Christian, quasi-Puritan culture of nineteenth-century New England in which Dickinson grew up, . . . the equation of divinity with maleness was so fundamental that it is hardly surprising to find Dickinson . . . blurring erotic with religious experience and imagery" (165).

But to spiritualize and internalize the erotic imagery is not, for Rich, enough. Are the erotic and spiritual terms "metaphors for each other, or for something more intrinsic to Dickinson?" (165). Rich's answer is that both sets of metaphors refer to "something more intrinsic," that something being Dickinson's "own interior power" as a poet: The poems that Rich has been discussing "are about the poet's relationship to her own power, which is exteriorized in masculine form" (165). Curiously enough, the transformations Rich suggests are precisely analogous to the historical development of the epic: from the physical and material epic (Homer) to the religious epic (Milton) to the interior epic of the poet's mind (Wordsworth). In other words, Rich puts Dickinson's poems through these transformations in order to make the poetry more accessible to the historical interpretive world Rich inhabits, to reduce if not eliminate significant difference—in short, to make Dickinson thoroughly and unproblematically a late modern figure.[3] When Rich says that "a woman's poetry about her relationship to her daemon—her own active, creative power—has in patriarchal culture used the language of heterosexual love or patriarchal theology" (170), she denies to heterosexual love and patriarchal theology any real and significant place in Dickinson's experience. They are merely ready-to-hand and uncontroversial sources of images and metaphors—they are *merely* metaphorical, odd though it is to hear a poet suggest such a thing.

One does not have to endorse the theories about Dickinson's supposed lovers that have been promulgated by people whom Rich rightly calls "legend-mongers" to recognize the problem with what Rich is doing here. It seems not to occur to Rich that Dickinson's views on certain important subjects might be different from Rich's own. For instance, Rich writes that "the terms she had been handed by society—Calvinist Protestantism, Romanticism, the nineteenth-century corseting of women's bodies, choice, and sexuality—could spell insanity to a woman genius" (161). Yet the available evidence suggests that Dickinson's attitudes toward at least some of these things (namely, Protestantism and Romanticism) might have been more complex and ambivalent than Rich's own easy rejection.[4] Similarly, Rich notes that Dickinson called Elizabeth Fry and Florence Nightingale "holy," only to comment that "one suspects she merely meant, 'great.'" But why should one suspect that? Surely Dickinson knew and cared about the difference between holiness and greatness; it is not as though she of all people was careless in her use of language.

Here is a case in which the embrace of a community of readers—women who are poets, and more particularly, lesbian poets—seems to require the exclusion of other readers (a topic we will have to explore more fully in Chapter 5). Having begun by rightly marking her differences from Dickinson, Rich comes in the end to a presumption of identity that disables her from certain productive forms of encounter with Dickinson's poetry. And this presumption of identity is achieved by relegating alternative interpretations to some more distant and utterly external sphere, where they need not be refuted or even encountered. (Rich doesn't *argue* with any of the interpreters of Dickinson whose work she thinks wrong-headed: She merely *asserts* what "the real question" is.[5]) But is this exclusion a contingent requirement of a particular historical situation—which is certainly the case with Woolf's claim that "[i]t is useless to go to the great men writers for help": The anticipated "hundred years" of the development of a women's tradition will open that door—or does it signify an ineradicable difference between the genders?

Much contemporary feminist criticism has faced and considered these alternatives. But how does the situation change if we take seriously Bakhtin's view that outsidedness—which, let me again stress, is *not* the Cartesian alienation against which much feminist criticism has rightly protested—is a key hermeneutical imperative? If we do take that view seriously, then the task for Rich becomes not just to acknowledge her differences from Dickinson but to consider how those differences can be productive of understanding. Moreover, readers (including male heterosexual readers) who offer to the reading of Dickinson different *kinds* of outsidedness could then be seen to make a valuable contribution to the understanding of her work. (This of course is not to say that all interpretations of Dickinson's poems are equally correct—that those who see "My life had stood—a Loaded Gun" as a poem about God, those who see it as a poem about a male lover, and those who see it as a poem about Dickinson's own poetic power are somehow *all* right—but, rather, that all these interpretations, when carefully and responsibly done, illuminate something in Dickinson's work and further the conversation toward its goal of ever-fuller understanding. It is in that sense that "every meaning will have its homecoming festival.")

In short, what I am invoking here, as a means of escaping the dilemma of choosing between an all-embracing universality of experience and an exclusionary enforcement of difference, is Milbank's overtly eschatological vision of Christianity as "something like 'the peaceful transmission of difference,' or 'differences in a continuous harmony'" (*Theology* 417). But, as I said back in Chapter 1, without the preservation of difference there can be neither transmission nor harmony. The key—and this is a central theme and problem of Milbank's theology—is to find difference that is purified of the violence of exclusion. This is one of the central tasks of Miroslav Volf's book *Exclusion and Embrace* (the language of whose title I have employed from time to time in this chapter and elsewhere):

> A judgment that names exclusion as an evil and differentiation as a positive good, then, is itself not an act of exclusion. To the contrary, such judgment is the beginning of the struggle against exclusion. . . . [T]he remedy for exclusionary judgments [is] certainly not "ironic stances." Instead, we need more adequate judgments based on a distinction between legitimate "differentiation" and illegitimate "exclusion" and made with humility. (68)

Volf goes on to say that it is the "self-giving love" of Jesus Christ that provides the center from which "judgments about exclusion must be made and battles against exclusion fought" (71). But of course, on my account this is a chimerically utopian, rather than an eschatologically hopeful, task outside the Christian Church. And Volf would, I think, agree: It is the Gospel as preached by the Church that alone can give him, a Croat, the strength to embrace his people's Serbian enemies. (Indeed, it is out of the collapse of Yugoslavia that this particular theological testimony came.) It is within the Church and only within the Church that Quixotic reading can become fully charitable reading. And in any case, what could a form of reading prompted and governed by "self-giving love" possibly look like?

KENOSIS

He left his Father's throne above,
(So free, so infinite his grace!)
Emptied himself of all but Love,
And bled for Adam's helpless race.

—Charles Wesley

The phenomenon of revering a text—bowing humbly before its wisdom and authority—is familiar to us chiefly through religious traditions. Its origins, perhaps, may be found in Jewish reverence for the Torah. In light of the previous discussion of love and knowledge, it may be worthwhile to consider this passage from the Zohar, that great text of Jewish mysticism:

> Torah may be compared to a beautiful and stately maiden who is secluded in an isolated chamber of a palace, and has a lover of whose existence she alone knows. For love of her he passes by her gate unceasingly and turns his eyes in all directions to discover her. She is aware that he is forever hovering about the palace and what does she do? She thrusts open a small door in her secret chamber, for a moment reveals her face to her lover, then quickly withdraws it. He alone, none else notices it; but he is aware it is from love of him that she has revealed herself to him for that moment, and his heart and soul and everything within him are drawn to her.

So it is with Torah, which discloses her innermost secrets only to them who love her. . . . Hence, people should pursue the Torah with all their might, so that they might come to be her lovers. (Holtz 29)

Perhaps it is in light of such an allegory that one should understand the striking words that the Talmud attributes to God: "So should it be that you would forsake me, but would keep my Torah"—a notion Emmanuel Levinas takes to mean that Jews should "love the Torah more than God."[1] This seems at first outrageous but perhaps extrapolates legitimately from the counsels of the Torah itself, in the *Shema* (Deut. 6:4–9). Such reverence finds its expression not only in familiar practices such as the use and wearing of phylacteries but also in less well-known but equally striking ceremonies such as the medieval one described by Alberto Manguel in *A History of Reading*:

On the Feast of Shavuot, when Moses received the Torah from the hands of God, the boy about to be initiated was wrapped in a prayer shawl and taken by his father to the teacher. The teacher sat the boy on his lap and showed him a slate on which were written the Hebrew alphabet, a passage from the Scriptures and the words "May the Torah be your occupation." Then the slate was covered with honey and the child licked it, thereby bodily assimilating the holy words. (71)

(Manguel does not note the Biblical echoes here, especially Psalm 19:10 and Ezekiel 3:3.) In the similar environment of the medieval Christian monastery, a like reverence toward holy or authoritative texts was practiced, also with the use of metaphorical encouragements: Jean LeClercq explains that when the common practices of *lectio* (reading) and *meditatio* (meditation) were combined, the result was sometimes referred to as *ruminatio*, the chewing of the word:

To meditate is to attach oneself closely to the sentence being recited and weigh all its words in order to sound the depths of their full meaning. It means assimilating the content of a text by means of a kind of mastication which releases its full flavor. It means, as St. Augustine, St. Gregory, John of Fécamp and others say in an untranslatable expression, to taste it with the *palatum cordis* or *in ore cordis*. (78)[2]

But of course, such reverence may be given to authors or works that are not in the usual sense either sacred or religious. George Steiner employs the same gustatory metaphor in recommending the careful memorization of great poems or pieces of music: "The private reader or listener can become an executant of felt meaning when he learns the poem or musical passage by heart. To learn by heart is to afford the text or music an indwelling clarity and life-force. Ben Jonson's term, 'ingestion,' is precisely right" (*Real* 9).[3] This ritual consumption of the holy or powerful text is not the only way in which passion and reverence can be expressed. Henri-Jean Martin comments that "Petrarch devoutly kissed his copy of Virgil before opening it; Erasmus did the same for his Cicero, and in the evening, when he had finished his day's work, Machiavelli put on his best clothes to read his favorite authors" (363). Petrarch's explanation of his frequent use of quotations from classical authors is particularly telling, and will be useful for our purposes:

> Nothing moves me so much as the quoted axioms of great men. I like to rise above myself, to test my mind to see if it contains anything solid or lofty, or stout or firm against ill-fortune, or to find if my mind has been lying to me about itself. And there is no better way of doing this—except by direct experience, the surest mistress—than by comparing one's mind with those it would most like to resemble. Thus, as I am grateful to my authors who give me the chance of testing my mind against maxims frequently quoted, so I hope my readers will thank me.

David Lyle Jeffrey, whose translation of this letter I have just quoted, singles out for close scrutiny one phrase here: "to find if my mind has been lying to me about itself." Writes Jeffrey, "This is a key phrase in Petrarch's remarks on the writer's dependence upon authorities, and it reveals a characteristic skepticism of the faithful Christian about the privatization of interpretation" (170–171). This is a notion to which we will return.

These examples indicate a straightforward reverence, but of course the dialogics of admiration and imitation is more complicated than that—more complicated, too, than Harold Bloom's tragic family romance in which aspiring sons endlessly slay their mighty fathers or are slain by them. In a sense, literary criticism—good literary criticism—has always been about discriminating among the various forms of admiration, though rarely has the critical task been formulated in that way. Do readers really love writers? Do they really revere them? Are love and reverence the same? If not, is reverence compatible with love? What other sorts of responses seem to be loving but in fact are not? In the "interludes" between chapters we have been exploring these questions, but we require one more term, or set of terms, with which to clarify our picture of charitable reading.

In an earlier chapter I explored Bakhtin's claim that self-love is impossible—along with a few of its manifold implications—in such detail because otherwise it might be tempting to assign a certain meaning to this claim that, though initially appealing, is ultimately unjustifiable. I refer to the idea that genuine love of others is *kenotic* in a particular sense of that word: Genuine love of others requires an emptying out of one's own self and a consequent refilling of the emptied consciousness with attention to the Other. This notion derives from St. Paul's account of Christ's *kenosis* or "self-emptying," "self-divestiture": "Have this mind among yourselves, which you have in Christ Jesus, who, though he was in the form of God, did not count equality with God a thing to be grasped, but emptied himself, taking the form of a servant, being born in the likeness of men" (Philippians 2:5–7 RSV).

Simone Weil believes a kenotic movement to be necessary for the love of others, as she explains in the continuation of a passage I quoted in Chapter 2: "This way of looking is first of all attentive. The soul empties itself of all its own contents in order to receive into itself the being it is looking at, just as he is, in all his truth" (115). Here again— now in her claim that real attentiveness to, and hence love for, the other depends upon an evacuation of the ego—Weil is a representative rather than a unique figure. Karl F. Morrison has identified this kenotic tradition as one of the great streams of ethical thought in the Western world: It describes, in his view, a "hermeneutics of empathy" that finds its most focused expression in the phrase "I am you." The self, in this picture, loses itself in the object of its contemplation. In Iris Murdoch's novel *The Unicorn*, a man in immediate danger of drowning finds his attentiveness to the world preternaturally intensified: He learns "to look and look until one exists no more"; with this death of self "the world becomes quite automatically the object of perfect love" (198). Here self-annihilation is the one thing needful for perfect attentiveness and perfect love.

Even Dostoevsky can partake of this tradition. Steven Cassedy, in an essay on Pavel Florensky, cites a passage from Dostoevsky's notebook, one written just after the death of Dostoevsky's first wife in 1864:

To love a person *as oneself*, according to Christ's commandment, is impossible. . . . After the appearance of Christ as *the ideal of man in the flesh*, however, it became as clear as day that the highest, the ultimate development of the individual person must progress precisely to the point . . . where man can find out, recognize, and, with all the force of his nature, be convinced that the highest use he can make of his individual person, of the fullness of the development of his self, is, as it were, to annihilate this self. (cited in Cassedy 96; original emphasis)

It would be surprising, given the weight of this testimony, if Bakhtin did not hold to a kenotic understanding of love. Yet the evidence suggests that Bakhtin directly rejects the kenotic tradition *as just described*—though, as we shall see, there is another sense in which the *kenosis* passage from St. Paul is utterly essential to his charitable hermeneutics, and ours.

Strong indications of that rejection may be found in Chapter 2, where we explored Bakhtin's emphasis on achieving a properly answerable "I-for-myself." To live "for oneself" in the answerable rather than the egotistical sense requires that one not engage in self-annihilation. One must place one's "signature" on the "emotional-volitional moment" of "I-for-myself" just as forcefully as one places it on the "I-for-another" moment. The clear implication is that the three key "emotional-volitional moments" (the third being "the other-for-me") are mutually reinforcing: No one of them can be reached in isolation from the others.

But Bakhtin goes further in saying that the loss or abdication of selfhood so prized by the interpretation of *kenosis* I have described, as well as by other forms of mysticism, leads also to the abdication of answerability and the refusal of self-activity—in short, to lose oneself is to assume an "alibi for Being."

Participation in the being-event of the world in its entirety does not coincide, from our point of view, with irresponsible self-surrender to Being, with being-possessed by Being. What happens in the latter case is that the passive moment in my participation is moved to the fore, while my to-be-accomplished self-activity is reduced. The aspiration of Nietzshe's philosophy reduces to a considerable extent to this possessedness by Being (one-sided participation); its ultimate result is the absurdity of contemporary Dionysianism. (*Toward* 49)[4]

The evacuation of the self in favor of Being, *or* of the other, actually *prevents* a genuinely answerable and self-active "I-for-another." As Bakhtin writes in "Author and Hero," in the Christ of the Gospels there appears for the first time in human history "an infinitely deepened *I-for-myself*—not a cold *I-for-myself*, but one of boundless kindness toward the other; an *I-for-myself* that renders full justice for the other as such, disclosing and affirming the other's axiological distinctiveness in all its fullness" (*Art* 56). (Christ is therefore the ultimate "other-for-me"—a point familiar to us from Bonhoeffer's famous claim that "Jesus is there only for others" [*Letters* 381].)

This is one of Bakhtin's most consistent themes. He would write much later in the set of notes titled "Toward a Reworking of the Dostoevsky Book" that what is required is "not merging with another, but preserving one's own position of *extralocality* and the *surplus* of vision and understanding connected with it" (*Problems* 299). In notes made near the end of his life, Bakhtin would define "understanding as the transformation of the other's into 'one's own/another's'"; the "principle of outsidedness" remains essential; neither the self nor the other is expendable, since self cannot be purely self nor other purely other (*Speech* 168). Perhaps the fullest and boldest exploration of this theme comes in "Discourse in the Novel," where Bakhtin explains that a "passive understanding of linguistic meaning"—or, it follows for Bakhtin, of personal actions more generally conceived—"is no understanding at all."

> Even . . . an understanding of the speaker's intention insofar as that understanding remains purely passive, purely receptive contributes nothing new to the word under consideration, only mirroring it, seeking, at its most ambitious, merely the full reproduction of that which is already given in the word—even such an understanding never goes beyond the boundaries of the word's context and in no way enriches the word. (*Dialogic* 281)

The failure to "enrich the word" is for Bakhtin an *ethical* failure: Passive reconstruction "leaves the speaker in his own personal context, within his own boundaries." An "active understanding" is "precisely what the speaker counts on" (*Dialogic* 282): To refuse it in the name of accurate reconstruction is to imprison one's interlocutor in a Cartesian fortress-self.[5]

But passive reconstruction damages the self of the interpreter as well as that of the speaker. One of the best accounts of this damage may be found in Solzhenitsyn's *The First Circle*, when State Counselor Innokenty Artemyevich Volodin reads forbidden books for the first time:

> It turned out that you have to know how to read. It is not just a matter of letting your eyes run down the pages. Since Innokenty, from youth on, had been shielded from erroneous or outcast books, and had read only the clearly established classics [of the Marxist-Leninist canon], he had grown used to believing every word he read, giving himself up completely to the author's will. Now, reading writers whose opinions contradicted one another, he was unable for a while to rebel, but could only submit to one author, then to another, then to a third. (344)

Solzhenitsyn here describes a universal ethical failure: Authors, teachers (including other mediators or transmitters of works), and readers alike engage in a simple hermeneutical system in which the word produced is authoritative and its reception purely passive. Innokenty's interpretive humility is a false humility: Having abdicated "self-activity," having claimed an "alibi for Being"—in obedience to authorities who demand just that from him—Innokenty has rendered himself incapable of achieving any of the three "emotional-volitional moments" that Bakhtin finds necessary to the truly answerable consciousness. At age thirty, he is beginning to learn for the first time what it might mean to be a responsible human being. And the first step, for him, is claiming the right to evaluate and respond to what he reads—to achieve an authentic "I-for-myself" that can then be the foundation for an authentic "I-for-another." Perhaps he will even be able to imagine an "other-for-me."[6]

So *kenosis* in the sense of self-evacuation or self-annihilation is forbidden by the Bakhtinian understanding of love. Thus one can see that by Bakhtin's lights Kierkegaard comes remarkably close to the true connection between love and knowledge but through a misplaced asceticism misses it:

> Christ says: The one I love, unto him I shall reveal myself. But that is a general truth: to the one who loves a thing, that thing reveals itself to him, to the one who loves truth, truth reveals itself, and so on. For we

generally think of the recipient as inactive and of the object to be revealed as conveying itself to him. But this is how it is: the recipient is the
lover, and then the loved one is revealed to him, for he himself is transformed in the likeness of the loved one. Becoming what one understands
is the only thorough way to understand, and one understands only according to what oneself becomes.

We see here, moreover, that to love and to know . . . are essentially
synonymous. And just as to love means that the other is revealed, so naturally it also means that one is revealed oneself. (*Papers* 343)

Kierkegaard comprehends the essential role played by the recipient
of the word; he understands that such receptivity is a form of love; but
he does not see that simply to "become what one understands" is to
give up something essential to understanding. Even in its humility, it
claims an end to wayfaring, a presumptuous assertion of the *status
comprehensor*—an assertion perhaps motivated by uneasiness with an
ongoing dialogical tension of self and other.[7]

Bakhtin's remarkable suggestion is that proper answerability requires not this Kierkegaardian ascesis, this self-evacuation, but rather
a self-*renunciation* that never loses or annihilates the self:

If I actually lost myself in the other (instead of two participants there
would be one—an impoverishment of Being), i.e., if I ceased to be
unique, then this moment of my non-being cannot become a moment in
the being of consciousness—it would simply not exist for me, i.e., being
would not be accomplished through me at that moment. Passive em-
pathizing, being-possessed, losing oneself—these have nothing in common with the *answerable* act/deed of self-abstracting or self-renunciation. In self-renunciation I actualize with utmost activeness and in full
the uniqueness of my place in Being. The world in which I, from my
own unique place, renounce myself does not become a world in which I
do not exist, a world which is indifferent, in its meaning, to my existence: self-renunciation is a performance or accomplishment that encompasses Being-as-event. (16)

What Bakhtin counsels here is an ascetic self-discipline that does
not eradicate the self but chastens it. It is very different from the kind
of *kenosis* recommended by Weil, Dostoevsky, and others in that tradition—but it owes its character to the passage from Philippians in
which the term *kenosis* appears. Immediately succeeding the sentences

just quoted is this comment: "A great symbol of self-activity, the descending [?] of Christ."[8] Mihailovic seems to think that Bakhtin refers here to Christ's descent into Hell (75), but if Sartre is wrong in thinking that "Hell is other people," it is more likely and more fitting that Bakhtin is referring to the passage from Philippians 2 mentioned earlier: the descent of the eternal Word from Heaven to Earth, his taking on of human flesh.

St. Paul's description of what happened in this *kenosis* is utterly germane to Bakhtin's description of genuine self-renunciation. Note that what Christ renounces in taking human form is an "equality with God" that is rightfully his: He sheds not false or prideful claims to superiority but, rather, the "form of God" that (in traditional Christian theology) is appropriate to his divine nature, in order to "take the form of a servant." He does not cease to exist, he does not eradicate his "I," but instead achieves true "self-activity," assumes a genuine "I-for-myself," precisely by virtue of his perfect servitude, his thoroughgoing commitment to "I-for-another." Let us recall again Bakhtin's description, in "Author and Hero," of Christ's "infinitely deepened *I-for-myself*—not a cold *I-for-myself*, but one of boundless kindness toward the other; an *I-for-myself* that renders full justice for the other as such, disclosing and affirming the other's axiological distinctiveness in all its fullness" (*Art* 56).

If this is, as already noted, quite unlike the *kenosis*-as-self-evacuation described by Weil and Dostoevsky, it bears a somewhat closer resemblance to what Clark and Holquist call the specifically "Russian kenotic tradition" (84), which emphasizes the ethical necessity of humbling oneself, of depriving oneself of all luxuries and even of that which might rightfully be said to belong to one, in order to "gain Christ" or "attain God." (This is a constant theme in the *Philokalia*, especially in the theology of St. Theodosius and in the much earlier texts attributed to St. Theodorus the Great Ascetic.) Yet this tradition doesn't quite fit either. Bakhtin's ethic shares the emphasis on humility, servitude, and the voluntary assumption of poverty, but, perhaps because it is an ethic rather than a theology as such, it focuses on love for the other rather than on "gaining Christ": "It should suffice to recall the inequality in principle between the *I* and the *other* with respect to value in Christian ethics: one must not love oneself, one must love the other; one must not be indulgent toward oneself, one must be indulgent toward the other; and in general, we must relieve the other of any burdens and take them upon ourselves" (*Art* 38). Bakhtin's view here is remarkably similar to that of Karl Barth, who preferred always to speak of genuine *agape* in terms of "self-giving" rather than "self-sacrifice," as Gene Outka has noted: "His preference . . . is more than fortuitous. He is preoccupied not so much with loss to the self as with gain for the other. At least references to self-giving seem always explicitly linked to other-regard; one gives by making oneself the other's guarantor rather than by virtue of abandoning one's own interests" (209).

Of course, Christian theology has always asserted that love of God and love of the neighbor are complementary rather than opposed, but the exact relationship between the two can in practice be hard to understand, still harder to realize—as we have seen in the case of George Eliot's Dinah Morris. One would not expect Bakhtin, in his early philosophical works, to explore this problem, but at one point in "Author and Hero" he seems to do just that. In the same passage in which he posits Christ's answerable or self-active "I-for-myself," he re-emphasizes the altruistic character of Christian ethical demand: "In all Christ's norms the *I* and the *other* are contraposed: for myself—absolute sacrifice, for the other—loving mercy" (56). But he then adds this crucial, even transformative, point: "But *I-for-myself* is the *other* for God. . . . God is now the heavenly father who is over me and can be merciful to me and justify me where I, from within myself, cannot be merciful to myself and cannot justify myself in principle, as long as I remain pure before myself. What I must be for the other, God is for me." This point is potentially transformative because it may explain how the demands of Bakhtin's ethics can me met. The suggestion here is first that God's "I-for-myself" and "I-for-the-other" find their perfect expression in the *kenosis* of Christ: "The Word became flesh" (John 1:14) is God's signature, in Bakhtin's sense, upon his love for us. But second, that divine signature, once recognized by me, provides the ground for, or source of, my own determination to act answerably, to "undersign" and "incarnate" my love for the other. Bakhtin verges here on the Solovyovian insistence that three—not two, as Bakhtin would say in his later notes (*Speech* 170)—is the "dialogical minimum." Solovyov claims that "I can only acknowledge the absolute significance of a given person, or believe in him (without which true love is impossible), by affirming him in God, and consequently by belief in God Himself, and in myself, as possessing in God the center and root of my own existence" (88). This is necessary because my fallen and sinful state deprives me of the power to acknowledge or believe in the other: "Man can restore formatively the image of God in the living object of his love, only when at the same time he restores that image in himself. However, he does not possess the power for this in himself, for if he possessed it he would not stand in need of restoration; and as he does not possess it in himself, he is obliged to receive it from God" (Solovyov 85–86).

The comments about Christian ethics I have cited from Bakhtin are brief passages in long works that otherwise make little or no mention of these issues. Still, those comments' resemblance to Solovyov's claims—which are themselves characteristic of traditional Christian ethics—strongly suggests that the early Bakhtin understood at least theism and perhaps even Christian belief to be necessary for anyone who hopes to love the other in the ethical or aesthetic spheres of interpretive activity. The *kenosis* of Christ establishes the pattern for our own answerable deeds: It is his "I-for-myself" and "I-for-another" that reveal to us the proper form of self-activity and empower us to pursue it persistently and faithfully.

At the beginning of this study I suggested that almost no one seems to have considered reading of non-Biblical texts a theologically significant activity. And yet only if reading *is* a theologically significant activity can many of the counsels I am making in this book be justified. The kenotic reading I have outlined makes little sense for a person who does not believe in the claims the Christian church has historically made for Jesus Christ, and who does not participate in the life of that church. Absent such faith and such participation, the humble, indeed sacrificial, nature of kenotic reading is pointless, for reasons that Reinhold Niebuhr explained many years ago:

> Sacrificial love . . . is an act in history; but it cannot justify itself in history. From the standpoint of history mutual love is the highest good. Only in mutual love, in which the concern of one person for the interests of another prompts and elicits a reciprocal affection, are the social demands of historical existence satisfied. . . .
>
> Sacrificial love thus represents a tangent towards 'eternity' in the field of historical ethics. It is nevertheless the support of all historical ethics; for the self cannot achieve relations of mutual and reciprocal affection with others if its actions are dominated by the fear that they may not be reciprocated. Mutuality is not a possible achievement if it is made the intention and goal of any action. Sacrificial love is thus paradoxically related to mutual love. (*Nature* II:69)

This is an acute comment on the mutuality that is foundational to Aristotle's understanding of love, especially the love called friendship. Though all genuine friendships in their full flower possess this mutuality, they had to *begin* by someone extending the offer of affection and attention without knowing whether the other would reciprocate. Given the evil that besets human life, it is no wonder that Milbank calls *kenosis* not just a risk but a "tragic risk" (*Word* 141), and though it is obvious that many people for many different reasons choose to take that risk—otherwise there would be no friendships, no loves at all—it seems almost cruel to *demand* that people do so. Yet Christianity makes just this demand, knowing, as Niebuhr says, that in merely human terms the demand is unjustifiable. And the only encouragement that Christianity can offer is that which comes from taking this "tragic risk" as a corporate endeavor, as the ever-repeated and never-perfected task of the hopeful church.

Interlude D:
Two Charitable Readers

1

As Adrienne Rich visited Emily Dickinson, so Jane Tompkins visited Buffalo Bill. Yet the visits were by necessity of very different character. Rich had every reason to believe that her pilgrimage to Dickinson's house would offer some opportunity, however imperfect, for "connection." But for Tompkins, a trip to the Buffalo Bill Museum involved a close encounter with a personification of the cultural and political imperialism that had shaped the American West in the nineteenth century. If Dickinson could appear to Rich as a deeply sympathetic figure who had much to say, quite directly, to "the mind of a woman poet in America today" (163), Buffalo Bill, we might imagine, could appear to Tompkins but as an apostle of violence toward and subjugation of the people and animals native to the West—a frightening figure at best. Yet what really happens is that, whereas Rich's essay chiefly enacts a confirmation of her hopes, records in interpretive form the achievement of valid connection, Tompkins's reflections on Buffalo Bill produce more surprising and complex conclusions.

Before we can assess these conclusions, we must understand the context of Tompkins's visit to Buffalo Bill's world. Tompkins begins *West of Everything*, the book of which the Buffalo Bill essay would ultimately become a part, with a bold statement: "I make no secret of the fact: I love Westerns" (3). But it very soon becomes clear that this love is a complex thing, mixed up with envy, loathing, and moral outrage—

113

among other emotions, all of which Tompkins makes it her business
to describe:

> I am simultaneously attracted and repelled by the power of Western
> heroes, the power that men in our society wield. I've been jealous of
> that power, and longed for it, wanted the experiences that accompany
> it, and seen the figures who embody it as admirable, worthy to emu-
> late, and sexually attractive. I have also been horrified by the male ex-
> ercise of power and, like most women, have felt victimized by it in my
> own life. . . .
> So I came to this project with a mixture of motives. . . . (18)

Tompkins notes that the Western—in whatever medium—provides a
model of character and behavior that quite explicitly is "not for
women but for men" (17). "Why does the Western harbor such ani-
mus against women's words?" she later asks—a woman, using words.
"Why should it be so extreme and unforgiving? . . . Why does the
Western hate women's language?" (64, 66) Tompkins is then an outsider to the Western's discursive world: It's not for her, it's not ad-
dressed to her. Her status as an academic critic, rather than a leisurely
reader, may alienate her still further from that world.

Later, returning to the theme of gender, Tompkins makes this
telling comment:

> In many Westerns . . . women are the motive for male activity (it's
> women who are being avenged, it's a woman the men are trying to res-
> cue) at the same time as what women stand for (love and forgiveness in
> place of revenge) is precisely what that activity denies. Time after time,
> the Western hero commits murder, usually multiple murders, in the
> name of making his town/ranch/mining claim safe for women and chil-
> dren. But the discourse of love and peace which women articulate is
> never listened to . . . , for it belongs to the Christian worldview the
> Western is at pains to eradicate. (41)

What makes this remark so telling—aside from its acute understanding of the incommensurability of Christianity and the moral framework of the Western—is its connection to the way Tompkins concludes her book. She has pointed to a scene in the movie *High Noon* in
which the Grace Kelly character cries out, just before the decisive
conflict between Gary Cooper and his enemies, "I don't care who's

right or who's wrong. There has to be some better way for people to live"; she has, moreover, noted the agonistic manner in which academic disputes are conducted, and has hinted at their structural likeness to conflicts in Westerns. Her book ends with these words:

> So instead of offering you a moral, I call your attention to a moment: the moment of righteous ecstasy, the moment when you know you have the moral advantage of your adversary, the moment of murderousness. It's a moment when there's still time to stop, there's still time to reflect, there's still time to recall what happened in *High Noon*, there's still time to say, "I don't care who's right or who's wrong. There has to be some better way for people to live." (233)

In the Western this voice is never listened to; can it be heard in the academy? It is a question we have pondered already in this book: Is there any alternative to the agonistic model of interpretation? Can, in Milbank's way of putting it, an "ontology of peace" replace the "metaphysics of violence"? Whatever answer we give, for our purposes now it is sufficient to note that, having begun her book by declaring her love for Westerns, Tompkins ends it by aligning herself with those voices within the discourse of the Western who *challenge* the validity of that discourse, that model of character and value.[1]

It is this complexity of response that governs her visit to the Buffalo Bill Museum—which is, and this is vital to Tompkins's essay, actually a series of museums: In addition to the one properly devoted to Buffalo Bill, there is the Whitney Gallery of Western Art, the Winchester Arms Museum, and the Plains Indian Museum. Together these constitute, Tompkins says, "one of the most disturbing places I have ever visited" (180). But the causes of the disturbance are not only the expected ones. It is true that many of Tompkins's expectations are confirmed: In the paintings and sculptures of Frederic Remington, for instance, she is struck both by "the brutality of their subject matter" and by the fact that the exhibit's written commentaries ignore that brutality. "In the face of unusual violence, or implied violence, their message was: what is important here is technique" (181). Much the same tendency shaped the Winchester Arms Museum, which celebrated the manufacturing procedures and commercial successes of gunmaking without any reference to the purposes for which those guns had been used, especially in the West (194). Moreover, the Buffalo Bill Museum itself was dominated by a display of the heads of animals the Great

White Hunters of Bill Cody's day had shot: "When I think about it I realize that I don't know why those animal heads are there. Buffalo Bill didn't kill them; perhaps they were gifts from the famous people he took on hunts. A different kind of jewelry" (186). But never acknowledged as such; indeed, as Tompkins notes, their link with Buffalo Bill is never explained at all.

This sort of suppression, or repression, is ideal grist for the many mills of suspicious hermeneutics: One could not expect any critic to refrain from noting the ideology at work and the lameness of the attempts to camouflage it. And Tompkins does not refrain from so noting. But her account does not stop there, for she must also visit the Plains Indian Museum. And for this she cherished higher hopes: "I had expected that the Plains Indian Museum would show me how life in nature ought to be lived: not the mindless destruction of nineteenth-century America but an ideal form of communion with animals and the land" (190). What she had hoped and thought to find was an Indian angel to counterbalance the cowboy demon. But what she saw documented instead was a Plains Indian culture whose

> mode of life was even more completely dedicated to carnage than Buffalo Bill's, dependent as it was on animals for food, clothing, shelter, equipment, everything. . . . What the museum seemed to say . . . was that cannibalism was universal. Both colonizer and colonized had had their hands imbrued with blood. The Indians had lived off animals and had made war against one another. Violence was simply a necessary and inevitable part of life. And a person who, like me, was horrified at the extent of the destruction was just the kind of romantic idealist my husband sometimes accuses me of being.

Here again—one could say that this is what Tompkins's marvelous book is really about—the protest against agonism and violence is coupled with the question of whether an alternative is possible.

Tompkins cannot answer this question. She doesn't even know if she has any real understanding of what she has seen in this museum—she considers various accounts of how the Plains Indians thought of animals, and wonders whether "Plains Indian culture, if representable at all, was simply not readable by someone like me" (190)—much less an ability to decide whether violence is indeed inevitable in human life. But in the end, though her confusion may not be immediately or evidently productive, her acknowledgment of her confusion is. She has been attentive, not only to the museums but to her own responses, and this attentiveness, as it always does, bears fruit:

> When I left the Buffalo Bill Historical Center, I was full of moral out-rage, an indignation so intense it made me almost sick, though it was pleasurable too, as such emotions usually are. But the outrage was un-dermined by the knowledge that I knew nothing about Buffalo Bill, nothing of his life, nothing of the circumstances that led him to be in-volved in such violent events. And I began to wonder if my reaction was-n't in some way an image, however small, of the violence I had been ob-jecting to. So when I got home I began to read about Buffalo Bill, and a whole new world opened up. I came to love Buffalo Bill. (195)

"I came to love Buffalo Bill." But this coming-to-love did not take the form of moral idealization, or the overcoming of otherness in a pre-sumptuous assertion of identity. Tompkins acknowledges all the vio-lence and cultural conquest and salesmanship in which Buffalo Bill was implicated, but cannot gainsay the universal and unanimous testi-mony of his contemporaries to his many virtues.

> Must we throw out all the wonderful qualities that Cody had, the spirit of hope and emulation that he aroused in millions of people, because of the terrible judgment history has passed on the epoch of which he was part? The kinds of things he stands for—courage, daring, strength, en-durance, generosity, openness to other people, love of drama, love of life, the possibility of living a life that does not deny the body and the desires of the body—are these to be declared dangerous and delusional although he manifested some of them while fighting Indians and others while representing his victories to the world? And the feelings he aroused in his audiences, the idealism, the enthusiasm, the excitement, the belief that dreams could become real—must these be declared mis-guided or a sham because they are associated with the imperialistic con-quest of a continent, with the wholesale extermination of animals and men? (201–202)

The rhetoric of this paragraph, I believe, testifies to my claim that Tompkins is a charitable reader. What is most noteworthy about it is that she does not stack the deck by imbalancing her clauses; she does not encourage us to love Buffalo Bill by diminishing or limiting her description of the evils with which he was associated; her concluding reference to "the imperialistic conquest of a continent, with the wholesale extermination of animals and men" ensures that her shining picture of Buffalo Bill's virtues will not obscure, even temporarily, "the epoch of which he was part" and on which history has pronounced such decisive and "terrible judgment." Tompkins's charity consists in the wholeness of her attention, her refusal to sacrifice attention to one truth so that another one may be privileged. Her own judgment is not so decisive, it is complex and ambivalent, and this is appropriate to the difficulty of the case at hand. If hard cases make bad law, they can also make good and charitable readers: Had Tompkins been more decisive, her essay perhaps would have been more coherent, but less charitable and less truthful. I refer once more to Iris Murdoch: "Coherence is not necessarily good, and one must question its cost. Better sometimes to remain confused" (*Metaphysics* 147).

Tompkins's willingness to admit her ambivalence has another notable effect as well: It encourages her to moral reflection, not just upon Buffalo Bill but also upon herself. She has evaluated not only the agonism of the West but also that of the academic world she inhabits; not only Buffalo Bill's violence but also her own. "Major historical events like genocide," she concludes,

> and major acts of destruction are not simply produced by impersonal historical processes or economic imperatives or historical blunders; human intentionality is involved and human knowledge of the self. Therefore, if you're really, truly interested in not having any more genocide or killing of animals, no matter what else you might do, if you don't first, or also, come to recognize the violence in yourself and your own anger and your own destructiveness, whatever else you do won't work. It isn't that genocide doesn't matter. Genocide matters, and it starts at home. (202–203)

Here Tompkins has appropriated, of course, the old notion that "charity begins at home," and indeed her reflections here are charitable not only toward Buffalo Bill as other—as neighbor, Kierkegaard would say—but toward herself, toward her own inner habitation. To acknowledge one's own potential for violence is to confront oneself with a devastating but necessary home truth.

At the end of Flannery O'Connor's great story "Revelation," Mrs. Turpin stares into a "pig parlor" full of hogs and contemplates the accusation that has been made that day against her: that she is an "old wart hog from hell." "Until the sun slipped finally behind the tree line," O'Connor writes, "Mrs. Turpin remained there with her gaze bent to them as if she were absorbing some abysmal life-giving knowledge" (508). To read one's neighbor charitably, and then to turn the same acute attention on oneself: This practice yields knowledge, knowledge that is always at first "abysmal"—no wonder we fear it— but always, in the end for which we hope, "life-giving."

2

One could argue that the achievement of Jane Tompkins's reading of Buffalo Bill lies in her hard-won ability to recognize the other as a neighbor: This, one could say, is a course that wisely avoids Cartesian alienation, in which the other is purely other, and a presumptuous Quixotic identification, in which the other becomes my mirror and is "other" only as my reflected image is "other." To be, as Bakhtin would have it, "outside" what you read but not alienated from it, so that you take up the responsibility of loving that newfound neighbor as yourself—that is the philosopher's stone of reading.

But we face this challenge in different ways. Tompkins had to bring an alien presence closer, had to achieve a dangerous intimacy with this poster boy for American domestic imperialism. But there are times when charity demands an opposite movement: a distancing, a distinguishing of the other from oneself so that the productive outsidedness can be achieved. Levinas perhaps makes the point too absolutely, but it is valuable in this context nonetheless: "The disproportion between the Other and the self is precisely moral consciousness" (*Difficult* 293). An understanding of this disproportion, I suggested, is what Adrienne Rich failed to achieve in her reading of Dickinson; but it can be done.

Interpretive charity does not come in a single form, and the other reader whose loving attentiveness I wish to praise enacts this productive distancing. The virtues I wish to identify in this reader's practice have been wittily described by Julian Barnes in his wonderful novel about a reader's attachment to a writer, *Flaubert's Parrot*:

> If you quite enjoy a writer's work, if you turn the page approvingly yet don't mind being interrupted, then you tend to like that author unthinkingly. Good chap, you assume. Sound fellow. They say he strangled an

entire pack of Wolf Cubs and fed their bodies to a school of carp? Oh
no, I'm sure he didn't: sound fellow, good chap. But if you love a writer,
if you depend upon the drip-feed of his intelligence, if you want to pursue him and find him—despite edicts to the contrary—then it's impossible to know too much. You seek the vice as well. A pack of Wolf Cubs,
eh? Was that twenty-seven or twenty-eight? And did he have their little
scarves sewn up into a patchwork quilt? And is it true that as he ascended
the scaffold he quoted from the Book of Jonah? And that he bequeathed
his carp pond to the local Boy Scouts? (127)

But of course "you" do not "seek the vice as well" unless "you" have
an uncommon honesty, and an uncommon commitment to loving attention. W. H. Auden was just such an uncommon reader, and we see
his charitable hermeneutics at work in the conversation he conducted
over many years with the writings of Søren Kierkegaard.

When Auden first came across the works of Kierkegaard in the late
1930s—when only a few were available in English translation—he was
utterly captivated. Many years later he would write a rather general
comment that encapsulates the reaction he had at the time:

> Like Pascal, Nietzsche, and Simone Weil, Kierkegaard is one of those
> writers whom it is very difficult to estimate justly. When one reads them
> for the first time, one is bowled over by their originality (they speak in a
> voice one has never heard before) and by the sharpness of their insights
> (they say things which no one before them has said, and which, hence-
> forward, no reader will ever forget). (*Forewords* 182–183)

As Kierkegaard's works appeared in English during the 1940s, Auden
made a point of reviewing them for major American periodicals: It
was his way of spreading the good news about this remarkable thinker
(whom indeed he played a major role in bringing before the public).
What is particularly interesting about these reviews, for our purposes
here, is their expository nature: Auden seems to think it his duty simply to present Kierkegaard's ideas with little comment or evaluation;
he takes the ideas' importance for granted. As intelligent—and, in the
circumstances, arguably appropriate—as these reviews are, one cannot
help thinking of Bakhtin's comment about the "purely passive, purely
receptive" understanding of an author's intentions that "contributes
nothing new to the word under consideration, only mirroring it, seeking, at its most ambitious, merely the full reproduction of that which

is already given in the word" (*Dialogic* 281) and that therefore constitutes something of an ethical failure of engagement.

It is not that Auden was ever unaware of Kierkegaard's personal limitations: In an introduction to a selection of Kierkegaard's writings that he edited in 1952, Auden noted that "[o]ccasionally, it must be confessed, Kierkegaard carried on like a spiritual prima donna" (*Forewords* 168), but even in this context he tended to accept Kierkegaard's own evaluation of himself and his place in society. This paragraph is almost a summary or précis of Kierkegaard's self-understanding as it develops in his journals:

> Every circumstance combined to make Kierkegaard suffer. His father was obsessed by guilt at the memory of having as a young boy cursed God; his mother was a servant girl whom his father had seduced before marriage; the frail and nervously labile constitution he inherited was further damaged by a fall from a tree. His intellectual precociousness combined with his father's intense religious instruction gave him in childhood the consciousness of an adult. Finally he was fated to live, not in the stimulating surroundings of Oxford or Paris, but in the intellectual province of Copenhagen, without competition or understanding. Like Pascal, whom in more ways than one he resembles, or like Richard III, whom he frequently thought of, he was fated to be an exception and a sufferer, whatever he did. (*Forewords* 169)

I believe that every sentence of this description could be traced to a sentence in Kierkegaard's journals, so completely subject is Auden's view to Kierkegaard's own.

Given Auden's enormous intelligence and the breadth of his reading, this state of affairs could not last. Eventually Auden came to realize that, despite Kierkegaard's evident and unquestionable brilliance, there were things, important things, he did not understand and perhaps was constitutionally incapable of understanding. In 1968 he had an opportunity to review the first volume of a new edition of Kierkegaard's *Journals and Papers*, and used it to express some "second thoughts" about this great thinker. Some of these second thoughts concerned Kierkegaard's character—for instance, his conviction that he was indeed "fated to be an exception and a sufferer, whatever he did," that he underwent a "unique tribulation" (Forewords 168). Auden agrees that Kierkegaard was never treated as a normal person, and that he was often made fun of: Yet now he says, "This must have been very disagreeable, but can it really be considered, as Kierkegaard himself considered it, an example of a righteous man's being martyred for the sake of the truth?" (184)

Likewise, Auden came to question Kierkegaard's view that his having been born into a provincial society was a kind of curse, especially since he was constantly denouncing the petty "worldliness" of Danish Christian society: "To condemn a society for being small and provincial," Auden points out, "is not to condemn it for being worldly, but for not being worldly enough: a provincial society lacks the worldly virtues of broad-mindedness and cynical tolerance exhibited by more cosmopolitan societies. As someone who had to write in Danish, Kierkegaard could reasonably complain that this severely limited the size of his potential audience, but this is a worldly objection" (186).

But it was not just Kierkegaard's interpretation of his circumstances that Auden came to question: He also saw the limitations of Kierkegaard's ideas.

> Given his extraordinary upbringing, it is hardly surprising that Kierkegaard should have become—not intellectually but in his sensibility—a Manichee. That is to say, though he would never have denied the orthodox doctrine that God created the world, and asserted that matter was created by an Evil Spirit, one does not feel in his writings the sense that, whatever sorrows and sufferings a man may have to endure, it is nevertheless a miraculous blessing to be alive. Like all heretics, conscious or unconscious, he is a monodist, who can hear with particular acuteness one theme in the New Testament—in his case, the theme of suffering and self-sacrifice—but is deaf to its rich polyphony. (191)

Auden does not deny the value, indeed the necessity, of Kierkegaard's work—later in the essay, he contends that on some subjects Kierkegaard speaks with "absolute authority" (197)—but he feels obliged to say that there are vital truths that Kierkegaard cannot tell us. Thus Auden goes on to argue that "Bonhoeffer, who speaks with the authority of someone who, unlike Kierkegaard, was actually martyred, has the proper corrective" to Kierkegaard's implicit Manicheanism (192). Auden then quotes a passage from Bonhoeffer's *Letters and Papers from Prison* on the spiritual value of physical and earthly affections—the very passage concerning the relationship of our human loves to the *cantus firmus* of heavenly love that we considered in Chapter 1 (and from which Auden draws his musical metaphor of polyphony).

But having so strictly indicated Kierkegaard's shortcomings—having distanced himself from Kierkegaard and established a Bakhtinian "outsidedness"—Auden then pivots his essay toward a renewed appreciation of Kierkegaard. Having noted Bonhoeffer's insistence that we be thankful for and appreciative of the "earthly" pleasures that God gives us, Auden continues:

> Kierkegaard could not honestly have said this about himself, but in his extraordinary portrait of the Knight of Faith one discovers to one's amazement that he knew—bless him!—that it was a defect, not a virtue, in him that he could not say it. The ideal Christian he describes is happily married, looks like a cheerful grocer, and is respected by his neighbors. "That," Kierkegaard says, "is what one should be, but, alas, to me he is incomprehensible: I only understand the Knight of the Doleful Countenance." [192]

"Bless him!" writes Auden: It is an exemplary instance of a proper hermeneutics of recovery. Kierkegaard's self-critique (in this case through the voice of Johannes de Silentio, the pseudonym that he used in *Fear and Trembling*) prompts Auden to a charitable recoupment of what Kierkegaard *does* offer: Having registered the inadequacies of Kierkegaard's thought, he is then free to turn to the Danish thinker's distinctive contributions: "Kierkegaard had, and always will have, an audience for whom it is imperative that they listen to him" (196). That audience, says Auden, is "the individual endowed with an exceptional talent for art or science or philosophy": At identifying the "spiritual dangers" for such a person, "Kierkegaard is better than anyone else; here, indeed, he is a prophet, calling the talented to repentance" (197). Auden is clearly speaking autobiographically, and acknowledging his gratitude to Kierkegaard for having revealed to him his own "pretensions," when he writes, "No person of talent who has read him can fail to realize that the talented man, even more than the millionaire, is the rich man for whom it is so difficult to enter the Kingdom of Heaven" (197).

The charity that Auden shows here is hard-won, for, as he explains at the beginning of his reconsideration of Kierkegaard, something often happens to the reader who is "bowled over" by the "originality" and "sharpness" of these writers who are "difficult to estimate justly": "But with successive readings one's doubts grow, one begins to react against their overemphasis on one aspect of the truth at the expense of all the others, and one's first enthusiasm may all too easily turn into an equally exaggerated aversion" (183). It is characteristic of Auden's charitable reading that he recognizes this danger, too: that one can become ashamed of one's own enthusiasms and determined to repudiate them—but at what cost? To be properly charitable, to strive in his reading to love God and love his neighbor, to continue to draw sustenance from what Julian Barnes's narrator would call the drip-feed of Kierkegaard's intelligence, Auden must be critical and discerning: He cannot fail to "seek the vice," to recognize the truth about the author that has meant so much to him. But he also cannot afford to pay the price of alienation: He must pass through discerning suspicion into the realm of potential recuperation. And this he does.

But one more thing is noteworthy. The finely calibrated moral rhetoric of Auden's reassessment of Kierkegaard suggests that Auden credits Kierkegaard himself for the concluding recuperation: Because Kierkegaard recognizes the limits of his imagination, because he holds forth for our admiration an ideal Christian life that he admits he cannot live, Auden is moved to respond with forbearance and a willingness to continue learning. Auden's charity, then, is also deeply, necessarily, humble. Bless him!

JUSTICE

In the Christian faith the final law in which all other law is ful-
filled is the law of love. But this law does not abrogate the laws of
justice, except as love rises above justice to exceed its demands.

—*Reinhold Niebuhr*

When W. H. Auden was a young schoolmaster, at the Downs
School in Cornwall, he had a very peculiar experience that caused him
to think long and hard about the relationship between love—in this
case the love of one's neighbor, what Auden would later call *agape*—
and justice.[1] He did not provide a full account of the experience until
1964, thirty years after it had occurred, and even then he did not
openly admit that the experience was his own. (It first appeared in his
Introduction to Anne Freemantle's anthology *The Protestant Mystics*,
and he referred to his story as "an unpublished account for the au-
thenticity of which I can vouch.") The account needs to be quoted at
some length:

> One fine summer night in June 1933 I was sitting on a lawn after dinner
> with three colleagues, two women and one man. . . . We were talking ca-
> sually about everyday matters when, quite suddenly and unexpectedly,
> something happened. I felt myself invaded by a power which, though I
> consented to it, was irresistible and certainly not mine. For the first time
> in my life I knew exactly—because, thanks to the power, I was doing it—
> what it means to love one's neighbor as oneself. I was also certain,
> though the conversation continued to be perfectly ordinary, that my

three colleagues were having the same experience. (In the case of one of them, I was later able to confirm this.) My personal feelings towards them were unchanged—they were still colleagues, not intimate friends—but I felt their existence as themselves to be of infinite value and rejoiced in it.

I recalled with shame the many occasions on which I had been spiteful, snobbish, selfish, but the immediate joy was greater than the shame, for I knew that, so long as I was possessed by this spirit, it would be literally impossible for me deliberately to injure another human being. I also knew that the power would, of course, be withdrawn sooner or later and that, when it did, my greed and self-regard would return. The experience lasted at its full intensity for about two hours when we said good-night to each other and went to bed. When I awoke the next morning, it was still present, though weaker, and it did not vanish completely for two days or so. The memory of the experience has not prevented me from making use of others, grossly and often, but it has made it much more difficult for me to deceive myself about what I am up to when I do. And among the various factors which several years later brought me back to the Christian faith in which I had been brought up, the memory of this experience and asking myself what it could mean was one of the most crucial, though, at the time it occurred, I thought I had done with Christianity for good. (*Forewords* 69–70)

Here indeed is a miniature Athens—perhaps even a tiny New Jerusalem. But when Auden wrote a poem about this experience, soon after it happened, his chief concern was to articulate his sense that the acceptance of such an excessively local culture was morally and politically indefensible.

The early stanzas of the poem, to which Auden would eventually give the title "A Summer Night," show no sign of uneasiness:

> *Equal with colleagues in a ring*
> *I sit on each calm evening*
> *Enchanted as the flowers*
> *The opening light draws out of hiding*
> *From leaves with all its dove-like pleading,*
> *Its logic and its powers:*
> *That later we, though parted then,*
> *May still recall these evenings when*

> *Fear gave his watch no look;*
> *The lion griefs loped from the shade*
> *And on our knees their muzzles laid,*
> *And Death put down his book.* (Collected Poems *117*)

But as the poem moves on, its center of interest shifts: What about those who are not so fortunate as to be enclosed within such an Edenic "ring"? How does an acknowledgment of their existence affect the comfortable insiders? Or is life in such an enchanted circle dependent on a studied ignorance of those outside? Perhaps the insiders, "whom hunger cannot move,"

> *do not care to know,*
> *Where Poland draws her eastern bow,*
> *What violence is done,*
> *Nor ask what doubtful act allows*
> *Our freedom in this English house,*
> *Our picnics in the sun.*
> *The creepered wall stands up to hide*
> *The gathering multitudes outside*
> *Whose glances hunger worsens;*
> *Concealing from their wretchedness*
> *Our metaphysical distress,*
> *Our kindness to ten persons.* (Collected Poems *118*)

This vision of love and community, then, may be not a free gift in which to rejoice but a dangerous temptation to social quietism: It is at best a "doubtful act." What the Auden of 1964 celebrates as a blessed inability to harm others, the Auden of 1933 fears as an insidious tendency to be satisfied with one's "kindness to ten persons" while the "gathering multitudes" outside starve. The perfect local understanding that the Auden even of 1940 celebrates as an incalculable gift, the Auden of 1933 finds scandalous precisely because it is local and not universal. It is only at the end of the poem, when "sounds of riveting" (138) betoken the rebuilding (presumably on more just and equitable foundations) of a ruined city, that the note of exaltation with which the poem began returns: Exaltation becomes possible again only when the little collegial circle of friends is incorporated, at least potentially, into a new city. As Edward Mendelson writes in the richest and wisest reading of this great poem, "Personal love . . . will have power to calm nations and grant even the murderer forgiveness and peace" only when it is "transfigured into public concord" (*Early* 170).

In other words, Auden believed, at the time, that the personal satisfactions of love could not be accepted as an alternative to, or a distraction from, the public demands of political justice. And it seems clear that the contemporary academy would largely agree with this view. Much contemporary criticism and theory—almost all varieties of feminism, Marxist and neo-Marxist criticism, ecocriticism, postcolonial criticism and theory, and so on—is motivated by an attempt to use the institutions and procedures of literary study to make some move, however trifling, in the direction of a more just social order. The tiny personal claims of love seem, many of us think, to carry little weight when compared to the sovereign demands of justice. But this apparent conflict bears a great deal of examination.

It is interesting to note that Auden's dilemma closely resembles that of Dinah Morris, in George Eliot's *Adam Bede*, whose sense of being torn between the love of Adam and the demands of universal charity we explored in Chapter 1. Auden would later call his experience a "vision of *agape*" because he was not bound to his colleagues by erotic or friendly attachments—"they were still colleagues, not intimate friends"—but "A Summer Night" suggests that at the time of the "vision" he understood his relationship with his colleagues in a way that closely resembles Aristotle's description of *philia* (not least because of their shared participation in a communal structure). But however we choose to define Auden's response to his colleagues, there is a *partiality* to this attraction that makes it "doubtful" to him in just the way that Dinah's love for Adam is "doubtful" to her.

But what is of greater interest here is the other half of each equation: For Dinah, as we saw, the partiality and the private satisfactions of her love for Adam are opposed by the universal claims of *charity;* but for Auden such private satisfactions are opposed by the universal claims of *justice*. Indeed, "A Summer Night" seems to reject not only the private loves (whether *eros* or *philia*) but also the kind of affection and attention that Dinah thinks it her spiritual mission to give to others. Throughout *Adam Bede* Dinah is eager to comfort those within her sphere of acquaintance who suffer, whether it be someone whom she knows fairly intimately (Hetty Sorrel in prison) or someone whom she barely knows at all (Lisbeth Bede after the sudden death of her husband). But this seems to be precisely the kind of care that Auden dismisses as "our kindness to ten persons," a kindness that scarcely deserves credit when there remain "gathering multitudes outside / Whose glances hunger worsens." In the young Auden's scheme of values, Dinah's kind of charity remains private and hence apolitical, even if it is not preferential.

What we see here, in the shift of the character of the felt general obligation from Dinah's charity to Auden's justice, is evidence of a slow but momentous social transformation, one that perhaps is best seen in England but that obtained all over Europe from the seventeenth century onward. This transformation had many causes, but two have particular significance for our argument here. First, the gradual constriction of the meaning of the word *charity* from "Christian love" to "benevolence toward the poor," a constriction that, as Raymond Williams points out, began in the Middle Ages: The narrower meaning was "probably already dominant" as early as the sixteenth century (*Keywords* 54). Second, the expansion of the notion of justice from the strictly aristocratic context that it finds in Aristotle—and therefore in most of his followers, among them many Christian thinkers—to a universal context. If justice is no longer relevant only to those who rule, but there are no widely recognized ways of redescribing justice as a virtue for everyone, then the practical result is that justice becomes a collective rather than a personal virtue, exhibited primarily in institutions rather than individuals.

These two developments are linked in interesting ways, for as charity comes to be identified with philanthropic benevolence it comes to be seen more and more as a work of supererogation—the fruit of personal graciousness, a free "gift" beyond what duty demands—rather than as an obligation due to others:[2] Only by making benevolence to the poor and oppressed a matter of justice rather than charity can the sense of obligation be effectively restored. The very constriction of the meaning of charity lessens its binding force: It retains that force only for people who retain some sense of the old meaning of the word, the love Christians should show to one another and to those outside the household of faith. As Gertrude Himmelfarb shows, notable among the groups who preserve that old meaning of the word, and who consequently remain extraordinarily active in personal charitable work, are the various followers of John Wesley (*Idea* 31–33); and of course, Dinah Morris is a Methodist.

But people do not like to be lectured about their obligations; that, coupled with the sense that justice is a political aspiration rather than a private virtue, makes it unsurprising that help for the poor takes on increasingly institutional forms—a trend commonly associated with the proliferation of charitable organizations in the nineteenth century, but which actually gains a great deal of momentum in the eighteenth.[3] The rise of charitable institutions renders charity less personal and more abstract, but also (consequently) binding in a way that residents of a bureaucratic society can feel the force of. In Himmelfarb's words,

> [T]he old kind of charity [represented, in my reading, by Dinah Morris] left it to each individual to alleviate, according to his means, the suffering he saw about him. The new kind . . . was less instinctive, more rational and systematic. It made of charity a matter for social action rather than the exercise of a private virtue, and it transformed it from a moral obligation to a legal right. (148–149)

Once the poor are understood to have the right to an alleviation of their suffering, the transformation of charity into justice is complete. Dinah Morris and Auden alike see private loves in tension with broader duties, but whereas Dinah fears that she may fail in her Christian "obligations" if she marries Adam Bede, Auden fears that his passive enjoyment of "our freedom in this English house, / Our picnics in the sun" will contribute, even if indirectly, to the denial of some oppressed people's rights.

The notion of a right to justice is of course an exceptionally powerful and probably indispensable one; it may even be present in the Hebrew Bible, if, as some have suggested, *mishpat* (usually "justice") can in some circumstances be translated as "right" (see, for example, O'-Donovan 247–248). But even if the notion has sound scriptural warrant, in the Biblical text rights do not displace the authority and centrality of love—indeed, one can plausibly contend that it is only in the context of God's love for us that our rights emerge and gain compelling force. But in political discourse of the last two centuries, the language of rights has supplanted the language of love, and interestingly enough, it is only in the world of literature that "the old kind of charity" has potent champions. (The irony of this fact will soon become evident.) Some of the consequences and costs of this supplanting of charity by justice—this move from an emphasis on the personal virtues of the rich to a proclamation of the public rights of the poor— may be seen with particular clarity in the work of Charles Dickens, nowhere more than in *Bleak House*.

One of the central themes of that novel is parental neglect of children, and particularly neglect by parents who think of themselves as engaged in "good works." The two most notable offenders in this respect are Mrs. Jellyby and Mrs. Pardiggle. Mrs. Jellyby is perhaps the better known, because she seems to us so characteristically Victorian a case and because Dickens associates her with that memorable phrase "telescopic philanthropy." She sits in the midst of a chaotic home, surrounded by her filthy and unheeded children, and explains that "the African project at present occupies my whole time. It involves me in correspondence with public bodies, and with private individuals anxious for the welfare of their species all over the country. I am happy to say that it is advancing" (86). Mrs. Jellyby thus serves as a kind of mediator between charitably minded individuals and the "public bodies," established institutions that are necessary to the success of any such far-flung ("telescopic") humanitarian enterprise.

Dickens spares little sympathy for these "public bodies," and indeed reserves some of his bitterest sarcasm for them. Much of this sarcasm is transmitted through the omniscient narrator's comments on Jo, the illiterate and sickly street sweeper:

> [H]e sits down to breakfast on the door-step of The Society for the Propagation of the Gospel in Foreign Parts, and gives it a brush when he has finished, as an acknowledgment of the accommodation. He admires the size of the edifice, and wonders what it's all about. He has no idea, poor wretch, of the spiritual destitution of a coral reef in the Pacific, or what it costs to look up the precious souls among the cocoanuts and bread-fruit. (274–275)

That last sentence calls into ironic question the motives of those who seek to propagate the Gospel in foreign parts, especially since they cannot be bothered even to teach the Jos of the world the Lord's Prayer. We learn this much later, when Jo is dying, and at this point in the narrative the irony becomes heavier and Dickens's contempt becomes, if possible, more pronounced:

> Jo is brought in. He is not one of . . . Mrs. Jellyby's lambs, being wholly unconnected with Borrioboola-Gha; he is not softened by distance and unfamiliarity; he is not a comfort or convenience to anyone, as a pretence afar off for leaving evil things at hand alone; he is not a genuine foreign-grown savage; he is the ordinary home-made article. Dirty, ugly,

disagreeable to all the senses, in body a common creature of the common streets, only in soul a heathen. Homely filth begrimes him, homely parasites devour him, homely sores are in him, homely rags are on him: native ignorance, the growth of English soil and climate, sinks his immortal nature lower than the beasts that perish. Stand forth, Jo, in uncompromising colours! From the soul of thy foot to the crown of thy head, there is nothing interesting about thee. (696)

It seems clear that for Dickens the institutionalization of charity is a major part of the problem here. Institutions such as "The Society for the Propagation of the Gospel in Foreign Parts" serve the twofold function of insulating us from the unpleasantness or mere "uninterestingness" of others who have some claim upon us (whether that claim is to be understood in terms of our obligations or their rights) and authorizing, by their public and institutional status, our charitable deeds.

The power of institutions to regulate and rationalize charitable activities is so great that it transforms even old-style private charitable work. Mrs. Pardiggle—Dickens's other neglectful mother (though neglectful in a very different way than Mrs. Jellyby, since she demands that her children participate in her beneficent work)—is no stranger to institutions: She and her family contribute to the "Tockahoopo Indians" and to the "Great National Smithers Testimonial," while one of her children is a member, however reluctant, of the "Infant Bonds of Joy"; moreover, she says, "I am on the local Linen Box Committee, and many general Committees" (152). Now, her encounters with the poor are far more direct than those of Mrs. Jellyby and, therefore, one might think, less subject to the Dickensian critique. But Mrs. Pardiggle has managed to discipline her personal encounters according to institutional canons of efficiency. Esther Summerson, the narrator of this part of the story, repeatedly uses a certain language to describe Mrs. Pardiggle's words and actions: Esther notes "her commanding deportment," her "mechanical way of taking possession of people," her "much too businesslike and systematic" voice. Esther links her with Mrs. Jellyby as persons of "rapacious charity"—a potent phrase, that. On a visit to one poor cottage, Mrs. Pardiggle "took the whole family into custody. I mean into religious custody, of course; but she really did it as if she were an inexorable moral Policeman carrying them all off to a station-house" (158). Clearly this is the capture of the virtue of charity by a rationalized, bureaucratic model of social organization.

Dickens clearly, in *Bleak House* and elsewhere, makes a plea for a return to the earlier model. Dickens is anything but a Methodist, and the Evangelicals—who were in a sense the Victorian-era heirs of the Methodists (whose social influence was fading even at the turn of the nineteenth century, the setting of *Adam Bede*)—receive incessant ridicule in his books and contempt in his letters. He fiercely repudiates the Evangelical conviction that charity is a gift of the Holy Spirit not fully available to people who do not know Jesus; but he certainly agrees with their sense that charity is primarily a virtue rather than a social achievement. Thus when Mrs. Pardiggle asks Esther to accompany her on her "rounds" of visiting, Esther demurs on grounds that we will find telling:

> I . . . said . . . that I was not sure of my qualifications. That I was inexperienced in the art of adapting my mind to minds very differently situated, and addressing them from suitable points of view. That I had not that delicate knowledge of the heart which must be essential to such a work. That I had much to learn, myself, before I could teach others, and that I could not confide in my good intentions alone. For these reasons, I thought it best to be as useful as I could, and to render what kind services I could, to those immediately about me; and to try to let that circle of duty gradually and naturally expand itself. (154)

These are of course precisely the lessons that Mrs. Pardiggle—who wishes to instruct, warn, and exhort rather than love—needs to learn, but she immediately dismisses Esther's concerns and never suspects that they might be relevant to her. Esther, by contrast, when confronted with the very people whose real suffering Mrs. Pardiggle ignores—to the point of not noticing that a child in the room where she preaches is dying—is able to respond naturally with appropriate words and, more important, deeds: Here once again we see the association of love with attentiveness, and the disabling consequences of inattentiveness. This happens just after Esther and her friend (Mrs. Pardiggle has continued on her "rounds") see the child die: "Presently I took the light burden from her lap; did what I could to make the baby's rest the prettier and gentler; laid it on a shelf, and covered it with my own handkerchief. We tried to comfort the mother, and we whispered to her what Our Saviour said of children. She answered nothing, but sat weeping—weeping very much" (160). (In that last sentence Dickens is refuting, as he often does, the then-familiar claim that the poor, having been hardened and calloused by their rugged lives, did not feel the loss of children as strongly as the delicately wrought persons of the "higher orders.") In the same way Allan Woodcourt, the physician who is to be Esther's husband, finds the dying Jo and tries to teach him the Lord's Prayer, which no one until that time had ever thought to teach him (705). Esther and Allan alike respond to the needs of those "immediately about" them, and as their knowledge of others grows in scope—at the beginning of the novel neither of them knows anyone like Jo or the poor women in the cottage—so too does their love.

These scenes could, of course, be cited as examples of Dickensian "sentimentality"; undoubtedly they have been.[4] But in light of the cultural history I have been tracing, that would be unfortunate. Dickens is attempting here a noteworthy task: to reclaim the affective and personal dimensions of a human relation that has become rationalized and thereby weakened. Again, the restriction of the notion of charity to "benevolence toward the poor" made charity supererogatory; its replacement by the vocabulary and concerns of justice restored the obligatory character of the relationship, but at the cost of systematizing and dehumanizing it. (The invocation of rights is thus necessary to recapture some of the force that the obligation had when it was a personal virtue.) Dickens is reaching back toward the older notion of charity as an individual virtue in hopes of preserving both the personal *and* the obligatory character of the relationship between rich and poor.

Dickens thus represents a point of view common in his time, and liable to be found among people of very different political convictions: that a society is strong and healthy not when people are bound to one another by law, contract, or utility, but rather when those bonds derive from personal intimacy and social and historical embeddedness in a given place. Thus Carlyle insists that the real well-being of the English laborer, indeed the real "condition of England," cannot be measured by the econometrics of (in a famous phrase) "cash payment as the sole nexus" of human relations: However well-paid a worker is, if he is related to his employer by "hostility, oppression, and chains of mutual necessity" his "condition" is not a good one. Only if employer and employee are linked by "bonds of friendliness and mutual help" will England be healthy (Carlyle 56). It is noteworthy that when Dickens decided to befriend a working man named John Overs, who wished to become a writer, he gave Overs a copy of the very work of Carlyle's from which I have been quoting, the pamphlet on *Chartism* (Ackroyd 302).

Likewise, William Cobbett waxed nostalgic about the England of his youth, before the Industrial Revolution had begun, when, as Gertrude Himmelfarb puts it (in a summary of Cobbett, with quotes), "a laborer would live out his whole life in the same cottage, just as he often worked for the same master . . . the whole of his life, without a contract but with the assurance of mutual good-will, 'the liberality and kindness of the employer . . . repaid by the respect and fidelity of the servant'" (208).[5] One need not endorse Cobbett's idealized history of England in order to recognize the appeal of this view of a healthy society, which—whether held by Cobbett, Carlyle, or Dickens—fits none of the conventional political categories.[6] Indeed, such a notion could fit none of these categories because it is not, in any commonly recognized sense, a political notion: It is, rather, the suggestion of an *alternative* to the usual political answers to social problems, the suggestion being that justice, as a political category, be superseded by the moral category of charity. As Michael Ignatieff writes, there is a domain of "human needs"—including, most prominently, love—that "test the limits of what politics can possibly offer." After all, "we cannot force someone to love us. We cannot claim love as a human right" (19). But this does not diminish the importance of love; rather, it indicates that the case for love cannot be made using the vocabulary of rights—nor, perhaps, any other argumentative vocabulary.[7] *Bleak House*, then, is in part an argument-through-narrative for the restoration of a comprehensive—but not, and we will soon explore the importance of this, a distinctively Christian—charity as a means for achieving the demands of justice, demands that the language of justice alone cannot support.

Even the most earnest and serious lovers of justice, at least in the last two centuries, can be puzzled by this move. It is the complexity of Dickens's picture of charitable social action and its defiance of categorization that make George Orwell, for instance, respond so ambivalently to Dickens. In his famous essay on Dickens, Orwell grapples with the peculiar position Dickens's novels occupy with regard to the political concerns of mid-Victorian England. Here is the key passage:

> The truth is that Dickens's criticism is almost exclusively moral. Hence the utter lack of any constructive suggestion anywhere in his work. He attacks the law, parliamentary government, the educational system and so forth, without ever clearly suggesting what he would put in their places. Of course it is not necessarily the business of a novelist, or a

satirist, to make constructive suggestions, but the point is that Dickens's attitude is at bottom not even *de*structive. There is no clear sign that he wants the existing order to be overthrown, or that he believes it would make very much difference if it *were* overthrown. For in reality his target is not so much society as "human nature." ... His whole "message" is one that at first glance looks like an enormous platitude: If men would behave decently the world would be decent. (51–52)[8]

One would expect a committed socialist like Orwell to eviscerate this moralism, and he can be sharply critical of it. But only a few pages later in the essay Orwell quite seriously reconsiders his distinction between moral criticism and constructive suggestion:

I said earlier that Dickens is not *in the accepted sense* a revolutionary writer. But it is not at all certain that a merely moral criticism of society may not be just as 'revolutionary'—and revolution, after all, means turning things upside down—as the politico-economic criticism which is fashionable at the moment. ... "If men would behave decently the world would be decent" is not such a platitude as it sounds. (64–65)

Of the morality that underlay these exhortations, Orwell makes this important statement: "Nearly everyone, whatever his actual conduct may be, responds emotionally to the idea of human brotherhood. Dickens voiced a code which was and on the whole still is believed in, even by people who violate it. It is difficult otherwise to explain why he could be both read by working people (a thing that has happened to no other novelist of his stature) and buried in Westminster Abbey" (103).

The question we must face now is whether the various intellectual movements typically grouped under the heading "postmodernism" have ensured that fewer people respond, and even then respond less strongly, to "the idea of human brotherhood." If so then there is all the more reason to insist that only a specifically and substantively Christian notion of charity can redeem what is best in Dickens's moral vision. After all, once one has said "If men would behave decently the world would be decent," and acknowledged the truth of the saying, what remains is to account for the very large problem that people often *do not* behave decently. What then? Christianity above all answers the "what then" question. Its purpose is not merely to critique: It has a prophetic witness that, to be sure, sometimes takes the form of denunciation, but, as Oliver O'Donovan writes, "the prophet is not allowed the luxury of perpetual subversion" (12). Nor is it the business of Christianity to define or promulgate virtues, and still less to concern itself with "values"; rather, it is to build up a community that embodies and proclaims the Kingdom of God. Thus John Milbank's assertion: "It is true that Aquinas, like Augustine, does not recognize any real justice that is not informed by charity, and that he has, in consequence, moved not very far down the road that allows a sphere of secular autonomy; nevertheless, he has moved a little, and he has moved too far" (*Theology* 407). On this account, merely to speak of justice as independent of charity is to invite the specter of secular autonomy, of a portion of the world independent of God's dominion. By speaking simply of justice, the Church cedes territory to the *imperium:* It renders unto Caesar what is manifestly not Caesar's.

It may not be perfectly clear, in light of the dismissals and avowals of the previous paragraph, what place this history of certain ideas about justice has in a book that claims to be a theology of reading. However, this whole cultural history deeply shapes and informs current academic debates about how to achieve or at least contribute to justice through the teaching and criticism of literature: For instance, Orwell is almost the inventor of "cultural studies"; he is the most often invoked model for a wide-ranging cultural criticism that serves political ends. But he is more honest than most current practitioners about the difficulties, and more committed than most to a belief that real political change is possible; therefore, he really provides not so much a model for as an alternative to contemporary cultural critique.[9] Moreover, he does not believe that one can move toward social justice by being unjust to the writers one interprets: Many socialists would never dream of granting Dickens's ideas as much respect as Orwell does, but Orwell is extremely wary of the idea that the personal practice of injustice can serve the achievement of social justice. Indeed, his critical but charitable reading of Dickens, seen as exemplary, can enable a critique of a contemporary academic political discourse that has exchanged Dickensian "sentimentality" for something of (paradoxically) far less political value.

Thus the story I have been telling bears not only a historical but a kind of allegorical relationship to contemporary literary and cultural studies: I understand much current political criticism to be fundamentally Pardigglean—the academy is full of "inexorable moral Policemen" whose big ideas about justice prevent them from receiving the kind of loving attention that would enable them to be truly just in their reading—whereas my position, shameful though it may be to say in the current context, is fully Summersonian. Esther's reply to Mrs. Pardiggle, properly considered and expanded, contributes to a theology of reading by showing how a concern for justice should be governed by the Christian commitment to charity. Having sketched out the historically available alternatives, and having noted that not only Auden's little story but also Dinah's dilemma in *Adam Bede* indicate the same sort of problem, I would suggest that a hermeneutics of love reveals these as false alternatives: We need not choose between a self-absorbed hedonism and a diligently politicized interpretation that gradgrindingly forces every text and every author into a fixed place in the political grid. A hermeneutics of love—as I hope we have seen, especially in Jane Tompkins's reading of Buffalo Bill—will be both flexible and responsible: It will have *universal obligations but highly particular forms of attention.* This is the road to justice, or as the Bible would have it, to *shalom.*

The problem is to find a conceptual vocabulary adequate to this goal—since, in the current environment, the Dickensian vocabulary is manifestly inadequate, and not only because it is insufficiently Christian. Vital to this search is Kathy Eden's book *Hermeneutics and the Rhetorical Tradition.* Eden begins by pointing to a concept that Aristotle develops in the fifth book of the *Nicomachean Ethics*: equity (*epiekeia*). Equity for Aristotle bears a curious relationship to justice: The two "are neither absolutely identical nor generically different" (Aristotle 1137a). Equity is different from and inferior to "absolute justice," which we don't in fact possess; but it is different from and superior to "legal justice," which we do possess. It more closely approximates absolute justice than legal justice ever can, because of the inevitable generality of legal justice: "All law is universal, and there are some things about which it is not possible to pronounce rightly in general terms; therefore in cases where it is necessary to make a general pronouncement, but impossible to do so rightly, the law takes account of the majority of cases, though not unaware that in this way errors are made" (1137b). It is because in a minority of cases errors are made that equity must be invoked as "a rectification of law in so far as law is defective on account of its generality" (1137c)[10]—precisely the way in which Mrs. Pardiggle is defective.

Eden demonstrates how, over a period of centuries, this legal principle of equity was adapted to the needs of interpretation: "Ancient rhetoricians . . . routinely elaborated the principles of interpretation alongside the arguments for an equitable judgment. . . . Designed, in contrast to legal statute, as a flexible measure, equity could take into account the infinite particularity of human events by investigating the agents' intentions"—very broadly conceived as the form or shape of an agent's whole life—"and thus could accommodate each individual case" (2). One cannot achieve interpretive justice by means of an inflexible application of rules and laws, any more than one can achieve political justice by the same means: In law and interpretation alike, the major thinkers of the ancient world recognized that even the best rules and laws cannot obviate the need for discerning judgment. Thus Gadamer—without referring to the ancient tradition that Eden delineates—sees immediately that Aristotle's ethical scheme offers "a kind of model of the problems of hermeneutics":

> The interpreter dealing with a traditionary text tries to apply it to himself. But this does not mean that the text is given for him as something universal, that he first understands it per se, and then afterward uses it for particular applications. Rather, the interpreter seeks no more than to understand this universal, the text—i.e., to understand what it says, what constitutes the text's meaning and significance. In order to understand that, he must not try to disregard himself and his particular hermeneutical situation. He must relate the text to this situation if he wants to understand at all. (324)

Thus the discerning judgment required by a commitment to equity involves, as a necessary part of understanding "the case," some understanding of oneself. (This seems to me precisely the point that Tompkins makes when she writes, "Genocide matters, and it begins at home.")

Thus, too, contemporary political criticism is Pardigglean by virtue of its refusal to consider the obligations of equity—which is to say, by virtue of its strict legalism; by virtue of its disregard of the need for the interpreter to be personally just, as well as to have accurate notions of what social justice is; by virtue of its lack of self-knowledge. It seems to me that one of the most important assumptions, and disabling illusions, of contemporary political criticism is the belief that one can seek political justice through one's literary criticism without seeking to be a just person. Critics simply *assume* that justice is conferred upon them by the justice of their cause, or that being just is something easily achieved—for instance, as Fred Inglis (a notable English proponent of the cultural studies model) argues, simply by doing cultural studies: As he puts it, with tongue only partially in cheek, "Cultural Studies will make you good" (229).

Let's unpack this claim. First of all, Inglis is quite straightforward about what is good, because he believes that we all know. That's why he's free to cite as his authority on the subject the "moral admonitions" that conclude the film *Monty Python's The Meaning of Life* (and that answer the question implicit in the title): "Nothing very special. Try to be nice to people. Avoid eating fat. Read a good book every now and again. Get some walking in. And try to live in peace and harmony with people of all creeds and nations. And finally here are some completely gratuitous pictures of penises to offend the censors" (Inglis 229). Inglis calls these "banal and welcome profundities," and gives his slightly edited version (minus the penises) later in his book: "Find a value; give it a history; see what may be done with it in human purposes. Be careful, bring all your sympathies to bear; hate what is hateful; be good" (240). For Inglis, *"this is the way the best and brightest of present-day students in the human sciences want to learn to think and feel. And having learned to think and feel thus, this is how they want to act and live"* (229; original emphasis).

Well, if we grant that these are admirable imperatives, how may we fulfill them? Far from showing that "Cultural Studies makes you good," Inglis has Cultural Studies *tell* you to be good. Surely the difference is significant. Even granted the assumption that "the best and brightest" students truly want to be so utterly liberal and tolerant—an assumption that no thoughtful person would readily make[11]—it is hard to see how a particular set of subjects for study will automatically and of themselves confer virtue upon their students. Inglis seems to have learned nothing from the collapse, in the Great War, of Arnoldian humanism.

Inglis is an unusually charming and funny proponent of these ideas, but in other respects a typical one. The untenability of the assumptions he shares with other cultural critics, coupled with the blithe confidence with which those assumptions are held, ensures that although the "moral Policemen" of current literary and cultural criticism are certainly inexorable, they are ineffectual as well. When Aristotle says that equity is not simply a desideratum but also a virtue that persons must practice, he is speaking a language that modern cultural criticism cannot understand.

So, once again we have seen the usefulness of Aristotelian ethical thought for hermeneutics. But of course we have also noted, elsewhere in this study, the limitations of Aristotelian schemes for a hermeneutics of Christian love: The virtues that Aristotle knew and celebrated may have contributed to justice in the political context of aristocratic Athens, but they are largely irrelevant to the quest for *shalom*. These conceptual limitations of Aristotelian thought make it all the more important that, as Eden explains, the ancient distinction between equity and "legal justice" passes easily into Christian thought and indeed has its greatest purchase upon us in its Christian form.

Eden sees this particularly clearly in the work of Basil the Great. Basil's favored opposition between *oikonomia* (economy) and *akribeia* (scrupulosity) inherits and develops the older distinction between equity and the rigidity of the legal statutes (Eden 45). But as Eden explains, what really governs Basil's continual employment of this distinction is its link with the Pauline contrast between the spirit and the letter. For Basil, the spirit (which gives life) is linked with "economical" and "equitable" reading: thus his argument that young Christians can benefit from the reading of pagan literature, but only if they do not read according to the killing letter of the law. By the strict terms of God's law these works can but be condemned—not because they are thoroughly erroneous but because their command of the truth is limited, defective.

We need to pause over this point for a moment. Werner Jaeger writes that in Basil's oration on Greek literature "the moral and religious content of ancient poetry is rejected, [whereas] the form is praised" (81), but this is manifestly wrong. Basil says quite explicitly that not only the great Homer, but indeed almost every pagan author with a high reputation, pursues wisdom and virtue. He is glad to be able to say this, because the education available to Christians in his time and place was largely pagan. As Edward Maloney, who edited Basil's oration, writes: Though the Roman Empire was officially Christian, pagans still controlled the "institutions of culture" (see Basil 12) and hence the texts in which young students were trained. Basil, therefore, advises Christian students to learn the skills of discernment that will enable them to recognize when the pagan writers are teaching wisdom and virtue, so that they may eat such good fruit as is available (section iii). In a pre-Mandevillian "fable of the bees," Basil encourages Christian students to follow the example of those insects by taking away, not whole flowers, but only the nourishment the flowers offer. And, in an ironically deft touch, he tells them that when the pagan writers teach sin or falsehood, the students should follow the example of Odysseus in the presence of the Sirens and stop their ears (section iv). As Eden points out, Odysseus is for Basil a recurrent model of prudence and good judgment (50–54).

Basil readily acknowledges that everything one can learn from pagan literature one can learn still better from Scripture (section x); but why not take every opportunity to grow in wisdom and virtue? The problem is to learn *how* to do so; and here we return to Eden's description of Basil's terminology. It is precisely a less "scrupulous" and more equitable reading of the pagan writers that releases them for our use, gives them a role in our school of virtue. By reading them according to the charitable spirit rather than the harsh and inflexible letter, we make them our own. The pagan writers can, when read in this way, be used even if they cannot strictly speaking be enjoyed—their dependence on false gods and inadequate understandings of human beings must not be ignored or minimized, but rather *overcome* by the determination to love God and neighbor better through reading them. For a certain kind of politically minded critic, the only proper response to a morally deficient text is to condemn its deficiencies: Basil's model provides a powerfully liberating alternative, in which even seriously wrong-headed books can provide *some* nourishment, nourishment for which we can be grateful.

Perhaps the most important point of all is that to read in this way is an act of charity to the works one reads *and* to oneself—an act of charity that includes and supersedes justice. In the *Confessions*, it is precisely this model that undergirds Augustine's reconfiguration, through *memoria*, of his literary education: The pagan scrupulosity that once had imprisoned him in Virgil's inadequate moral world is, after his conversion, replaced by an equitable, "spiritual" re-interpretation that can make even the reading of Virgil and other pagans useful and beneficial. When Augustine talks as though the only valuable thing he learned from his literary education was how to read and write (*Confessions* I.xiii), he seems not to realize this point; only in the discussion of *memoria* in Book X does he approach the freedom and confidence of Basil.

So far, so good. But, as we have seen in earlier chapters, these questions cannot be fully explored without reference to the social and ecclesial context of interpretation. It is practically impossible simply to *decide* to read for justice and the charity that surpasses justice—to read for *shalom.* Thus Basil, knowing that the schools are pagan, assumes that the students to whom he writes will be nurtured by the counter-institution of the Church; it is the sound teaching of the Church that provides the students with the resources necessary to reconfigure, properly and healthily, the ideological world of the pagan writers and teachers. It is with similar thoughts in mind that Augustine, in the *City of God,* challenges the definition of a "people" or a "community" offered by Scipio in Cicero's dialogue *De Republica:* "The community [is] an association united by a common sense of right and a community of interest" (Augustine, *City* I.73). At this stage in his argument (II.21) Augustine offers no alternative to Scipio's definition; he contents himself with noting that, by this definition, "that commonwealth never existed, because there never was real justice in the community." Much later (XIX.21), having completed his deconstruction of the pagan political order and having developed his notion of the two coexistent cities, Augustine returns to Scipio's definition and explains in greater detail what is wrong with it: "If a soul does not serve God"—and it will not serve a God it does not love—"it cannot with any kind of justice command the body, nor can a man's reason control the vicious elements in his soul. And if there is no justice in such a man, [then] there is no justice in a gathering which consists of such men" (XIX.883).

How then can justice be infused into the persons who make up a "gathering" or community? This indeed is the key question. Augustine answers (in XIX.23):

> Justice is found where God . . . rules an obedient city according to his grace . . . so that just as the individual righteous man lives on the basis of faith which is active in love, so the association, or people, of righteous men lives on the same basis of faith, active in love, the love with which a man loves God as God ought to be loved, and loves his neighbor as himself. But where this justice does not exist, there is certainly no "association of men united by a common sense of right and by a community of interest." (XIX.890)

Here we circle back to a problem invoked repeatedly in this book, and indeed in this chapter: In Augustine's politics and Basil's hermeneutics alike, such comprehensive and just charity can be achieved only in the life of the Church. The Church is the school for virtue—for charity as the architectonic virtue—and it is within the communal practice of the Church that equitable, "economic" reading makes sense. Though rejecting scrupulosity in interpretation, Basil insists that the local congregation be scrupulous (he uses just that word) in its obedience to Scripture and to the dictates of the Catholic Church. As Eden points out, it is no accident that the argument for equitable interpretation flourished in the age of the great ecumenical councils, which had the function of prescribing the boundaries beyond which orthodox believers may not go. For Basil, it is this framework of faithful obedience to the Gospel witness that liberates the reader to read more generously, according to the spirit rather than the letter. Absent such faithful obedience, such reading would exemplify license rather than liberty, antinomianism rather than the freedom of Christian charity.

The lessons are, I believe, clear, though daunting: no justice without the precedence and governance of charity; no charity without the guidance of the faithful and obedient church; no church without the Gospel that constitutes and inspires it.[12] Charitable readers, equitable and just readers, will always be found here and there—one hopes—but a potent and fully articulated hermeneutics of love will arise only from a healthy community of believers. "Our kindness to ten persons" can be made righteous only in that context; only that context can teach us how to make our "circle of duty gradually and naturally expand itself." In the life of the Church these become the common and quotidian elements of justice. Such fully charitable reading, in a just association of persons, will be an ecclesial, not a personal, achievement; and certainly not the achievement of this book.

POSTLUDE

"It theemth to prethent two thingth to a perthon, don't it, Thquire?" said Mr. Sleary, musing as he looked down into the depths of his brandy and water: "one, that there ith a love in the world, not all Thelf-interetht after all, but thomething very different; t'other, that it hath a way of ith own of calculating or not calculating, which thomehow or another ith at leatht ath hard to give a name to, ath the wayth of the dogth ith!"

Mr. Gradgrind looked out of window, and made no reply.

—Dickens, Hard Times

But this is all too solemn. In my first chapter I wrote these words: "Like all good theology, then, a theology of reading will require an emphasis on discerning judgment: But it will also find its place as part of a theology of gift and recreation." And though I have indeed had something to say about gifts, there has been a great deal more about obligations and precious little about recreation. This imbalance was perhaps necessary, but nevertheless somewhat unfortunate: For the best Christian theology has always understood love to be the fullest liberation, and has found love best exemplified in play. It is worth noting that *perichoresis*—the doctrine of the loving interrelations of the persons of the Trinity, which I discussed in Chapter 2—takes its name from Greek words meaning "to dance around." Dance is one of the most elemental and universal forms of play.

Thus it is particularly appropriate that the words I have cited as the epigraph to this concluding section are spoken, in *Hard Times*, by the owner of a circus. Sleary has actually hit upon three, not just two, key ideas that quite forcibly present themselves to a person: first, that whereas self-interest is pervasive it is not ubiquitous, so there can be genuine love between and among people; second, that that love is not utterly chaotic, but has at least sometimes its own peculiar structure, its own habitual manner of working, its own "way of calculating or not calculating"—though, to be sure, a way inaccessible to Gradgrind's utilitarian calculus; and third, that that "way of calculating or not calculating" is difficult to specify: An adequate vocabulary for it is extremely elusive.

I would like to think that writing a book like this one—that is, making an academic case for governing interpretation by the law of love—bears some analogy to running a circus. To those who would label the project naive, childish, frivolous, foolish, the ringmaster can do little more than simply shrug and continue the game. Indeed, this is the best form of argument available to the circus-owner or the advocate of charitable interpretation. To Gradgrind's Benthamite arguments Sleary has no response except to continue the circus's performances, and merely to say, as he does more than once, "People mutht be amuthed" (32, 222)—which is not an argument but a kind of imperative declaration: Sleary politely refuses to enter the dialectical arena where Gradgrind brandishes his Benthamite weaponry, but instead contents himself with (a) doing something else and (b) proclaiming that he is doing something else. "People mutht be amuthed" bears the whole content of Sleary's kerygma.

Sleary, then, is an evangelist of *play*—a notion requiring reflection. In J. Huizinga's famous *Homo Ludens*, he suggests three criteria that distinguish true play. First, he says, "play is a voluntary activity" (7). Second, play "is a stepping out of 'real' life into a temporary sphere of activity with a disposition all of its own" (8). Third, play is characterized by "secludedness . . . limitedness. It is 'played out' within certain limits of time and place. It contains its own course and meaning. Play begins, and then at a certain moment it is 'over'" (9).

Sleary's circus is certainly a voluntary activity: No one *has* to go to the circus. It also stands apart from the regular forms of life. In fact, Dickens explicitly disconnects it from the agricultural labor of the countryside and the industrial labor of Coketown: It was set up in "the neutral ground upon the outskirts of the town, which was neither town nor country" (8). He goes on to say of that ground, "and yet was either spoiled"—that is, this neutral ground could be considered a "spoiled" form of countryside or cityscape. Sleary's circus redeems the spoiled ground by transforming it from a shapeless and purposeless place, neither this nor that, into an environment for the distinctive human activity called play, an environment set apart from the labors of both country and city. And the circus obviously has its beginning and its ending—in terms of not only its performances but also its residence in a town, since it is a traveling circus (is there any other kind?)—and thus would seem to fulfill Huizinga's third criterion as well.

But if Sleary's circus perfectly embodies playfulness, what may be said of its relation to that other distinctive human activity of which Sleary speaks, as though he were a kind of authority—namely, love? It is interesting that some of Dickens's critics have identified the connection between Sleary's circus and love, though they have not been able to explain it. Monroe Engel writes of Sleary as an embodiment of fancy, and contends that "[f]ancy is the progenitor of charity, in the Christian rather than the philanthropic sense" (174). Likewise, J. Hillis Miller writes that "[i]n *Hard Times* Dickens dramatizes in strikingly symbolic terms the opposition between a soul-destroying relation to a utilitarian, industrial civilization . . . and the reciprocal interchange of love. If the perpetually clanking machinery of the Coketown mills . . . is the symbol of one, the 'horse-riding,' as in Picasso's *Saltimbanques*, is the dominant symbol of the other" (226). Circuses and love are alike unnecessary from a material and utilitarian point of view, and perhaps from other points of view as well: As Auden once wrote, "Thousands have lived without love, not one without water" (*Collected Poems* 584). In this respect, circuses and love meet Huizinga's first criterion for play.

But it is not clear that love can be said to fulfill these latter two criteria. It will not remain in its place; it spills over into territory where it does not belong and where often it is not welcome; indeed, if it does not do these things it is not love. Charitable interpretation, were anyone to pursue it, would certainly be like this: It could scarcely be welcome in the academic practice of criticism, given its unpredictable and disruptive character—unpredictable and disruptive in terms familiar to critical practice, that is, though I have been at pains to argue here

that, as Sleary would have it, "it hath a way of ith own of calculating or
not calculating" that is legitimate and rational, though it may be "hard
to give a name to." (I have suggested earlier that one appropriate
name may be *hope:* Charitable readers do not calculate the likelihood
of reward for their loving attention, but their commitment to hope is
a kind of calculation, a wager on the graciousness of God and on the
imago dei present in the writers of books.)

And indeed, despite what we have said about the circus as a fine illustration of Huizinga's notions of play, the same proves to be true of
Sleary's circus. Near the end of *Hard Times* the boundaries between
the circus and the "real world" become wonderfully permeable. I am
not one of those who think of *Hard Times* as a masterpiece—though
that group includes Ruskin, Shaw, and F. R. Leavis, with the most recent of this noteworthy company apparently being Martha Nussbaum—but surely one of the most remarkable scenes in all of Dickens
comes here, after a performance of the circus:

> . . . Mr. Gradgrind sat down forlorn, on the Clown's performing chair in
> the middle of the ring. On one of the back benches, remote in the sub-
> dued light and the strangeness of the place, sat the villainous whelp,
> sulky to the last, whom he had the misery to call his son.
>
> In a preposterous coat, like a beadle's with cuffs and flaps exaggerated
> to an unspeakable extent; in an immense waistcoat, knee-breeches, buck-
> led shoes, and a mad cocked hat; with nothing fitting him, and everything
> of coarse material, moth-eaten and full of holes; with seams in his black
> face, where fear and heat had started through the greasy composition
> daubed all over it; anything so grimly, detestably, ridiculously shameful as
> the whelp in his comic livery, Mr. Gradgrind never could have by any
> other means believed in, weighable and measurable fact though it was.
> And one of his model children had come to this! (215)

In the book's third chapter, Gradgrind had been horrified to find his
children peeking at the circus through cracks and holes in the wall of
boards: Now his son is, though but temporarily, a participant in the
circus, and the "eminently practical" Mr. Gradgrind himself sits on a
clown's chair, smack in the middle of the ring. Yet only in this absurd
environment can the reconciliation of the two Gradgrinds begin.

Moreover, when Bitzer suddenly appears on the scene to take Tom
Gradgrind into custody—fulfilling, as he explains, every principle
taught him by Gradgrind *pere*—Tom can be rescued only by the tricks

of the circus: Sleary's trained horse and learned dog are essential to
the enterprise of getting Tom onto a ship and beyond the reach of the
English law. The circus has ceased to be (as J. Hillis Miller had called
it) a "symbol" of charity: The members of the circus have come to incarnate charity. In his discourse on the strange ability of dogs to find
their masters and the indescribable movements of love, Sleary was not
talking about himself—indeed, he was trying to suggest to Gradgrind
that Tom would someday return home (as indeed he eventually tries
to do, though unlike Merrylegs the dog, he dies before he can get
back)—but his words apply perfectly to the energy and cleverness he
has just expended in trying to help Mr. Gradgrind, until then no
friend of his: "[T]here ith a love in the world, not all Thelf-intereth
after all, but thomething very different." Gradgrind cannot think of a
way to repay Sleary for the loving gift he has received: Sleary tells him
that if he will "only give Horthe-riding a bethpeak, whenever you can,
you'll more than balanthe the account." It is difficult to see how the
occasional word of praise for the circus could "more than balanthe the
account"—but then, love "hath a way of ith own of calculating or not
calculating."[1]

The economy here is, simply, the economy of grace. Charity is gracious—one might also say gratuitous, with all the implications of that
complex root-word *gratia*. But this is always a hard notion to get at,
still harder to incorporate into the fabric of our lives. Thus, although
it may seem odd that Martha Nussbaum, in her book *Poetic Justice*, in
giving extended consideration to *Hard Times* as a book that could be
very useful in shaping public discourse about justice and political goals
more generally, has almost nothing to say about Sleary's circus, it is
not really odd. For what Nussbaum wants to say is that *Hard Times*
can shape and contribute to our political discourse without changing
it in really fundamental ways—without reconfiguring it beyond all
recognition—and indeed she has to make this argument if she is going
to get public-minded people even to consider the public uses of literature. But if this argument is going to be successful Sleary and his
horse-riding need to be kept well out of the picture, because his commitment to play and his belief in love will appear wildly impractical
and indeed anarchic in any imaginable modern political model, even if
that model isn't completely utilitarian. Dickens actually offers us a
more radical set of choices than Nussbaum does, as Raymond
Williams explains in a passage I quoted in Chapter 5: Dickens's "positives do not lie in social improvement, but rather in what he sees as

the elements of human nature—personal kindness, sympathy, and forbearance. It is not the model factory against the satanic mill, nor is it the humanitarian experiment against selfish exploitation. It is, rather, individual persons against the System. In so far as it is social at all, it is the Circus against Coketown" (*Culture* 94–95).

Dickens operates here under the auspices of the distinction between head and heart: That's what Coketown and circus, respectively, mean for him. It is this distinction that Gradgrind uses to enable his own moral awakening:

> "Some persons hold . . . that there is a wisdom of the Head, and that there is a wisdom of the Heart. I have not supposed so; but, as I have said, I mistrust myself now. I have supposed the head to be all-sufficient. It may not be all-sufficient; how can I venture this morning to say it is! If that other kind of wisdom should be what I have neglected, and should be the instinct that is wanted, Louisa—"
>
> He suggested it very doubtfully, as if he were half unwilling to admit it even now. (170)

The word *instinct* pursues the familiar contrast: instinct versus conscious decisionmaking, intuition versus reason, emotion versus intellect—these are the notions that underlie the division between heart and head, and however dear they may have been to Dickens, they have clearly lost any usefulness they may once have had, which is why until this point in the book I have not referred to them. Sleary's formulation—love "hath ith own way of calculating or not calculating"—is better, acknowledging as it does that whereas love can be freely and indiscriminately bestowed ("not calculating") it also possesses its own "calculating" logic of exchange and reciprocity that, however inaccessible to Cartesian or utilitarian schemes of rationality, is a logic nonetheless. This is the point of Pascal's much-abused phrase "the heart has its reasons which the reason cannot know," and it is Sleary's point, too. It is more accurate and useful than Gradgrind's binary opposition of head and heart.

But Sleary's point is ultimately an outrageous one, too disruptive to be embraced by even so earnest a reformer as Martha Nussbaum. And Dickens, the supposed arch-sentimentalist himself, gives us this plea for love in Sleary's lisping voice, thus situating it in a comic context that not only deflects its sentimentality but eliminates its aura of threat. That Dickens had to do this, and why he had to, is well understood by Auden, who contends that "the voice of *Agape*, of Holy Love," can in this world speak only in the comic mode (*Dyer's* 145). Love, like the Cross—but then Love is the Cross, and the Cross Love—can be nothing but foolishness in the eyes of this world, and we laugh at foolishness. We laugh mockingly, or we laugh warmly—according to our disposition—but we laugh, because laughter is the natural human response to incongruity. And what could be more incongruous than the claim, in the midst of our misery, that "there ith a love in the world, not all Thelf-interetht after all, but thomething very different"? What could be more incongruous than the conjunction of love and interpretation?

Notes

Prelude

1. The question of whether Aristotelian ethical thought can survive transplantation from the Athenian *polis* is a vexed and important one. Alasdair MacIntyre thinks it can work, though not automatically or easily: "So theories of justice and practical rationality confront us as aspects of traditions, allegiance to which requires the living out of some more or less systematically embodied form of human life, each with its own specific modes of social relationship, each with its own . . . evaluative practices. This does not mean that one cannot be an Aristotelian without membership in an actual *polis*. . . . Were this so, the study of . . . Aristotelian . . . theory could be only of antiquarian interest. What it does mean is that it is only insofar as those features of the *polis* which provide an essential context for the exercise of Aristotelian justice . . . can be reembodied in one's own life and that of one's time and place that one can be an Aristotelian. . . . So also and correspondingly with other traditions of enquiry" (*Whose* 391). Bernard Williams also explores this question: See especially *Ethics* 35.

2. "Be sure of it," says the Moor to "honest Iago," his lieutenant; "give me the ocular proof" (III.iii.366).

3. Stanley Cavell's reading of *Othello* runs strictly parallel to my argument here, concerned as it is with Othello's manifest lack of knowledge of Desdemona and his consequent transformation of her—first in his mind and then physically, by killing her—from a human being into a stone, a piece of "monumental alabaster" (V.ii.5): "A statue, a stone, is something whose existence is fundamentally open to the ocular proof. A human being is not" (*Disowning* 141).

4. That there are propositions that cannot be doubted, and therefore cannot be argued for, is the impetus for Wittgenstein's *On Certainty*, which is immensely relevant here, as can be seen in Cavell's Wittgensteinian exploration of Othello's certainties: See *Disowning* (ch. 3) and the last section of *The Claim of Reason*.

Chapter 1

1. This is as good a time as any to note that certain christological presuppositions underpin my argument. A proper understanding of the twofold commandment requires a proper understanding of who Jesus is. For the authority of Jesus' summation of the law derives from his personal stature as the embodiment of God's love. One sees this idea at work in Paul's writings, especially in Romans, where he says both that "Christ is the end [*telos*] of the law" (10:4) and that "love is the fulfilling [*pleroma*] of the law" (13:10). In these passages Paul clearly has in mind not only the twofold commandment but also Jesus' claim that he came not to abolish the law but to fulfill it (Mt. 5:17): It is *as* the embodiment of God's love that Jesus *becomes* that fulfillment. Jesus as Love, through his teaching and healing, brings good news to sinners, and through his death makes that good news effective to save and to reconcile. Thus the authority of the twofold commandment, and a proper interpretation of it, depends upon orthodox doctrines of Incarnation and Atonement. (On these points I am indebted to the section of Kierkegaard's *Works of Love* called "Love Is the Fulfilling of the Law" [99–136]).

2. The last phrase of this passage is translated very differently by R. P. H. Green in his recent edition of *De Doctrina* (under the title *On Christian Teaching*): Instead of "has not been deceived," Green gives us "has not made a fatal error." But this is to neglect the force of the phrase in Augustine's Latin: *non perniciose fallitur*, meaning literally "is not perniciously led astray." Green perhaps is relying on the etymology of *error*, which invokes the notion of straying (or being caused to stray) from the right path, an image that Augustine develops later in this very section. But the common modern use of *error* to mean *mistake* tends to obscure the emphasis that D. W. Robertson's word *deceived* captures. Augustine's point is not that the law of love prevents the interpreter from making mistakes but, rather, that it keeps the interpreter on or close to the right road, which is to say the road that (in Bunyan's potent formulation) leads to the Celestial City.

A further note: The chief notion expressed in this passage, that God's grace enables an interpreter to profit from reading a text even if that interpreter mistakes the author's meaning, may be found elsewhere in Augustine's work, for instance in *The Confessions*: "What harm does it do me if different meanings, which are nevertheless all true, can be gathered from these words? What harm can it do me if my view of what Moses meant is different from someone else's view? Certainly all of us who read are endeavoring to find out and to grasp what the man whom we are reading meant to say, and when we believe that he is a man who tells the truth we dare not imagine that he said anything which we ourselves know or believe to be false. So while we are all trying in our reading of the Holy Scriptures to grasp what it was that the author of them meant to say, what harm can it do if a man grasps hold of something which you, who are the light of all truthful minds, show him is true, even if the author whom he is reading did not grasp this truth—though the author did of course express a truth, but a different one?" (xii.18). David Glidden takes this passage to be saying that "the first sentence of Genesis is open to rival readings, each of which might itself be true, notwithstanding authorial intent" (138). Glidden does not seem to be aware of Augustine's treatment of the issue in *De Doctrina;* but even his treatment of the passage from *The Confessions* is dubious, since it hinges on the adjective *rival:* Augustine would certainly have agreed that textual meaning can be polyvalent, but certainly *not* that those meanings or levels of meanings can be at odds with one another, since truth cannot be at odds with truth.

3. Among the scholars to approach the issue, though not in my view to offer serious and thorough consideration of the Augustinian understandings of either love or interpretation, are Baer, Fortin, Glidden, Morrison (ch. 6), and Shafer.

4. Kevin Vanhoozer recognizes just the point I am making here, the point that undergirds my entire project: "General hermeneutics is inescapably theological. Our polluted cognitive and spiritual environment darkens understanding—of *all* texts. . . . Understanding—of the Bible or of any other text—is a matter of ethics, indeed, of spirituality. Indeed, interpretation ultimately depends upon the theological virtues of faith, hope, and love" ("Spirit" 161). Vanhoozer develops these ideas, but in the context of Biblical interpretation only, in his book *Is There a Meaning in This Text?* For other approaches to Biblical interpretation that pursue some of the same questions I pursue here, see Fowl and Hauerwas.

5. See Jerome's Epistle 29, as quoted in Jeffrey (76). Jeffrey's third chapter, "Secular Scripture: The Beautiful Captive," is a lucid and concise summary of patristic views on the uses of pagan literature. I am indebted to him in the paragraphs that follow.

6. Quoted in Pelikan, *Jesus* (43). Pelikan goes on to comment that "[d]uring the Byzantine period various Christian commentators on both the *Iliad* and the *Odyssey* carried out this image and in the process helped to protect the ancient classics against the misplaced zeal of religious bigotry."

7. In this context it does not matter whether Augustine in speaking of the "author" of a biblical text means God or the human but divinely inspired author. The degree of authority possessed and the reader's obligations remain the same in either case.

8. Here, Green's translation is much better and clearer: "Anyone with an interpretation of the scriptures that differs from that of the writer is misled, but not because the scriptures are lying" (27). Note that Green retains the sense of deception or misleading in *fallitur* that he neglects in the earlier passage.

9. Augustine provides a detailed analysis of the kinds and causes of error in *De Utilitate Credendi*, which was written in 391 (perhaps five years before the

parts of *De Doctrina* we have been considering). See the thorough summary of his conclusions in Stock, *Augustine* (169–173).

10. On this particular kind of sadness-cum-enjoyment, see A. D. Nuttall's fine book, *Why Does Tragedy Give Pleasure?* Augustine is interested primarily in the *immediate* pleasures of reading, and he assumes that those pleasures will fade when subjected to reflective scrutiny; but on the penultimate page of his book Nuttall makes it clear that the problem is more complex than that: "Aristotle's interest was engaged not by the initial thrill experienced by the audience as they sat in the theatre but by their state of mind when the play was over, after the lucid demonstration of a probable or necessary sequence of events leading to the dreadful death of the protagonist. Tragedy, unlike fairground rides, operates not only at the level of arousal but also at the level of conclusion or closure. . . . There is no doubt that tragedy makes use of [the pleasure of arousal]. But in tragedy the irresponsible pleasure of arousal is joined with bonds of iron to the responsibilities of probable knowledge and intellectual assent" (104).

11. Stanley Fish's comment on this passage is useful: "Raphael's lesson extends beyond the present example to a general instruction for reading the world: whatever you encounter, either in nature or in the society of men, read it—see it—as a manifestation of godly power and beneficence. To proceed in the other direction and look for meaning in the phenomena themselves, as if they were their own cause and the independent determinants of their own value, is to mistake that which has been created for the creator, and the name of that mistake is idolatry" (*Surprised* xvi).

12. To be fair to Augustine, he was not always so trepidatious. There is much justice in Jean Bethke Elshtain's comment that "he remains deeply—to his own mind, at times, even dangerously—in love with the world" (117). In order to counter the reductive and unfair picture of Augustine as a world-hating ascetic, Elshtain prefaces her book with this beautiful quotation from *De Trinitate* (VIII.iii): "Behold, and see again if you can. Certainly you love only the good, because the earth is good by the height of its mountains, the moderate elevation of its hills, and the evenness of its fields; and good is the farm that is pleasant and fertile; and good is the house that is arranged throughout in symmetrical proportions and is spacious and bright; and good are the animals, animate bodies; and good is the mild and salubrious air; and good is the food that is pleasant and conducive to health; and good is health without pains and weariness; and good is the countenance of man with regular features, a cheerful expression, and a glowing color; and good is the soul of a friend with the sweetness of concord and the fidelity of love; and good is the just man; and good are riches because they readily assist us; and good is the heaven with its own sun, moon, and stars; and good are the angels by their holy obedience; and good is the lecture that graciously instructs and suitably admonishes the listener; and good is the poem with its measured

rhythm and the seriousness of its thoughts." There are passages like this throughout Augustine's work, in which his attentiveness is truly extraordinary as he considers the beauty of worms, the remarkable variety of human faces (given the limited number of elements to be arranged), and the possible functions of men's nipples. Indeed, Garry Wills refers to just these passages when enlisting Augustine in the service of a "theology of erotica" (*Under* 293). Wills so much likes Augustine's contemplation of the "glories of the worm"—in the latter's early treatise *De vera religione*—that he quotes it again in his biography of Augustine (*Saint Augustine* 138).

13. This point has particular relevance for reading. It is common enough for us to think of children being "ready" or "unready" for certain books, but we rarely apply this criterion to adults. Consider Alasdair MacIntyre on the reading of Thomas Aquinas: "The question of what the *Summa* is . . . forces us back upon the question of what kind of persons we will have to be or become, either in the thirteenth century or now, in order to read it aright. The concept of having to be a certain sort of person, morally or theologically, in order to read a book aright—with the implication that perhaps, if one is not that sort of person, then the book should be withheld from one—is alien to the assumption of liberal modernity that every rational adult should be free and is able to read every book" (*Three* 133).

14. This is precisely the method often used by Milton in *Paradise Lost*, as Stanley Fish demonstrated some years ago in *Surprised by Sin:* "In the course of the poem . . . the reader (1) is confronted with evidence of his corruption and becomes aware of his inability to respond adequately to spiritual conceptions, and (2) is asked to refine his perceptions so that his understanding will be once more proportionable to truth the object of it" (lxxi).

15. On *studiositas*, see Stock, *Augustine* (261). The distinction between curiosity and studiousness is not unique to Augustine. Hans Robert Jauss begins his account of the nature of aesthetic experience with this report: "At a time when the symbolic representation of nature began to flourish on the capitals of Romanesque cathedrals, Bernard of Clairvaux complained in a letter to Abbot William that monks now preferred reading 'in marmoribus' to reading 'in codicibus' [reading marble to reading books] and would rather spend the whole day marveling at the incredible profusion of animals and fabulous beasts than meditate on God's own text, the Bible. . . . He finds that his brethren are being led astray because they are curious, and he accounts for that curiosity by their amazement at the abundance of figures and the variety of forms. What Bernard rejects here is, from the point of view of a devout rigorism, an illegitimate form of curiosity which, along with the symbolic object, also enjoys its sensuous appearance which ensnares. This criticism makes clear that even religious art can never wholly guard against eliciting an aesthetic attitude that will be more encompassing than dogma allows" (3–4).

16. Thus Dante's picture of the distractions of art at the beginning of the *Purgatorio:* As the redeemed souls gather around Casella to hear him sing, forgetting for that moment their need to purge themselves on the mountain, Cato the guardian rushes to them and chastises them for their neglect of their duty (Canto 2. ll, 106–133).

17. An important, if not (in my view) fully adequate philosophical treatment of these issues may be found in Singer (chs. 13 and 14).

18. Compare Adam's argument with Alasdair MacIntyre's statement in *After Virtue:* "Virtues are dispositions to act in particular ways, but also to feel in particular ways. To act virtuously is not, as Kant was later to think, to act against inclination; it is to act from inclination formed by the cultivation of the virtues. Moral education is an *'education sentimentale'*" (149).

19. My attention was called to the importance of this essay by Rosemary Ashton, in her biography of George Eliot (144–146). Ashton is also very good on the character of Eliot's debt to Feuerbach, a recurrent theme in the biography and one that will be discussed shortly.

20. Gilbert Meilaender, in his *Friendship: A Study in Theological Ethics,* investigates this tendency among Christian thinkers to see ethical dangers in the "preferential" nature of friendship. Meilaender quotes Jeremy Taylor, the seventeenth-century Anglican divine: "When friendships were the noblest things in the world, charity was little." In other words, when the ancient Greeks and Romans emphasized the great virtue of friendship, they neglected to care for those who stood outside *philia's* charmed circle. Samuel Johnson, as was his wont, formulated the potential problem with exemplary clarity (though in a way perhaps inconsistent with his own great capacity for friendship): "All friendship is preferring the interest of a friend, to the neglect, or, perhaps, against the interest of others. . . . Now Christianity recommends universal benevolence, to consider all men as our brethren; which is contrary to the virtue of friendship, as described by the ancient philosophers." Kierkegaard's too-harsh Cumming-like distinction between *agape* and all other forms of love—on the grounds that everything except *agape* makes distinctions and holds preferences—may be found in *Works of Love* (64–67). Barth's response to this tendency may be found in the *Church Dogmatics* (IV/2:818–120). His position is nicely summarized by Gene Outka: "While Barth distinguishes agape and friendship, he does not just oppose them as Kierkegaard is inclined to do. All of us clearly 'like' some persons more than others and may be prepared because of this to be kind and generous toward them. It is unnecessary and actually unwise to denounce in the strongest possible terms all such bonds. One must simply be concerned with agape's independence from, not its condemnation of, every relation presupposing liking" (210). Outka also discusses at some length Barth's unwillingness to identify *agape* with universality (210–214).

21. In a later letter Bonhoeffer says of the Song of Songs, "I should prefer to read it as an ordinary love song, and that is probably the best 'Christological' exposition" (315). This fascinating connection between the Chalcedonian definition of Jesus Christ and musical polyphony—put in service of an interpretation of human affections—is not unique to Bonhoeffer: As we shall see in later chapters, it is fundamental to the early philosophical work of Mikhail Bakhtin. Alexandar Mihailovic's book on Bakhtin develops this claim in detail, though without reference to Bonhoeffer.

22. Jean Grondin, like some other scholars, is at pains to claim that Augustine's hermeneutics, as articulated in *De Doctrina*, was important for Gadamer and Heidegger alike (ch. 7). And this is true, but largely because Gadamer and Heidegger were intrigued by Augustine's theories of signification and language. On the role played by charity or the will in interpretation they have little if anything to say.

Interlude A: the Illuminati

1. A brilliant and funny contemporary take on these very issues—complete with a story of a writer's burned letters that echoes "The Aspern Papers"—is Julian Barnes's *Flaubert's Parrot*. However, Geoffrey Braithwaite, the book's narrator, is too fine an example of pure *curiositas*, too lacking in malice, for my purposes in this chapter. As it happens, Barnes is a great delineator of curiosity: The protagonist of his novel *Staring at the Sun*, Jean Serjeant, is also an excessively and charmingly curious person, who "used to ask [herself] questions in bed . . . instead of praying" (149). She wondered, among other things, "whether there was a sandwich museum, and if so where it was. And why Jews didn't like golf. And how Mussolini knew which way the paper folded. And whether heaven was up the chimney. And why the mink is excessively tenacious of life."

2. James's comments on "The Figure in the Carpet" are curious and perhaps instructive. He says, first, that he was concerned to explore in this story "our so marked collective mistrust of anything like close or analytic appreciation—appreciation, to *be* appreciation, implying of course some such rudimentary zeal" (*Literary Criticism* 1234). The narrator may possess a kind of zeal, but not the kind that would produce "close or analytic appreciation." James continues: "What I most remember of my proper process is the lively impulse, at the root of it, to reinstate analytic appreciation, by some ironic or fantastic stroke, so far as possible, in its virtually forfeited rights and dignities." He pities Vereker for his inability to achieve an appreciative audience: He says that "the poor man" depends, "for the sake of being understood and enjoyed, on some responsive reach of critical perception that he is destined never to waylay with success" (*Literary Criticism* 1234–1235). Does this mean that no one actually discovers the "secret"? Or, perhaps, that there *is* no

secret, that Vereker concocted the story as a way of commanding "appreciation"? In any event, of the unnamed narrator James says, in bizarrely phallic language, that he possesses but "limp curiosity" that "at a given moment begins vaguely to throb and heave"; as a result of this throbbing, "acuteness . . . struggles to enter the field" (1235). Whether "acuteness" is able to retain its erection long enough actually to "enter the field," or whether it subsides back into "limpness," James coyly refuses to say: "The reader is, on the evidence, left to conclude" (1236). My reading, "on the evidence," opts strongly for detumescence.

Chapter 2

1. MacIntyre in making this argument relies heavily on the work of Albrecht Dihle: "The Greeks had no word of this kind in their language to denote will or intention as such" (Dihle 20). Dihle affirms repeatedly that the Greeks explained actions as consequences of reason or emotion, period: "the two kinds of motivation, that from reasoning and that from emotion" (26). "The twofold psychology that explains human behavior on the basis of the interaction of rational and irrational forces and has no room for the concept of will prevails throughout the Greek tradition from the time of Homer onwards" (27). Dihle's book does not take account of Anthony Kenny's *Aristotle's Theory of the Will*, published three years earlier, and this is unfortunate, because Kenny strongly contests the claim that Aristotle lacked a theory of the will. However, it is not clear to me that Kenny's detailed comparative analysis of Aristotle's ethical writings challenges the key point made by MacIntyre, which is that Augustine's notion of *voluntas* as something prior to reason or passion is unprecedented in ancient thought. For instance, near the beginning of his book Kenny focuses on the key categories in Aristotle that help us to understand the difference between voluntary and involuntary action: They are "some affective state, . . . some cognitive state," and a third state that is "a combination of both cognition and desire" (13). Thus reason and passion remain the basic categories. Perhaps the key interpretive issue here is what we are to make of the central Aristotelian term *akrasia*, often translated as "weakness of will" (see Dahl, especially ch. 9). What makes one's will weak? Kenny does not show that the cause lies elsewhere than in malformation of the reason and the passions.

2. Nussbaum explains why she translates *philia* simply as "love": Aristotle's use of it "includes many relationships that would not be classified as friendships. The love of mother and child is a paradigmatic case of *philia*; all close family relations, including the relation of husband and wife, are so characterized. Furthermore, our 'friendship' can suggest a relationship that is weak in affect relative to some other relationship, as in the expression 'just friends.' Aristotle deals with relationships of varying degrees of intimacy and depth; a

few of them may be weak in affect. But *philia* includes the very strongest affective relationships that human beings form; it includes, furthermore, relationships that have a passionate sexual component" (*Fragility* 334). What the
various forms of *philia* have in common, Nussbaum continues, is mutuality,
reciprocity—a theme to which we will return in later chapters.

3. Lewis quotes the phrase as the epigraph to his *Problem of Pain*.

4. Milbank's description of Augustine's position is certainly very sympathetic, and not surprisingly, since Milbank tends to refer to his theological
stance as "postmodern critical Augustinianism." He writes: "Antique ethics,
therefore, were not really, for Augustine, 'ethical,' because not finally about
the realization of community as itself the final goal. They failed to arrive at an
'interpersonal' perspective and therefore, when deconstructed, finished up by
celebrating the greater strength shown by the *polis* or the *soul* in its control of
its members or its body. From the viewpoint of antiquity, then, it must appear
that, in heaven, where there is only harmony and tranquillity, there is no scope
for virtue at all, whereas for Augustine, it is only here that virtue, and the full
range of human powers, will be properly displayed. All the antique virtues are
for him ambiguously virtuous, because each is necessitated by an absence of
charity and peace" (*Theology* 410–411). Though Milbank is contending with
Alasdair MacIntyre in this portion of his book, MacIntyre makes the same
point with equal force: "Charity is not of course, from the biblical point of
view, just one more virtue to be added to the list. Its inclusion alters the conception of the good for man in a radical way; the community in which the
good is achieved has to be one of reconciliation" (*After* 174).

5. In Wilken's translation, Origen employs a familiar distinction, but in
language that is inverted from the English norm. What Origen/Wilken calls
understanding is mere basic comprehension: a matter, one might say, of having a strictly grammatical understanding of what is being said. What Origen
calls *knowledge* is much fuller and deeper. In English it is more common to
celebrate *understanding* as the deeper comprehension and to use *knowledge* as
a relatively dismissive term.

6. I do not know that Bakhtin anywhere makes explicit the claim that consciousness is linguistic and, therefore, that hermeneutics has universal applicability in the human sciences. However, such a conviction seems to me implicit
in everything Bakhtin writes. Gadamer of course does, often, make this express
claim. The potential problems with this claim are treated by Jürgen Habermas
in his well-known essay "On Hermeneutics' Claim to Universality."

7. As is almost always the case with Bakhtin, his comments in *Toward a Philosophy of the Act* apply equally well to what is usually called "ethics" (involving relations among persons), on the one hand, and what is usually called
"hermeneutics" but what Bakhtin called "aesthetics" (involving persons' encounters with texts), on the other. For Bakhtin, and this is true at any stage of
his career, acts of interpretation are always ethically fraught, whereas ethical

questions always assume hermeneutical form. This is why Bakhtin can move so easily between literary criticism and moral philosophy—or rather, erase the boundaries between the two, overtly so in "Author and Hero in Aesthetic Activity" (*Art* 4:257)—and why Alexandar Mihailovic (ch. 1) focuses on the importance of the concept of "discourse" (*slovo*) for Bakhtin: "Discourse" is how we live as well as what we read.

A lovely account of the rewards of attentiveness may be found in Henry James's preface to *The Golden Bowl:* "The sense of receiving has borne me company without a break; a luxury making for its sole condition that I should intelligently attend. The blest good stuff, sitting up, in its myriad forms, so touchingly responsive to new care of any sort whatsoever, seemed to pass with me a delightful bargain, and in the fewest possible words. 'Actively believe in us and then you'll see!'—it wasn't more complicated than that, and yet was to become as thrilling as if conditioned on depth within depth" (*Literary Criticism* 1334).

8. "One can imagine Derrida as very modest, entirely occupied by reading and re-reading his predecessors with minute attention, determined to spend the time it takes over the slightest detail, the slightest comma, guardian of the letter of the old texts, putting nothing forward that he has not already found written by an other, scarcely our contemporary—and this is true. But one can also imagine him, on the contrary, as immodesty itself, forcing these same old texts to say something quite different from what they had always seemed to say . . . —and this is not false" (Bennington, in Bennington and Derrida 6–7).

9. For Weil, here and elsewhere in her work, human particularity is best grasped through personal suffering coupled with the recognition of suffering in others. She would surely agree with Tolstoy's famous opening line of *Anna Karenina:* "Happy families are all alike, but each unhappy family is unhappy in its own way." A liberal-ironist version of the same contention—that human solidarity is best based on a common suffering—turns up in the work of Richard Rorty (*Contingency*, ch. 9). An interesting question is why St. Paul's injunction to "weep with those who weep" is received so enthusiastically by such a wide range of thinkers, whereas scarcely anyone acknowledges the other half of the saying: "Rejoice with those who rejoice" (Rom. 12:15).

10. For interesting reflections on the "problematics of vision" in the early Bakhtin, see Caryl Emerson (110–111).

11. Bakhtin's concerns, then, are substantial, and his tendency to avoid the language of "human nature" and "common humanity" is an understandable one. But let me argue with Mikhail Mikhailovich for a moment. We should not forget that Alyosha uses his belief in the common humanity that he shares with Captain Snegiryov to formulate judgments not only about the Captain but also about himself. Understanding himself to be in a definable

analogical relationship with the Captain, Alyosha comes to believe that the Captain will take the money, but he also comes to see the "sensitivity" of the Captain's soul, the pettiness of his own, and the certainty that he too would take the money were he in the Captain's place. In other words, Alyosha puts his self-concept at risk in the very way that Bakhtin thinks essential to the understanding of persons as persons rather than as "cognized things": "The genuine life of the personality is made available only through a dialogic penetration of that personality, during which it freely and reciprocally reveals itself" (59). This is precisely what Alyosha does. Therefore, despite the dangers that Bakhtin properly identifies, the analogical understanding of persons rooted in Christian doctrines of creation and sin *can* be a powerful tool in the growth of love for one's neighbor.

12. Bakhtin is so insistent that this abstracting and objectifying of the "I" is "absolutely alien to the ethical event of being" because of his belief, noted briefly above but repeatedly expressed throughout Bakhtin's early work, that ethics is properly understood only in relation to the "answerable act" (*postupok*), and that the truly answerable act is always historically concrete and particular (in this regard, see especially *Toward* 30). This is the sense in which Bakhtin's early work is most thoroughly anti-Kantian: It understands the abstracting and universalizing of ethical decisionmaking inherent in Kant's categorical imperative as utterly inimical to true ethical—that is, answerable—action. On this point see Mihailovic (65ff).

Interlude B: Transfer of Charisma

1. As Brian Boyd has written in a recent essay on the novel, "Kinbote thinks himself devoted to Shade and Shade's poem ('Such hearts, such brains, would be unable to comprehend that one's attachment to a masterpiece may be utterly overwhelming'), yet he cannot make the effort to understand the particulars of Shade's imaginative world (words, things, customs, allusions, intentions), so that his performance as editor becomes an exact image of all moral myopia, all failure to make the effort to respect the sheer difference of another individual" ("Shade" 2). Kinbote's "attachment" requires none of the attentiveness that I have identified as the first requirement of charitable reading.

2. Boyd points out in his great biography of Nabokov that, although Kinbote does not know the "pale fire" passage, he echoes it twice, once in a way that would make himself the moon and Shade the sun: "I have reread, not without pleasure, my comments to his lines, and in many cases have caught myself borrowing a kind of opalescent light from my poet's fiery orb, and unconsciously aping the prose style of his own critical essays" (81). And once the other way around, in the passage I cited earlier in which Kinbote sees in the poem "a long ripplewake of [his] glory" (297). I am indebted here to Boyd's whole chapter on *Pale Fire* (425–456).

Chapter 3

1. "Essai sur le don" originally appeared in the 1925 volume of *Année Sociologique*, a journal devoted to sociology in the Durkheimian mode (Mauss was Durkheim's nephew).

2. There are, of course, different kinds of struggles, and even if thinkers agree upon the enemies that require resistance, they may counsel different forms of resistance. As Lester H. Hunt points out, Nietzsche's emphasis on the need for "overcoming" can sound Kantian, but the kind of overcoming Nietzsche has in mind is very different than Kant's (80).

3. In the preface to his stimulating collection *A Nietzsche Reader*, R. J. Hollingdale assembles a set of Nietzsche's reflections on how he should be read, how he actually is read, and why he is read so badly. A profound tension between the desire to be understood and the desire to remain impervious to understanding is evident in almost every passage.

4. Some scholars have questioned whether Aristotle really endorses the portrait of magnanimity that he sketches in the *Ethics*, in part because it seems to clash with his emphasis on the need for friendship: The magnanimous man can seem to be quite self-sufficient in a way that Aristotle, as we have seen, criticizes. But this need not be the case. For the magnanimous man there are few potential friends, because he has few equals, fellow citizens with whom he can have a genuinely mutual and symmetrical relationship. But this is not to say that he can or would wish to live without friends altogether. It may simply be that his possession of many virtues—"Magnanimity seems to be a sort of crown of the virtues, because it enhances them and is never found apart from them. This makes it hard to be truly magnanimous, because it is impossible without all-round excellence" (*Ethics* 1123b35)—enables him better to survive what Nussbaum would call the bad luck of not coming into contact with many equals. What is curious about this form of bad luck, of course, is that one is put in danger of it precisely by being exceptionally virtuous: On the other hand, the virtuous person is better able to withstand the blows of misfortune than the less virtuous. (The peculiarity of this situation perhaps helps to explain Aristotle's confusing and apparently inconsistent comments on the magnanimous person's response to both the bestowal and the denial of external rewards.) So Aristotle is not, on this matter, as Platonic as he may sound: The magnanimous person is not really self-sufficient. But it is the *apparently* Platonic character of Aristotle's picture of magnanimity that appeals to Nietzsche.

5. Immensely relevant here are W. H. Auden's reflections on the difference between classical comedy (Aristophanes, Plautus, Terence) and Christian comedy (Shakespeare): "Comedy . . . is not only possible within a Christian society, but capable of a much greater breadth and depth than classical comedy. Greater in breadth because classical comedy is based upon a division of

mankind into two classes, those who have *arete* and those who do not, and only the second class, fools, shameless rascals, slaves, are fit subjects for comedy. But Christian comedy is based upon the belief that all men are sinners; no one, therefore, whatever his rank or talents, can claim immunity from the comic exposure and, indeed, the more virtuous, in the Greek sense, a man is, the more he realizes that he deserves to be exposed. Greater in depth because, while classical comedy believes that rascals should get the drubbing they deserve, Christian comedy believes that we are forbidden to judge others and that it is our duty to forgive each other. In classical comedy the characters are exposed and punished: when the curtain falls, the audience is laughing and those on stage are in tears. In Christian comedy the characters are exposed and forgiven: when the curtain falls, the audience and the characters are laughing together" (*Dyer's* 177). To receive a gift is, in Nietzsche's scheme, to acknowledge oneself to be without *arete*; it renders comical any claims one might make to virtue, at least the great virtues.

6. The most brilliant portrayal I know of the presumption that would annul the need for hope is found in W. H. Auden's poem "Under Sirius." Auden envisions a late-Roman poet and rhetorician named Fortunatus who fails to perceive his fortunate state and instead mopes about listlessly—"Lying in bed till noon, . . . [his] much advertised epic not yet begun"—wishing that "Some earthquake would astonish / Or the wind of the Comforter's wing / Unlock the prisons and translate / The slipshod gathering." But Auden warns Fortunatus of the dangers accompanying such triumphalist presumption: "It is natural to hope and pious, of course, to believe / That all in the end shall be well, / But first of all, remember, / So the Sacred Books foretell, / The rotten fruit shall be shaken. . . . / How will you answer when from their qualming spring / The immortal nymphs fly shrieking, / And out of the open sky / The pantocratic riddle breaks:— / "Who are you and why?" (*Collected Poems* 545–546).

Interlude C: Quixotic Reading

1. One recalls here Nicholson Baker's confession that "Updike is a better writer than I am *and* he is smarter than I am" (134). It is a humbling confession; on the other hand, it justifies the loving attention he has given to Updike. The same can be said for Rich's attitude toward Dickinson. Some of this language will seem merely formal, a nod in the direction of humility rather than the thing itself; perhaps even hypocritical. But gestures of this kind are important as reminders of our limitations—reminders to ourselves and to our readers. It is extremely important that the little constellation of rhetorical gestures made by Rich has almost completely disappeared from critical discourse, so that we no longer even pretend to humility. Hypocrisy may well be the tribute that vice pays to virtue, but when vice ceases to pay virtue any tributes

at all, we have a problem. Auden is useful here: "If good literary critics are rarer than good poets or novelists, one reason is the nature of human egoism. A poet or a novelist has to learn to be humble in the face of his subject matter which is life in general. But the subject matter of a critic, before which he has to learn to be humble, is made up of authors, that is to say, of human individuals, and this kind of humility is much more difficult to acquire. It is far easier to say—'Life is more important than anything I can say about it'—than say—'Mr. A's work is more important than anything I can say about it' (*Dyer's* 8).

2. For a historical exploration of this theme, see the first chapter of Elaine Showalter's *A Literature of Their Own*, "The Female Tradition" (3–36). Someone could perform a great service for scholarship by showing how this construction of a female tradition resembles and differs from earlier projects in the text-centered building of communities—for instance, the medieval projects described by Brian Stock in *Listening for the Text*, especially his seventh chapter, on "Textual Communities."

3. At one point Rich writes, "I know that for me, reading her poems as a child and then as a young girl already seriously writing poetry, she was a problematic figure" (167). But Rich attributes the "problematic" nature of the encounter to the "heavily edited" and bowdlerized editions in which the poetry was then available, not to any distance—fertile or otherwise—between herself and Dickinson.

4. This complexity of response is sensitively traced throughout Roger Lundin's excellent biography of Dickinson.

5. In an important essay, Donald Marshall shows how a model of knowledge gained through "conceptual rationality" can come to displace, even obviate the need for, interpretation: "If truth is to come to us through interpretation, conceptual rationality cannot be what we are seeking. In the turn to reflection here, we are no longer listening to the text but making it the mere occasion to reiterate what we have legitimated on other grounds. Where the text resists this imposition, it will be condemned or ignored, but that collapse of interpretation calls into question not the text but the attempt to control it in this way" (75–76). What Rich appeals to is not "conceptual rationality" but experience, feeling, and intuition; however, her appeal has precisely the same effect of causing her, at times, to stop "listening to the text" and to make Dickinson's complicated poems "the mere occasion to reiterate" what she has learned from that experience, feeling, and intuition.

Chapter 4

1. See Susan Handelman's masterful discussion of this topic in *The Slayers of Moses* (171–178). She is commenting both on Levinas's "Loving the Torah More than God" (*Difficult* 142–145) and on Derrida's "Violence and Metaphysics: An Essay on the Thought of Emmanuel Levinas" (*Writing* 79–153).

2. Likewise, for Cardinal Newman, the vital move from "notional" to "real" assent (a distinction I mentioned in Chapter 2) is enabled by the practice of meditation: "To the devout and spiritual, the Divine Word speaks of things, not merely of notions. And, again, to the disconsolate, the tempted, the perplexed, the suffering, there comes, by means of their very trials, an enlargement of thought, which enables them to see in it what they never saw before. Henceforth there is to them a reality in its teachings, which they recognize as an argument, and the best of arguments, for its divine origin. Hence the practice of meditation on the Sacred Text; so highly thought of by Catholics. Reading, as we do, the Gospels from our youth up, we are in danger of becoming so familiar with them as to be dead to their force, and to view them as a mere history. The purpose, then, of meditation is to realize them; to make the facts which they relate stand out before our minds as objects, such as may be appropriated by a faith as living as the imagination which apprehends them" (79).

3. On the role of memorization and reminiscence in the monastery—which involve the continual pronunciation of the words, so that learning by heart is also "learning by mouth"—see LeClercq (24, 78–80). This kind of reading is to be contrasted with the purely silent reading to which Steiner implicitly refers, the origins and character of which are much debated: For a brief account of the debate, see Martin, *History* (67–73); for a provocative argument about "the invention of silent reading," see Svenbro, ch. 9.

4. One finds a similar argument being made by Solovyov, who has sometimes been put forth as an influence upon Bakhtin (see, for example, Mihailovic 70). Solovyov says bluntly that "the meaning of human love, speaking generally, is *the justification and salvation of individuality through the sacrifice of egoism*" (42; original emphasis). Notice that the elimination of egoism is the salvation of individuality, which remains. Thus Solovyov distrusts the mystical dissolution of the self, because "in mystical love the object of love comes in the long run to an absolute indistinction, which swallows up the human individuality. Here egoism is abrogated only in that very insufficient sense in which it is abrogated when a person falls into a state of very deep sleep" (47). Solovyov wants to preserve the integrity of both the lover and the loved one, but to have them joined together in what he calls a "living *syzygetic* relation" (113)—a term derived from the Greek word *syzygy* meaning (says Solovyov) "close union." The whole picture resembles the early Bakhtin's notions of love in several ways.

5. An excellent example of this false and dangerous kenosis comes at the end of Ibsen's *Hedda Gabler*, when George Tesman and Thea Elvsted decide to reconstruct the papers of the dead genius Eilert Løvborg. Says Tesman, "Setting other people's papers in order—it's exactly what I can do best" (300).

6. Another brilliant illustration of the consequences of this abdication comes in Dostoevsky's *Demons*, in the bone-chilling but utterly penetrating

remark Peter Verkhovensky makes to Kirillov regarding the latter's belief—buttressed by what appears to Kirillov to be an ineluctable set of logical steps—that he must commit suicide in order to be truly free and thereby to become God: "I only know it was not you who ate the idea, but the idea that ate you" (558).

7. Even the ascesis preached by the later Foucault—the loss of self in "boundary experiences"—operates according to the logic that governs Weil's and Kierkegaard's understanding of *kenosis*. At the heart of this position is a fear and loathing of oneself. On Foucault's asceticism, see Harpham.

8. The bracketed question mark indicates the editor's uncertainty about the word translated as "descending." The manuscript now titled *Toward a Philosophy of the Act* is not only fragmentary but also damaged by decades of neglect after it was hidden away. The sentence about the "descending of Christ" is immediately followed by thirty-two indecipherable words—though some attempts at conjectural reconstruction of those words have been made (see *Toward* 90, note 54). The reading "descending" (which the editors were confident enough about to put in the text rather than recording it as indecipherable) is perfectly consistent with the theme of the passage. Here is an English translation of the reconstructed passage (provided to me by Caryl Emerson and Alexandar Mihailovic, to whom I am grateful): ". . . through communion, through the separation of his blood and flesh as he suffers a permanent death, alive and active in the world of events. It is through his non-immanence in the world that we are alive and commune with it, are attached to it."

Interlude D:
Two Charitable Readers

1. It is interesting to note that no one has argued more forcefully and compellingly for the inevitable agonism of interpretation, indeed intellectual discourse more generally—indeed, more generally still, *political* discourse—than Stanley Fish, who happens to be Jane Tompkins's husband. An especially noteworthy example is his recent essay "Mutual Respect as a Device of Exclusion," in which Fish contends that the influential model of "deliberative democracy" articulated by Amy Gutmann and Dennis Thompson claims to get us beyond the harshness of agonism but in fact does no more than mask agonism: We may pretend to care about building procedural safeguards that will ensure "mutual respect" among citizens, but what we really care about is "particular outcomes." We should simply admit that we want what we want, and simultaneously admit that struggle, conflict, is the only way to achieve our goals (whatever they may be).

Chapter 5

1. The argument that follows in the first few pages of this chapter appears, in longer and different form, in Chapter 4 of my book *What Became of Wystan: Change and Continuity in Auden's Poetry* (Fayetteville: University of Arkansas Press, 1998).

2. I will be using the terms *duty* and *obligation* often in the following pages, but let it not be thought that I understand either charity or justice in purely deontological terms. I agree with Bernard Williams that *duty* is one of the types of ethical consideration, but not the only one (see *Ethics* 16–17, 179). Duty is prominent in this chapter because it is prominent in the minds of the characters and writers I am discussing.

3. One can see the confusions about charity and justice, private and public virtue, in the emergence of the word *charity* as a noun describing an institution. As Raymond Williams says, the use of the word in this way was in place by the seventeenth century, particularly (I would think) in reference to the establishment of "charity schools" for poor children. The first example cited in the OED is from a 1697 entry in John Evelyn's diary: "I went this evening to see Christ's Hospital . . . having never seen a more noble, pious, and admirable charity." Christ's Hospital, in London, was the most famous of these schools; Coleridge and Charles Lamb were educated there.

4. Many critics over the years have singled out Jo as a figure whose ignorance and poverty are exaggerated for polemical purposes, but, as Peter Ackroyd points out in his biography of Dickens, Dickens had "read in the *Examiner* an account of the cross-examination of a fourteen-year-old boy, George Ruby, who earned his living by sweeping the mud and manure from the streets of London." Ackroyd quotes the account, in which George Ruby says that he does not know what prayers are or what God is, though he also says "I've heard of the Devil, but I don't know him." Dickens later reprinted this exchange in one of the periodicals he edited. Ackroyd simply says, "And there are still those who accuse Dickens of melodramatic exaggeration" (583).

5. Raymond Williams makes the point that Cobbett's idealizing of the past extended even to his view of the Middle Ages, and that Cobbett's *History of the Protestant Reformation in England and Ireland* (1824–1827) may have been a major source of the medievalism that would become so popular later in the century (*Culture* 19).

6. Cobbett, widely thought of as one of the most radical political thinkers of his time, insisted that "I want to see no innovation in England. . . . We want *great alteration*, but we want *nothing new*" (quoted in Himmelfarb 214; also in Raymond Williams, *Cobbett* 39, where Williams comments that "this was not only Cobbett's view. It was widely shared by many of the most radical reformers. . . ." Williams is right, in the first chapter of his *Culture and Soci-*

perhaps significant for the discussion at hand that Dickens gives us a good indication of the characteristic dangers of what would strive to be "equitable" judgment: not the overly rigid implementation of overly general statutes, but a tendency to get lost in a sea of unforeseen complexities, special cases, and mitigating circumstances—with the ultimate consequence that judges who cannot envision what a truly equitable decision would be end up making no decision at all. Equity cannot, therefore—and Aristotle of course understood this—be a replacement for legal statutes, only a supplement to them. This caution applies to hermeneutics as well.

11. As is so often the case, Inglis is blithely unaware of the boundaries of his tolerance. He insists that his model of Cultural Studies "in no way instructs or commands a way of thought: it is part of its genteel liberalism not to." He has not noticed, it appears, that in the immediately preceding paragraph he said that "we had better accept as a straight truism that the study of culture, as of nature, teaches atheism" (231).

12. An inability to recognize this chain of necessary relations weakens the argument of Martha Nussbaum's provocative essay "Equity and Mercy." Lacking a grounding in Christian charity, the equitable mercy Nussbaum rightly counsels as a legal principle also lacks persuasive power. Why must we be merciful, especially to the unmerciful? How can the will to vengeance be replaced by merciful impulses? Moreover, Nussbaum can offer only a negative definition of mercy; centering her argument on the Latin form (*clementia*), she cites as authoritative Seneca's definition: "the inclination of the mind toward leniency in exacting punishment." This mercy, unlike the mercy that flows from Christian love, apparently can be characterized only by what it refrains from doing.

Postlude

1. These reflections might encourage us further to reconsider the usefulness of Huizinga's definition of play. His points seem to me generally sensible, and yet to contain something of the purism of Derrida's definition of the gift. Play cannot simply be identified with leisure: It is one of the things we do with our leisure time, though not the only thing—think of Chesterson's essay "In Praise of Idleness," idleness being leisure but not play. Play certainly does require a measure of freedom from obligation and responsibility, and therefore is strongly voluntaristic—thus the absurdity of Miss Havisham, in Dickens's *Great Expectations,* ordering Pip and Estella to play so she can watch them—and it does have its own rules. But really, it never remains hermetically sealed off from the rest of life: The rules of play bear close resemblance to other kinds of rules, indeed are often derived from nonleisurely practices, and what we do and learn when we play is always being compared

ety, to link Cobbett with Edmund Burke, whom in some ways he closely resembles.

7. Similarly, I have contended elsewhere that the nineteenth-century novel simply *is* the philosophical discourse of Liberalism, which is constitutionally unamenable to dialectical defense. See my review of *Existentialists and Mystics*, by Iris Murdoch, in *First Things* (January 1999), 40–44.

8. Orwell's point about Dickens's failure to make positive recommendations is, interestingly, recapitulated in Himmelfarb's judgment about Carlyle: "His readers . . . looked to him for a moral critique of institutions, policies, and doctrines which they themselves subscribed to, for which they (and perhaps Carlyle himself) had no practical alternatives, but which they suspected were morally dubious and even dangerous" (204). Orwell's view of Dickens's politics is shared by Raymond Williams: Dickens's "positives do not lie in social improvement, but rather in what he sees as the elements of human nature—personal kindness, sympathy, and forbearance. It is not the model factory against the satanic mill, nor is it the humanitarian experiment against selfish exploitation. It is, rather, individual persons against the System. In so far as it is social at all, it is the Circus against Coketown" (*Culture* 94–95). ("The System" is of course Cobbett's characteristic way of referring to the whole socioeconomic order against which he protests in the name of an older more "organic" order—though sometimes he offers the still simpler designation "It." I will have more to say about Coketown and the Circus in the last pages of this book.

9. Terry Eagleton has made this point very nicely: "There are some kinds of criticism—Orwell's would do as an example—which are a good deal more politically radical than their bluffly commonsensical style would suggest. For all his dyspepsia about shockheaded Marxists . . . Orwell's politics are much more far-reaching than his conventionally-minded prose would suggest. With much post-colonial writing, the situation is just the reverse. Its flamboyant theoretical avant-gardism conceals a rather modest political agenda. Where it ventures political proposals at all, which is rare enough, they hardly have the revolutionary élan of its scandalous speculations on desire or the death of Man or the end of History. This is a feature shared by Derrida, Foucault and others like them, who veer between a cult of theoretical 'madness' or 'monstrosity' and a more restrained, reformist sort of politics, retreating from the one front to the other depending on the direction of the critical fire."

10. It is a fascinating if bitter irony that the Court of Chancery that Dickens satirizes so powerfully in *Bleak House* is a key branch of what in England is called "equity law": Courts like Chancery were devised specifically for the purpose of remedying the deficiencies, due to generality, of the common law courts. This task, needless to say, they did not invariably accomplish. It is

with what we do and learn in the rest of our lives. Habits of mind and temperament formed in hours of play are not automatically suspended when play is suspended. In the end we may have no more success in separating play from "real life" than Derrida had in distinguishing the gift from reciprocal exchange.

WORKS CITED

Ackroyd, Peter. *Dickens*. New York: HarperCollins, 1990.

Aristotle. *Ethics*. [Nicomachean Ethics.] Trans. J. A. K. Thomson, revised by Hugh Tredennick. Harmondsworth, Eng.: Penguin, 1976.

Ashton, Rosemary. *George Eliot: A Life*. London: Allen Lane/Penguin, 1996.

Auden, W. H. *Collected Poems*. Ed. Edward Mendelson. Revised edition. London: Faber, 1991.

_____. *The Dyer's Hand and Other Essays*. London: Faber, 1962.

_____. *Forewords and Afterwords*. New York: Random House, 1973.

Augustine. *The City of God*. Trans. Henry Bettenson. Harmondsworth, Eng.: Penguin, 1972.

_____. *The Confessions*. Trans. Rex Warner. New York: New American Library, 1963.

_____. *The First Catechetical Instruction*. Ed. and Trans. Joseph P. Christopher. New York: Newman, n.d.

_____. *On Christian Doctrine*. [De Doctrina Christiana.] Trans. D. W. Robertson Jr. Indianapolis: Bobbs-Merrill, 1958.

_____. *On Christian Teaching*. Trans. R. P. H. Green. Oxford: Oxford University Press, 1997.

_____. *On the Trinity*. [De Trinitate.] *Select Library of Nicene and Post-Nicene Fathers of the Christian Church*. Ed. Philip Schaff. http://ccel.org/fathers2/NPNF1-03/TOC.htm

Baer, Helmut David. "The Fruit of Charity: Using the Neighbor in *De Doctrina Christiana*." *Journal of Religious Ethics* 24, no. 1 (spring 1996): 47–64.

Baker, Nicholson. *U and I*. New York: Random House, 1991.

Bakhtin, Mikhail. *Art and Answerability: Early Philosophical Essays*. Ed. Michael Holquist and Vadim Liapunov. Trans. Vadim Liapunov. Austin: University of Texas Press, 1990.

_____. *The Dialogic Imagination: Four Essays*. Ed. Michael Holquist. Trans. Caryl Emerson and Michael Holquist. Austin: University of Texas Press, 1981.

_____. *Problems of Dostoevsky's Poetics*. Ed. and Trans. Caryl Emerson. Minneapolis: University of Minnesota Press, 1984.

_____. *Speech Genres and Other Late Essays*. Ed. Caryl Emerson and Michael Holquist. Trans. Vern W. McGee. Austin: University of Texas Press, 1986.

_____. *Toward a Philosophy of the Act*. Ed. Vadim Liapunov and Michael Holquist. Trans. Vadim Liapunov. Austin: University of Texas Press, 1993.

Barnes, Julian. *Flaubert's Parrot*. New York: Knopf, 1985.

_____. *Staring at the Sun*. New York: Knopf, 1987.

Barth, Karl. *Church Dogmatics*. IV/2. Trans. G. W. Bromiley. Edinburgh: T. & T. Clark, 1968.

Basil, St. *St. Basil the Great to Students on Greek Literature*. Ed. Edward R. Maloney. New York: American Book Company, 1901.

Bennington, Geoffrey, and Jacques Derrida. *Jacques Derrida*. Trans. Geoffrey Bennington. Chicago: University of Chicago Press, 1992.

Berlin, Isaiah. *The Magus of the North: J. G. Hamann and the Origins of Modern Irrationalism*. New York: Farrar, 1993.

Blake, William. *The Complete Poetry and Prose*. Ed. David V. Erdman. Revised edition, Garden City, N.Y.: Anchor, 1982.

Blumenberg, Hans. *The Legitimacy of the Modern Age*. Trans. Robert M. Wallace. Cambridge, Mass.: MIT Press, 1983.

Bonhoeffer, Dietrich. *Letters and Papers from Prison*. Enlarged edition. New York: Macmillan, 1971.

Booth, Wayne. *The Company We Keep: An Ethics of Fiction*. Berkeley: University of California Press, 1988.

Boyd, Brian. "Shade and Shape in Pale Fire." *Nabokov Studies* 4 (1977). http://www.libraries.psu.edu/iasweb/nabokov/boydpf1.htm

_____. *Vladimir Nabokov: The American Years*. Princeton: Princeton University Press, 1991.

Brown, Peter. *Augustine of Hippo*. Berkeley: University of California Press, 1967.

Bruns, Gerald L. *Hermeneutics Ancient and Modern*. New Haven: Yale University Press, 1992.

Buechner, Frederick. *Now and Then*. New York: Harper, 1983.

Burke, Kenneth. *The Philosophy of Literary Form*. Baton Rouge: Louisiana State University Press, 1941.

Caputo, John D. *The Prayers and Tears of Jacques Derrida: Religion Without Religion*. Bloomington: Indiana University Press, 1997.

Carlyle, Thomas. "Chartism." In *Critical and Miscellaneous Essays*, Vol. 4 (pp. 36–117). New York: American Publishers Corporation, 1869.

Cassedy, Steven. "P. A. Florensky and the Celebration of Matter." In *Russian Religious Thought* (pp. 95–111). Ed. Judith Deutsch Korngold and Richard F. Gustafson. Madison: University of Wisconsin Press, 1996.

Cavell, Stanley. *The Claim of Reason: Wittgenstein, Skepticism, Morality, and Tragedy*. New York: Oxford University Press, 1979.

———. *Disowning Knowledge in Six Plays of Shakespeare*. Cambridge, Eng.: Cambridge University Press, 1987.

Cervantes, Miguel de. *"The Deceitful Marriage" and Other Exemplary Novels*. Trans. Walter Starkie. New York: New American Library, 1963.

Clark, Katerina, and Michael Holquist. *Mikhail Bakhtin*. Cambridge, Mass.: Belknap/Harvard, 1984.

Crites, Stephen. "The Narrative Quality of Experience." In *Why Narrative? Readings in Narrative Theology* (pp. 65–88). Ed. Stanley Hauerwas and L. Gregory Jones. Grand Rapids, Mich.: Eerdmans, 1989.

Davidson, Donald. "Radical Interpretation." In *Inquiries into Truth and Interpretation*. Oxford: Clarendon, 1984.

Davie, Donald (Ed.). *The New Oxford Book of Christian Verse*. Oxford: Oxford University Press, 1980.

Dahl, Norman O. *Practical Reason, Aristotle, and Weakness of the Will*. Minneapolis: University of Minnesota Press, 1984.

Derrida, Jacques. *Dissemination*. Trans. Barbara Johnson. Chicago: University of Chicago Press, 1981.

———. *Given Time*. Vol. 1; *Counterfeit Money*. Trans. Peggy Kamuf. Chicago: University of Chicago Press, 1992.

———. *Writing and Difference*. Trans. Alan Bass. Chicago: University of Chicago Press, 1978.

Dickens, Charles. *Bleak House*. 1853. Harmondsworth, Eng.: Penguin, 1971.

———. *Hard Times*. 1854. New York: Norton, 1966.

Dihle, Albrecht. *The Theory of the Will in Classical Antiquity*. Berkeley: University of California Press, 1982.

Dostoevsky, Fyodor. *The Brothers Karamazov*. Trans. Richard Pevear and Larissa Volokhonsky. New York: Vintage, 1990.

———. *Demons*. Trans. Richard Pevear and Larissa Volokhonsky. New York: Vintage, 1994.

Eagleton, Terry. "In the Gaudy Supermarket." *London Review of Books*, May 31, 1999. http://www.lrb.co.uk/v21/n10/eagl2110.htm

Ebeling, Gerhard. *Introduction to a Theological Theory of Language*. Trans. R. A. Wilson. London: Collins, 1973.

Eden, Kathy. *Hermeneutics and the Rhetorical Tradition*. New Haven: Yale University Press, 1997.

Edwards, Jonathan. *A Jonathan Edwards Reader*. Ed. John E. Smith, Harry S. Stout, and Kenneth P. Minkema. New Haven: Yale University Press, 1995.

Eliot, George. *Adam Bede*. Harmondsworth, Eng.: Penguin, 1980.

———. *Essays of George Eliot*. Ed. Thomas Pinney. New York: Columbia University Press, 1963.

Elshtain, Jean Bethke. *Augustine and the Limits of Politics*. Notre Dame, Ind.: Notre Dame University Press, 1995.

Emerson, Caryl. "Keeping the Self Intact During the Culture Wars: A Centennial Essay for Mikhail Bakhtin." *New Literary History* 27, no. 1 (1996): 107–126.

Emerson, Ralph Waldo. *Essays and Lectures*. New York: Library of America, 1983.

Engel, Monroe. *The Maturity of Dickens*. Cambridge, Mass.: Harvard University Press, 1959.

Fish, Stanley. "Mutual Respect as a Device of Exclusion." *Deliberative Politics*. Ed. Stephen Macedo. New York: Oxford University Press, 1999.

_____. *Professional Correctness: Literary Studies and Political Change*. Oxford: Clarendon, 1995.

_____. *Surprised by Sin: The Reader in* Paradise Lost. 2nd edition. Cambridge, Mass.: Harvard University Press, 1997.

Fortin, Ernest. "Augustine and the Hermeneutics of Love: Some Preliminary Considerations." In *The Birth of Philosophic Christianity: Studies in Early Christian and Medieval Thought* (pp. 1–21). Lanham, Md.: Rowman & Littlefield, 1996.

Fowl, Stephen. *Engaging Scripture: A Model for Theological Interpretation*. Oxford: Blackwell, 1998.

Freemante, Anne, ed. *The Protestant Mystics*. Boston: Little, Brown, 1964.

Gadamer, Hans-Georg. *Truth and Method*. 2nd edition. Translated and revised by Joel Weinsheimer and Donald G. Marshall. New York: Crossroad, 1992.

Gay, Peter. *The Enlightenment: An Interpretation*. Vol. 1, *The Rise of Modern Paganism*. New York: Norton, 1966.

Glidden, David. "Augustine's Hermeneutics and the Principle of Charity." *Ancient Philosophy* 17 (1997): 135–157.

Grondin, Jean. *Sources of Hermeneutics*. Albany: SUNY, 1995.

Grube, G.M.A. *Plato's Thought*. London: Methuen, 1935.

Habermas, Jürgen. "On Hermeneutics' Claim to Universality." In *The Hermeneutics Reader*, ed. Kurt Mueller-Vollmer (pp. 294–319). New York: Continuum, 1994.

Handelman, Susan A. *The Slayers of Moses: The Emergence of Rabbinic Interpretation in Modern Literary Theory*. Albany: SUNY Press, 1982.

Harpham, Geoffrey Galt. *The Ascetic Imperative in Culture and Criticism*. Chicago: University of Chicago Press, 1988.

Hauerwas, Stanley. *Unleashing the Scripture: Freeing the Bible from Captivity to America*. Nashville: Abingdon, 1993.

Havel, Vaclav. *Letters to Olga*. Trans. Paul Wilson. New York: Holt, 1989.

Heidegger, Martin. *Nietzsche*. Vol. II, *The Eternal Recurrence of the Same*, trans. David Farrell Krell. San Francisco: Harper, 1984.

Himmelfarb, Gertrude. *The Idea of Poverty: England in the Early Industrial Age*. New York: Knopf, 1983.

Holtz, Barry, ed. *Back to the Sources: Reading the Classic Jewish Texts*. New York: Summit, 1984.

Huizinga, Johan. *Homo Ludens: A Study of the Play-Element in Culture*. 1950. Reprint, Boston: Beacon,1972.

Hunt, Lester H. *Nietzsche and the Origin of Virtue*. London: Routledge, 1991.

Hyde, Lewis. *The Gift: Imagination and the Erotic Life of Property*. New York: Vintage, 1983.

Ibsen, Henrik. *Four Major Plays*. Trans. Rolf Fjelde. New York: New American Library, 1965.

Ignatieff, Michael. *The Needs of Strangers*. Harmondsworth, Eng.: Penguin, 1984.

Inglis, Fred. *Cultural Studies*. Oxford: Blackwell, 1992.

Jaeger, Werner. *Early Christianity and Greek Paideia*. New York: Oxford University Press, 1961.

James, Henry. *Complete Stories 1892–1898*. New York: Library of America, 1996.

———. *Literary Criticism*. Vol. II, *French Writers, Other European Writers, The Prefaces to the New York Edition*. New York: Library of America, 1984.

Jauss, Hans Robert. *Aesthetic Experience and Literary Hermeneutics*. Trans. Michael Shaw. Minneapolis: University of Minnesota Press, 1982.

Jeffrey, David Lyle. *People of the Book: Christian Identity and Literary Culture*. Grand Rapids, Mich.: Eerdmans, 1996.

Jüngel, Eberhard. *God as the Mystery of the World*. Trans. Darrell L. Guder. Grand Rapids, Mich.: Eerdmans, 1983.

Kenny, Anthony. *Aristotle's Theory of the Will*. New Haven: Yale University Press, 1979.

Kermode, Frank. *The Genesis of Secrecy: On the Interpretation of Narrative*. Cambridge, Mass.: Harvard University Press, 1979.

Kierkegaard, Søren. *Fear and Trembling. Repetition*. Trans. Howard V. Hong and Edna H. Hong. Princeton: Princeton University Press, 1983.

———. *Papers and Journals: A Selection*. Ed. and Trans. Alastair Hannay. Harmondsworth, Eng.: Penguin, 1996.

———. *Works of Love*. Trans. Howard and Edna Hong. New York: Harper, 1964.

Knowles, David. *The Evolution of Medieval Thought*. New York: Vintage, 1962.

LeClercq, Jean. *The Love of Learning and the Desire for God*. New York: Mentor, 1961.

Levinas, Emmanuel. *Difficult Liberty: Essays on Judaism*. Trans. Séan Hand. Baltimore: Johns Hopkins University Press, 1990.

Lewis, C. S. *The Four Loves*. 1960. London: HarperCollins/Fount, 1977.

_____. *Metaphysics as a Guide to Morals*. Harmondsworth, Eng.: Penguin, 1992.

_____. *The Unicorn*. New York: Viking, 1987.

Nabokov, Vladimir. *Pale Fire*. 1962. Reprint, New York: Vintage, 1989.

Newman, John Henry. *An Essay in Aid of a Grammar of Assent*. 1870. Garden City, N.Y.: Doubleday, 1955.

Niebuhr, Reinhold. *The Nature and Destiny of Man*. 2 vols. New York: Scribner, 1943.

Nietzsche, Friedrich. *Beyond Good and Evil*. Trans. R. J. Hollingdale. Revised edition. Harmondsworth, Eng.: Penguin, 1990.

_____. *Ecce Homo*. Trans. R. J. Hollingdale. Harmondsworth, Eng.: Penguin, 1992.

_____. *A Nietzsche Reader*. Ed. and Trans. R. J. Hollingdale. Harmondsworth, Eng.: Penguin, 1977.

_____. *Thus Spoke Zarathustra*. Trans. R. J. Hollingdale. Harmondsworth, Eng.: Penguin, 1969.

_____. *Twilight of the Idols; and The Anti-Christ*. Trans. R. J. Hollingdale. Harmondsworth, Eng.: Penguin, 1968.

Nussbaum, Martha C. "Equity and Mercy." *Philosophy and Public Affairs* 22, no. 2 (Spring 1993): 83–125.

_____. *The Fragility of Goodness: Luck and Ethics in Greek Tragedy and Philosophy*. Cambridge, Cambridge University Press, 1986.

_____. *Love's Knowledge: Essays on Philosophy and Literature*. New York: Oxford University Press, 1990.

_____. *Poetic Justice: The Literary Imagination and Public Life*. Boston: Beacon, 1995.

Nuttall, A. D. *Why Does Tragedy Give Pleasure?* Oxford: Clarendon, 1996.

Nygren, Anders. *Agape and Eros*. Trans. Philip S. Watson. London: SPCK, 1953.

O'Connor, Flannery. *The Complete Stories*. New York: Farrar, 1971.

O'Donovan, Oliver. *The Desire of the Nations: Rediscovering the Roots of Political Theology*. Cambridge, Eng.: Cambridge University Press, 1996.

Orwell, George. "Charles Dickens." In *A Collection of Essays* (pp. 48–103). San Diego: Harcourt, 1981.

Outka, Gene. *Agape: An Ethical Analysis*. New Haven: Yale University Press, 1972.

Pelikan, Jaroslav. *The Christian Tradition: A History of the Development of Doctrine*. Vol. 2, *The Spirit of Eastern Christendom (600–1700)*. Chicago: University of Chicago Press, 1974.

_____. *Jesus Through the Centuries: His Place in the History of Culture*. New Haven: Yale University Press, 1985.

_____. *The Problem of Pain*. London: Macmillan, 1940.

Lundin, Roger. *Emily Dickinson and the Art of Belief*. Grand Rapids, Mich.: Eerdmans, 1998.

MacIntyre, Alasdair. *After Virtue*. 2nd edition. Notre Dame, Ind.: Notre Dame University Press, 1984.

_____. *Three Rival Versions of Moral Inquiry*. Notre Dame, Ind.: Notre Dame University Press, 1990.

_____. *Whose Justice? Which Rationality?* Notre Dame, Ind.: Notre Dame University Press, 1988.

Manguel, Alberto. *A History of Reading*. New York: Viking, 1996.

Marion, Jean-Luc. *God Without Being*. Trans. Thomas A. Carlson. Chicago: University of Chicago Press, 1991.

Marshall, Donald. "Truth, Universality, and Interpretation." In *Disciplining Hermeneutics: Interpretation in Christian Perspective*, ed. Roger Lundin (pp. 69–84). Grand Rapids, Mich.: Eerdmans, 1997.

Martin, Henri-Jean. *The History and Power of Writing*. Trans. Lydia G. Cochrane. Chicago: University of Chicago Press, 1994.

Mauss, Marcel. *The Gift: Forms and Functions of Exchange in Archaic Societies*. Trans. Ian Cunnison. New York: Norton, 1967.

Meilaender, Gilbert. *Friendship: A Study in Theological Ethics*. Notre Dame, Ind.: University of Notre Dame Press, 1981.

Mendelson, Edward. *Early Auden*. Cambridge, Mass.: Harvard University Press, 1981. (Reprinted in 1983.)

Mihailovic, Alexandar. *Corporeal Words: Mikhail's Bakhtin's Theology of Discourse*. Evanston, Ill.: Northwestern University Press, 1997.

Milbank, John. *Theology and Social Theory: Beyond Secular Reason*. Oxford: Blackwell, 1990.

_____. *The Word Made Strange: Theology, Language, Culture*. Oxford: Blackwell, 1997.

Miller, J. Hillis. *Charles Dickens: The World of His Novels*. 1958. Reprint, Bloomington: Indiana University Press, 1969.

Milton, John. *Paradise Lost*. Ed. Alastair Fowler. London: Longman, 1968.

Moltmann, Jürgen. *Theology of Hope*. Trans. James W. Leitch. New York: Harper, 1967.

Morrison, Karl F. *"I Am You": The Hermeneutics of Empathy in Western Literature, Theology, and Art*. Princeton: Princeton University Press, 1988.

Morson, Gary Saul. "Bakhtin and the Present Moment." *The American Scholar* 60, no. 2 (Spring 1991): 201–222.

Morson, Gary Saul, and Caryl Emerson. *Mikhail Bakhtin: Creation of a Prosaics*. Palo Alto, Calif.: Stanford University Press, 1990.

Murdoch, Iris. *Existentialists and Mystics: Writings on Philosophy and Literature*. Ed. Peter Conradi. London: Allen Lane/Penguin, 1998.

Pieper, Josef. *On Hope.* Trans. Mary Frances McCarthy. San Francisco: Ignatius, 1986.

Remnick, David. *Lenin's Tomb: The Last Days of the Soviet Empire.* New York: Vintage, 1994.

Rich, Adrienne. *On Lies, Secrets, and Silence: Selected Prose 1966–1978.* New York: Norton, 1979.

Ricoeur, Paul. *Freud and Philosophy.* Trans. Denis Savage. New Haven: Yale University Press, 1970.

_____. *The Symbolism of Evil.* Trans. Emerson Buchanan. Boston: Beacon, 1967.

Rolle, Richard. "The Law of Love." In *The Law of Love: English Spirituality in the Age of Wyclif,* ed. David Lyle Jeffrey (pp. 155–162). Grand Rapids, Mich.: Eerdmans, 1988.

Rorty, Richard. *Contingency, Irony, and Solidarity.* Cambridge. Cambridge University Press, 1989.

Schweickart, Patrocinio. "Reading Ourselves: Toward a Feminist Theory of Reading." In *Gender and Reading,* ed. Elizabeth Flynn and Patrocinio Schweickart. (pp. 31–62). Baltimore: Johns Hopkins University Press, 1986.

Shafer, Ingrid H. "From the Senses to Sense: The Hermeneutics of Love." *Zygon* 29, no. 4 (December 1994): 579–602.

Shakespeare, William. *The Riverside Shakespeare.* Ed. Herschel Baker. 2nd edition. Boston: Houghton Mifflin, 1997.

Showalter, Elaine. *A Literature of Their Own: British Women Novelists from Brontë to Lessing.* Expanded edition. Princeton: Princeton University Press, 1999.

Singer, Irving. *The Nature of Love.* Vol. 1, *Plato to Luther.* 2nd edition. Chicago: University of Chicago Press, 1984.

Solovyov, Vladimir. *The Meaning of Love.* Revised translation by Thomas R. Beyer Jr. Hudson, N.Y.: Lindisfarne, 1985.

Solzhenitsyn, Aleksandr. *The First Circle.* Trans. Thomas H. Whitney. New York: Harper, 1968.

Steiner, George. "Critic/Reader." In *George Steiner: A Reader.* New York: Oxford, 1984. 67–98.

_____. *Real Presences.* Chicago: University of Chicago Press, 1989.

Stock, Brian. *Augustine the Reader.* Cambridge, Mass.: Harvard University Press, 1996.

_____. *Listening for the Text: On the Uses of the Past.* Baltimore: Johns Hopkins University Press, 1990.

Svenbro, Jesper. *Phrasikleia: An Anthropology of Reading in Ancient Greece.* Trans. Janet Lloyd. Ithaca, N.Y.: Cornell University Press, 1993.

Tompkins, Jane. "At the Buffalo Bill Museum—June 1988." In *The Best American Essays 1991*. Ed. Joyce Carol Oates. New York: Ticknor & Fields, 1991.

_____. *West of Everything: The Inner Life of Westerns*. New York: Oxford University Press, 1992.

Trollope, Anthony. *Phineas Finn*. 1869. World's Classics edition. Oxford: Oxford University Press, 1982.

Vanhoozer, Kevin. *Is There a Meaning in This Text? The Bible, the Reader, and the Morality of Literary Knowledge*. Grand Rapids, Mich.: Zondervan, 1998.

_____. "The Spirit of Understanding: Special Revelation and General Hermeneutics." In *Disciplining Hermeneutics: Interpretation in Christian Perspective*, ed. Roger Lundin (pp. 131–166). Grand Rapids, Mich.: Eerdmans, 1997.

Volf, Miroslav. *Exclusion and Embrace: A Theological Exploration of Identity, Otherness, and Reconciliation*. Nashville: Abingdon, 1996.

Webb, Stephen H. *The Gifting God: A Trinitarian Ethics of Excess*. Oxford: Oxford University Press, 1996.

Weil, Simone. *Waiting for God*. Trans. Emma Craufurd. New York: Harper, 1951.

Wesley, Charles. "And Can It Be That I Should Gain." In *A Burning and a Shining Light: English Spirituality in the Age of Wesley*, ed. David Lyle Jeffrey (p. 262). Grand Rapids, Mich.: Eerdmans, 1987.

Wilken, Robert L. *Remembering the Christian Past*. Grand Rapids, Mich.: Eerdmans, 1995.

Williams, Bernard. *Ethics and the Limits of Philosophy*. Cambridge, Mass.: Harvard University Press, 1985.

Williams, Raymond. *Cobbett*. Oxford: Oxford University Press, 1983.

_____. *Culture and Society: 1780–1950*. New York: Columbia University Press, 1958. (Reprinted in 1983.)

_____. *Keywords: A Vocabulary of Culture and Society*. Revised edition. New York: Oxford University Press, 1983.

Wills, Garry. *Saint Augustine*. New York: Viking, 1999.

_____. *Under God: Religion and American Politics*. New York: Simon and Schuster, 1990.

Wittgenstein, Ludwig. *On Certainty*. Ed. G E. M. Anscombe and G. H. von Wright. Trans. Denis Paul and G. E. M. Anscombe. New York: Harper, 1969.

Woolf, Virginia. *A Room of One's Own*. 1929. New York: Harcourt, 1989.

Wordsworth, William. Preface to *Lyrical Ballads*. In *Selected Prose*, ed. John O. Hayden. Harmondsworth, Eng.: Penguin, 1988.

Index

CPSIA information can be obtained at www.ICGtesting.com
Printed in the USA
BVOW071133030313

314541BV00001B/98/A

9 780813 365664